STRATEGIES FOR GUIDING CONTENT READING

RELATED TITLES OF INTEREST

Content Reading and Literacy: Succeeding in Today's Diverse Classrooms
Donna E. Alvermann and Stephen F. Phelps
ISBN: 0-205-15164-7

Teaching Content Reading and Writing
Martha Rapp Ruddell
ISBN: 0-205-14003-3

Reading in the Content Areas for Junior High and High School
Judith A. Cochran
ISBN 0-205-13404-1

A Sourcebook of Interactive Methods for Teaching with Texts
David A. Hayes
ISBN: 0-205-13306-1

Teaching in Content Areas with Reading, Writing, and Reasoning
Harold L. Herber and Joan Nelson Herber
ISBN: 0-205-14158-7

Reading and the Middle School Student: Strategies to Enhance Literacy
Judith L. Irvin
ISBN: 0-205-11958-1

Teaching Literature in Middle and Secondary Grades
John S. Simmons and H. Edward Deluzain
ISBN: 0-205-13195-6

Second Edition

STRATEGIES FOR GUIDING CONTENT READING

Sharon J. Crawley
Florida Atlantic University

Lee Mountain
University of Houston

ALLYN AND BACON

Boston   London   Toronto   Sydney   Tokyo   Singapore

Library of Congress Cataloging-in-Publication Data

Crawley, Sharon J.
   Strategies for guiding content reading / Sharon J. Crawley, Lee
Mountain. — 2nd ed.
      p.   cm.
   Includes bibliographical references (p.) and index.
   ISBN 0-205-14886-7
   1. Content area reading.   2. Language arts—Correlation with
content subjects.   I. Mountain, Lee Harrison.   II. Title.
LB1050.455.C73   1995
428.4' 07--dc20   94-42835
                                                      CIP

Printed in the United States of America
10 9 8 7 6 5 4 3 2 1   99 98 97 96 95

CONTENTS

PREFACE

A student once asked her instructor, "Why did you become a teacher?"

"Because I enjoy helping people learn," the teacher replied.

"What is the most important thing you do in helping people learn?" the student inquired.

"The most important thing I do?" the teacher repeated, pausing to think for a moment. "I help my students understand and use what they read. Books are the main instructional tool for learning. And reading is the main skill for learning. So I help my students get the most out of reading their textbooks."

The major instructional tool in most classrooms is the textbook, so this teacher was speaking for many teachers when she described the most important thing she did. Content area teachers increasingly are becoming aware of the need to help students understand and use the content of their subject area textbooks.

Strategies for Guiding Content Reading is a concise, direct, "how-to" book for preservice and inservice teachers in middle and secondary schools. Middle schools begin as early as grade 4 in some states.

You will immediately become involved with the content of each chapter through prereading activities. These activities include discussing anticipation questions and then preorganizing and predicting content. Following each chapter is a postreading section. You will respond to contents through writing activities, reviewing vocabulary and concepts from the chapter by categorizing, and completing the practice activities located in Appendix A and suggested for reinforcing the content of the chapter.

Modeling is done throughout the textbook. Strategies are first described, then illustrated by examples and discussions. An array of strategies, from very easy to more challenging, is provided because of the wide diversity of achievement levels in our classrooms. Our classrooms have students ranging from academically gifted students to those who have never attended school because of social and economic conditions in their native countries.

In Chapter 1 we focus on the reading process. This provides you with background regarding reading as a visual, decoding, thinking, psycholinguistic, metacognitive, and technological process.

Chapters 2 and 3 describe the evaluation process. How can we determine the difficulty of a textbook before it is purchased? How can we identify those students who will be able to read the textbook and those who will have difficulty reading it once it has been purchased?

Chapter 4 presents vocabulary development. Because we know that understanding content area vocabulary is a prerequisite to comprehension, it is imperative that we introduce and reinforce the vocabulary of our subject area. Vocabulary growth, mental imagery, categorizing, contextual analysis, morphemic analysis, and word play activities are topics discussed.

The questioning skills of teachers are important to the development of comprehension, study skills, writing, and cooperative learning. Questioning taxonomies and guidelines for improving students' responses to questions are presented in Chapter 5.

Prereading strategies of building background and predicting are presented in Chapter 6. Silent reading and postreading strategies are described in Chapter 7.

Use of study skills is important for any student who wishes to organize and retain content materials. What specific study strategies are available for students to use with content area materials? What are some of the outlining, note taking, and memory aids available to assist students in the independent learning process? What test-taking guidelines can you present to your students? Answers to these questions are covered in Chapter 8.

Integrating writing into the content areas, Chapter 9, is a concern of teachers. What are some guidelines for including writing in the content areas? What general frameworks or structures can you follow in teaching? How can you get students' "creative juices" flowing? How can you utilize writing to have it reinforce the content of your subject area?

Not all students' needs will be met by teaching vocabulary, comprehension, and study skills. Some students will learn better by working in groups, some by listening, and others may still need specific materials adjustments. These topics are discussed in Chapter 10.

Students' interests, along with the role of multicultural literature in content areas, are a major theme in Chapter 11. Questioning strategies, ideas for using literature, and ways students can be directed toward books are topics of Chapter 11. Chapter 11 also presents an extensive list of multicultural books.

Finally, the days of students coming from two-parent homes and cozy houses with white picket fences have passed. Chapter 12 addresses the topics of students at risk, the multicultural backgrounds of students, and students who are classified as "exceptional."

Teachers who are interested in students' progress will make variations in their teaching styles and strategies to meet the needs and interests of students. We hope that as you read this book, you will be motivated to incorporate these strategies into your content area program in order to help your students understand and use what they read.

We are indebted to the many students who contributed their creative ideas and constructive editorial criticism to this manuscript while it was in preparation. To these students, who are too numerous to mention, appreciation is expressed.

We also are indebted to the authors and publishers who gave us permission to quote from their publications. We wish to express our appreciation to Susan Hutchinson of Allyn and Bacon for her extensive assistance. We would also like to express our appreciation to the following reviewers for their insights and suggestions: Sandra Baker, teacher, School Town of Munster, Indiana; Shirley Crenshaw, Research and Training Associates, Inc., Overland Park, Kansas; and Judith Irvin, Florida State University. Many thanks to all!

ABOUT THE AUTHORS

Dr. Sharon Crawley, professor of education at Florida Atlantic University, is co-author of the *Jamestown Heritage Readers,* senior author of *Remediating Reading Difficulties*, and the author of many professional articles. Dr. Crawley has taught and served as a reading consultant in schools in Connecticut. She earned her doctor of education degree from the University of Houston, Texas. She served on the faculty at Augusta College, Georgia, and the University of Texas, El Paso, before moving to her present position at Florida Atlantic University. Dr. Crawley is a frequent presenter at the conventions of the International Reading Association.

Dr. Lee Mountain, professor of education at the University of Houston, Texas, is the author of over a hundred texts, articles, software programs, videotex materials, math/reading simulations, and children's books. After being selected for Phi Beta Kappa at George Washington University, she taught in public schools in Virginia, Colorado, and New Jersey. She then earned her doctorate at Pennsylvania State University and served on the faculty of Rutgers University until moving to her present position at the University of Houston. She has long been a frequent presenter at the conventions of the International Reading Association.

STRATEGIES FOR GUIDING
CONTENT READING

1

THE NATURE OF
READING

New Reading / Math Program Makes a Difference!
Teachers Make Reading Relevant
Students in Japan Read Better Than Students in USA
SAT Scores Are Down

After reading those headlines aloud, Leslie turned to the next section of the newspaper. "Shall I go on?" she asked the other teachers.

"Those headlines are confusing," said Matt. "We're math, science, social studies, English, home economics, and music teachers. We're not reading teachers."

"Students are supposed to be taught reading in grades 1 through 6," Peggy added. "We teach our subjects, not reading."

"Reading is important in my math class," said Leslie. "Remember, we can't expect students to learn everything in six years of school. Students read words, symbols, and problems in my class."

"I wonder if those headlines are accurate?" questioned Phil. "I wonder if students in our classes are reading better or worse than students of fifty years ago."

"Let me go on with these articles," said Leslie. "I bet they'll answer your question."

DISCUSS

Do content area teachers have any responsibility for teaching reading? How does the reading of students today compare with the reading of students in other countries? with the reading of students thirty years ago?

PREORGANIZE

Go through the chapter and make a skeletal outline of the major headings and subheadings. This will provide you with a chapter organizer. Predict the contents of the text under one of these subheadings.

1

OBJECTIVES

After reading this chapter, you should be able to

1. explain a rationale for teaching reading in the content areas.
2. identify problems students face in reading content area materials.
3. describe how you decode printed words that are unfamiliar to you.
4. describe how your eyes operate while you read.
5. describe the dimensions of recognition, literal comprehension, interpretation, and critical/creative reading.
6. describe reading as a psycholinguistic process.
7. describe reading as a metacognitive process.
8. describe reading as a technological process.
9. define the following terms related to the reading process:

decoding	schemata	regression
symbol	pitch	eye span
fixation	juncture	semantic knowledge
literal comprehension	syntactic knowledge	phonological
interpretation	miscue	knowledge
critical/creative	psycholinguistics	stress
saccadic movements	return sweep	morpheme
graphic cues	word recognition	metacognitive

THE NATURE OF READING IN THE CONTENT AREAS

As we entered Juanita's classroom, we observed a social studies lesson in progress. The students had their books open and were taking turns reading orally. John read a paragraph fluently. Then Kim stumbled through her paragraph.

At the end of oral reading Juanita asked many comprehension questions. Several of the questions she asked were: "In what year was the Declaration of Independence signed? Who were the signers of the Declaration of Independence? In what city was the Declaration signed?" All of her questions required the recall of facts that had just been read aloud.

After the students left the room, we talked with Juanita.

SHARON: You asked many questions during your lesson.

JUANITA: Yes, I believe in keeping a fast pace in my classroom. But my students don't seem to think too long before answering my questions.

SHARON: Do you have a lot of material to cover in a year?

JUANITA: Too much! That's why I have my students read aloud. Then I know they're covering the material.

SHARON: Do your students enjoy reading aloud?

JUANITA: Only a few of them do. Some are awful at oral reading. A lot of the time, my students don't listen to each other very carefully.

SHARON: If your students aren't listening, are they actually covering the material?

JUANITA: I guess not. But I want to make sure they learn what's in the textbook. And the material's too hard for them to handle in silent reading assignments. So if oral reading isn't the way, what is?

If you are teaching (or if you intend to teach) in the content areas, you may be echoing Juanita's question. Many of your students will have trouble with silent reading assignments. For many, the textbook may be too difficult.

There is a constant need for you to help your students cope with their content area reading. Herber (1970) identified curriculum pressures, content area materials, and students' competence as the three major problem areas in content reading instruction.

Curriculum pressures are increasing because the amount of information in content area subjects is growing at phenomenal rates. For example, Spivack (1982) identified 50,000 journals and 200,000 publications a year in science and technology fields. More information was printed between 1970 and 1980 than in all previous history. This knowledge explosion creates pressure for you to provide your students with the most relevant information. You need to separate important instructional objectives from those that are less important.

Content area materials themselves pose problems for your students. Many texts appear to be encyclopedic. Chapters contain a high density of concepts and facts presented very quickly. Because of this rapid presentation of information, the material may appear to be difficult and dull, and students may not be able to learn from it.

Students' competence is a third area of concern. You face a wide range of reading levels in your class. In a typical sixth grade class, you might have students at eight different reading levels. Your students may not have the background of experiences to understand the material. Their vocabularies may be meager. They may not retain the information you are trying to teach. Your students may not use their previously acquired reading and study skills at higher levels within the same subject. For example, students may not use their map-reading skills from ninth grade social studies when reading tenth grade social studies materials. Students may not transfer their reading and study skills from one subject to another. That is, students may not utilize the reading skills they apply in social studies when reading science materials. Students tend to view each classroom and each subject in isolation.

The reading achievement of students deserves our attention; however, research presents mixed results. Overall, students in the United States are reading better today than students of ten to fifty years ago (Linn, Graue, & Sanders, 1990; Micklos, 1980; and Mullis & Jenkins, 1990).

From another perspective, the reading skills of students and young adults can be interpreted as being weak. Researchers have found that students are weak in utilizing inferential reading skills (Applebee, Langer, & Mullis, 1988; Kirsch & Jungeblut, 1986). Concern was also heightened by the Commission on Reading report, *Becoming a Nation of Readers* (1985). When the reading achievement of students in the United States was compared with that of students in fifteen other countries, U.S. students' achievement ranked below the international average.

Researchers have also addressed an apparent decline in literacy in America. Ravitch and Finn (1987) present the results of the National Assessment of Educational Progress (NAEP), in which students were asked 141 questions in history and 121 questions in literature. The average scores of students were 54.5 percent correct in history and 51.8 percent correct in literature. E. D. Hirsch (1987) contends that American students do not have the necessary knowledge to communicate and have a cohesive society.

With past performance in mind, will our students be able to compete in the future? Will our students be able to gain the reading skills necessary to survive in an ever-increasingly technological environment?

The most logical place to incorporate reading and thinking skills is in the content subjects. The complexity of the reading process requires you to help students plan for the reading task, assess their backgrounds of information and experiences and develop purposes for reading, and check to see if they actually have learned the material. In other words, you need to help your students before, during, and after a reading assignment.

Let's consider now what your students actually do during the complex process called reading.

THE NATURE OF THE READING PROCESS

> *A centipede ran happily*
> *Until a frog in fun*
> *Asked, "Pray, which leg comes after which?"*
> *This threw his mind in such a pitch*
> *He stood distracted in the ditch*
> *Considering how to run.*

You're as experienced in reading content area materials as that centipede was in running. But can you tell "which leg comes after which" in the reading process? Can you identify some of the difficulties teachers experience in assisting students to comprehend their content area textbooks? This section of the chapter will help you discover what happens during the complicated process called reading. It also will help you identify some of the difficulties connected with teaching content area subjects that depend on reading.

Reading as a Decoding Process

Most primary grade pupils, and students who have difficulty reading, regard reading as decoding. These pupils often define *reading* as "sounding out words." Actually, the decoding process involves mentally moving from symbols (letters) to sounds to words. To get the feel of reading as decoding, try reading the following passage.*

> But the vampire was faster. It leaped at Hal and sent him sprawling. As Hal rolled onto his back, the vampire was upon him. Its red lips curled back, showing sharp white teeth. The creature held Hal down and lowered its face over his throat. Hal struggled and kicked. He thrashed from side to side. The vampire's teeth touched Hal's neck.
>
> In an instant Lynn struck. She beat on the vampire's back with her fists. Howling, the creature let go of Hal and turned on her. Lynn leaped back and picked up a stick with a sharp point. "On my planet a stake through the heart kills a vampire," she shouted, thrusting it into his chest.

Were you successful at reading backward and upsidedown? What happened as you tried to decode these words? Did you look at individual letters? Did you say the letters of the words to yourself? Did you try to connect sounds to these letters? Maybe you broke the words into syllables or used your sense of structure and context to identify the words. Even if you were able to decode the words, the passage would be meaningless if the words were not in your vocabulary. Merely sounding out words is *not* reading.

Reading as a Visual Process

Many reading clinicians and eye specialists view reading as a visual process. They know from photographing eye movements that a reader's eyes make a series of stops, called fixations, on each line of print. The reader's eyes jump from fixation to fixation in tiny, jerky movements called saccadic movements. Some people read only one word (or even one syllable) per fixation.

Suppose a reader is averaging five fixations per line on text with about ten words per line. This reader's eye span—the number of words the reader can read in one fixation—is about two words.

You may occasionally notice a small backward eye movement that is not as pronounced as the return sweep to the next line. This shorter movement is a regression. During a regression, a reader looks back at the word or words just read.

To get the feel of reading as a visual process, try this experiment. Have a partner hold a textbook so that the top of the book is straight out from your partner's nose. Then watch the eye movements as your partner reads. The return sweep at the end of each line is easy to spot, like the return of a typewriter carriage

---

* From *Attention Span Stories: Star Trip* by Lee Mountain, Ed. D., p. 23. Copyright 1978 by Jamestown Publishers, Providence, Rhode Island. Reprinted by permission.

or a computer cursor. The saccadic movements are harder to see; they resemble tiny muscular twitches between fixations. If you watch a television news commentator reading from the teleprompter, you may see these eye movements.

Reading as a Thinking Process

Many teachers regard reading as a thinking process involving word recognition skills, literal comprehension skills, interpretation skills, and critical/creative thinking skills. These four kinds of skills can be thought of as the four dimensions of reading.

If you stare at the following optical illusion, you will notice that your perspective on it seems to shift. Similarly, your perspective on the reading process shifts as you view it with an emphasis on word recognition, literal comprehension, interpretation, or application.

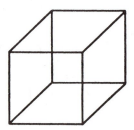

Let's consider the four dimensions of reading one by one.

Word Recognition

To experience the first dimension of reading, word recognition, glance at the word in this oval. If you recognize it, do what it says to do.

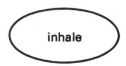

If you just took a deep breath, you demonstrated that you recognized the word without sounding it out through phonics. You recognized it without recourse to the dictionary. You read the word instantly and perfectly on the first dimension of reading—word recognition.

Now, glance at the word in this rectangle. If you recognize it, do what it says to do.

expatiate

This word may be within the recognition boundaries of your vocabulary, but it poses a recognition problem for most adults. Perhaps this experiment gives you a feeling for the recognition difficulties that content area students have with many words in their textbooks.

Literal Comprehension

Literal comprehension is the second dimension of reading. To comprehend textbook material, students need to both recognize the words and understand their meaningful groupings into phrases, clauses, sentences, and paragraphs.

Consider the word in this square on the two dimensions of recognition and literal comprehension.

lead

You can recognize it, can't you? You have seen it hundreds of times before. But can you comprehend it? No, not until you see it in context—that is, in a meaningful group of words.

Now consider these two sentences, both of which contain the word *lead:*

1. You take the *lead,* and I'll follow.
2. You take the *lead,* and I'll follow with the copper and zinc.

Did you change your mind about the pronunciation of *lead* when you finished reading the second sentence? If so, you made good use of the context to help with literal comprehension. You comprehended *lead* in terms of the rest of the sentence (especially "copper and zinc").

When you comprehend at the literal level, your mind operates like a warehouse, taking in and storing the author's material. But the mind of an efficient reader does much more than that. At higher levels of comprehension, your mind operates more like a production plant. It takes in the raw materials presented, and it processes them to create a new product—your own interpretation of the reading material.

A student who gives back exactly what was in the book is demonstrating literal comprehension. That student is mentally warehousing the author's material. But you want your students to do more than that. So you want to help your students reach the third dimension of reading—interpretation.

Interpretation

When you interpret reading material, you stop to think about what you have comprehended. You mentally process the author's ideas. Your mind becomes a production plant forming your own opinions, reactions, and conclusions about the material you have read.

The difference between literal comprehension and interpretation becomes obvious in this reading situation: Suppose both a thief and a victim see a car pull up beside them with the word *police* printed on it. In that context both the thief and his victim would literally comprehend the word *police* in the same way, as a word meaning "law enforcement officer." But would they interpret the word *police* in the same way? Hardly. The thief's interpretation would be "I'm caught." The victim's interpretation would be "I'm saved."

Critical/Creative Reading

Critical/creative reading, the fourth dimension of reading, involves producing individual ideas. Readers relate what an author says with their unique interpretation of the author's message to produce original ideas. In this dimension of reading the reader asks, "What can I do with the information I understand?"

Let's go back to our analogy of the dimensions of reading to a factory system. The literal comprehension dimension was similar to the factory warehouse. Interpretation was a new product produced from the material in the warehouse. During the critical/creative dimension, new uses are developed for the product that was manufactured during the interpretation dimension.

Reading as a Psycholinguistic Process

From birth, we develop schemata. These schemata, or frameworks of thinking and knowledge, serve as a structure for comprehension. They represent broad aspects of knowledge rather than definitions. To understand the schema (singular of schemata) of *bakery*, a student must understand many other schemata, such as *cashier, purchasing, baking, ingredients, customer,* and *goods*.

We develop meaning by using schemata. These schemata affect comprehension. They provide "file folders" for assimilating or storing new information. They help us identify what is important. They help us summarize because they can separate important ideas from nonessential. And they help us remember because we remember our interpretations, not the book. (McNeil, 1984)

We expand schemata through actual and vicarious experiences. Schemata help us construct meaning from these experiences. At the heart of many of these experiences is language. The phonological, semantic, and syntactic features of our language help us communicate and interpret messages. Let us briefly look at each of these features.

Phonology

The *phonological* feature of language is made up of phonemes and suprasegmental phonemes. *Phonemes* are the smallest significant units of sound in our language. For example, examine the word *mat.* How many sounds do you hear in it? You hear three sounds: /m/, /a/, /t/. Now look at the word *fish*. How many sounds do you hear? You see four letters; but you hear only three sounds: /f/, /i/, /sh/.

Suprasegmental phonemes, or the elements of our intonational system, give our language rhythm and melody. The three suprasegmental phonemes are pitch, stress, and juncture, described as follows:

1. Pitch refers to how high or low a sound is made. Read these sentences: READY. READY? READY! How did the meaning change as your pitch changed?

2. Stress refers to the amount of emphasis given to various words in a sentence. Read these sentences: I LOST ten dollars. I lost TEN dollars. I lost ten DOLLARS. Can you detect the different emphases?

3. Juncture refers to the slight breaks or pauses between words or sentences. Say these pairs of words: *eyelash—I lash; beatnik—beat Nick; I scream—ice cream.* The sounds are the same, but the junctures are different. Do the words in each pair have different meanings? Now say these two sentences: "Kim!" shouted Terry. Kim shouted, "Terry!" These sentences contain exactly the same words. But do they have different meanings?

Semantics

The *semantic* feature of language refers to the meanings of words or word parts and the way they are used in sentences. Morphemes are an important element when we speak about semantics. Morphemes are the smallest significant units of meaning in our language. The word *doors* has two morphemes: *door* and *s,* which makes the word plural. We call *door* a free morpheme because it has meaning by itself. We call *s* a bound morpheme because it has to be connected to another morpheme before it takes on meaning.

Because of your semantic knowledge you can identify which of the following can happen: The lake swam across the dog. The dog swam across the lake.

Syntax

The *syntactic* feature of language refers to the arrangement of words in sentences. To be meaningful, a sentence must follow a grammatical pattern. One of the grammatical patterns in English is noun-verb (e.g., Dogs bark.) Which of the following sentences follows a grammatical pattern in English?

> The painted was house.
> The was painted house.
> The house was painted.
> House painted was the.

You were able to identify the sentence that follows a grammatical pattern in English because of your experience with language. You probably were able to rearrange the words into the correct pattern in your own mind. The redundancy of the pattern in our language made this task easy for you.

As we grow and mature in our linguistic competence, we meet many redundancies. We hear the same language patterns used over and over again. The same sounds are used repeatedly when speaking. Words and word parts are used often with the same meaning. As we move into reading, the same redundancies appear on the printed page.

According to psycholinguists, because of previous experience with nonprint language and redundancies in printed language, experienced readers can get meaning from printed symbols (graphic cues) without saying all the words to themselves. They do not have to view all the letters in a word or the entire configuration of all letters in a word to read. Efficient readers select only those printed cues they need to arrive at meaning. They use their syntactic knowledge and semantic knowledge to reduce the amount of print-to-speech (graphophonic) information they need to arrive at meaning or comprehension.

Now try to read the following two sentences. Each "sentence" contains only minimal cues in each word. Yet as an efficient reader you will be able to read the material.

1. Th_ bl_ck st_ll_ _n q_ _ckl_ g_ll_p_d thr_ _gh th_ gr_ _n f_ _ lds.
2. It is evident that the jury did not have all the facts in the case.

Were you able to read these sentences? Undoubtedly, you were able to read them. You did not have to see all the letters in each word or the complete letter configurations in all words in order to read the sentences. You were able to read using minimal cues. Consonants and the skyline of letters provide us with important minimal cues when we read.

Compare this to yourself as an efficient listener. Do you have to listen to every word a speaker is saying in order to understand the message? No, you probably listen only to those auditory cues you need to arrive at the speaker's message.

Kenneth Goodman refers to the reading process as a psycholinguistic guessing game. *Psycholinguistics* is the interaction between thought and language. The reader's eyes focus on the printed material, and the reader makes guesses about the meaning of the material being read. The reader confirms or rejects the meaning. If meaning is confirmed, the reader understands the author's message. If meaning is not confirmed, the reader regresses and rereads the material.

Efficient reading does not require perfect word-by-word identification. Researchers such as Goodman have analyzed the oral reading of students. They found that errors or *miscues* (oral reading responses different from the graphic presentation of the material) often did not interfere with comprehension. Readers understood the author's messages, but changed the words or word patterns. A second type of miscue indicated that some readers did not understand the author's messages.

The following examples will help you understand the difference between the two types of miscues. In this miscue, comprehension is not affected:

Original sentence: The dog ran into the house.
Read by student: The dog ran into the home.

Comprehension *is* affected, however, by a miscue like this:

Original sentence: The dog ran into the house.
Read by student: The dog ran into the horse.

In summary, reading as a psycholinguistic process is a procedure by which the reader strives for understanding. Reading is a process of deriving meaning from the smallest number of printed cues possible. Reading is not the act of plodding from one word to the next, focusing on exact word recognition.

Reading as a Metacognitive Process

Before we identify the elements of metacognition, let's consider the following situation: Your telephone rings. When you answer it, the person at the other end tells you that you are the winner of a ten-minute shopping spree at your neighborhood supermarket.

Your task is to obtain the items you desire in ten minutes. So you write a list of the kinds and number of items you want. Obtaining these items becomes your *plan*.

Your next step is to develop a *strategy* for obtaining these items. You identify where the items are located in the store and determine the quickest and easiest way to get around the store.

You arrive at the store. All eyes are on you and your ten minutes begins. You follow your strategy and keep track of, or *monitor,* how you're doing.

Finally, when your time has elapsed, you check, or *evaluate,* to see how well you did. Did you obtain all the items you wanted? Were you missing any items? What items were you missing?

Spring (1985) provides us with a description of the metacognitive process. Metacognition has four components: planning, forming a strategy, monitoring, and evaluating.

Metareaders plan. They identify the type of text, what they already know about the topic, what they expect to learn, and what they need to do on completion of the reading assignment.

Metareaders form strategies. They set purposes for reading based on objectives, their own knowledge about the topic, and the requirements of the assignment.

Metareaders monitor how well they are doing. They are aware of whether or not they understand the material. They answer purpose-setting questions, summarize, and identify new information they have learned.

Finally, metareaders evaluate. They evaluate what they learned and how well they learned it. Metareaders may use self-testing.

The following classroom scene depicts Mr. Splot encouraging his students to verbalize their study techniques. Mr. Splot is passing back a set of tests and initiates the discussion based on a note Bob wrote at the end of his test.

Mr. Splot: Bob wrote me an interesting note at the end of the test: "The spirit is willing, but the concentration is weak." What did you mean by that, Bob?

Bob: Well, I can prove my spirit was willing to study for this test. When I was reviewing, I stayed off the phone for two hours. I went through the whole chapter. But I didn't concentrate very well, especially that second hour.

MR. SPLOT: You've spotted your problem. What can you do about it?

BOB: Take a break after an hour. I concentrate best when I first sit down to study.

MICHELLE: That's not my way. It takes me a while to get into a chapter. When I first start reading, I'm usually still thinking about what I want to buy at the mall.

MR. SPLOT: Then you've noticed how your mind works too, Michelle. How can you make it work better for you?

MICHELLE: I could read the first page twice since I know my concentration isn't that great when I start.

MR. SPLOT: Good. When you monitor yourself well, you ask yourself at the end of every page whether you have concentrated and comprehended.

TERRY: That's too general for me. I can't just ask myself if I've comprehended. I have to make myself write some notes on the material to be sure I've remembered the important points.

JONATHAN: I've noticed that I have to sit at the table, have my favorite radio station playing softly in the background, and have a bottle of my favorite soft drink on the table before I can even begin studying. Notes don't help me as much as highlighting. With highlighting, I'm marking what's important *while* I'm reading, and that really keeps me on the job when I study.

TERRY: I have to sit at my desk and have the room completely quiet. I can't stand eating or drinking anything when I study. My best technique is to try to read the teacher's mind the night before the test. I think to myself as I'm reviewing, "If I were the teacher, what questions would I ask?"

MR. SPLOT: *(handing back the tests)* You're identifying your own best methods of learning. Knowing this will help you study during the rest of this class and in other classes.

The following day Mr. Splot continued his discussion on study techniques. This time the discussion centered on study aids featured in the textbook.

MR. SPLOT: Open your books to the beginning of the next chapter, page 22. As you look at page 22, does anything stand out?

TERRY: Yes. I see words in dark print at the beginning of each section.

MR. SPLOT: What information do you think this dark print gives you?

JONATHAN: I'm not sure, but it looks like topics. And the topics seem to be organized.

MR. SPLOT: What can you do to find out if the topics are organized?

TERRY: We probably could list these topics on paper and see if we can organize them.

MR. SPLOT: That's a good idea. Try doing that and see what happens.

BOB: *(ten minutes later)* When I organized these topics, I ended up with something like an outline. I didn't even have to change the order of anything in the chapter.

MR. SPLOT: Does knowing this help you with your studying?

TERRY: Yes.

MR. SPLOT: How does it help you?

TERRY: If I look at these headings, I'll know the important topics and how the chapter is organized.

MR. SPLOT: Good. Is there anything else you notice on page 22 or in the rest of Chapter 2?

(The discussion continued with students identifying words in italics, definitions in the margins on the page, and questions at the beginning and end of each subsection.)

There are many examples of metacognitive discussions with students in educational literature. Several you might be interested in reading include Duffy and Roehler (1987, 1986), Lindquist-Sandmann (1984), Palincsar (1986), and Schwartz and Sheff (1975).

Reading as a Technological Process

Instructional technologists view reading as an interactive literacy process. Reading via computers may involve interacting with print on a monitor or logging on a telecommunications network to bring print onto a screen.

Once print is visible, electronic technology can offer the reader a variety of support systems not always available with traditional books. The computer keyboard allows the reader to interact with the print in different ways. For example, if a reader does not recognize a particular word, the reader can point to the word and the computer will say it aloud. If the word is not in the student's listening vocabulary, the student can access a definition. The student may also have the option of having the computer read a whole story aloud, varying the voices of the characters. Other options might be to explore the story's landscape, to hear a translation of the story in another language, or to hear commentary about the selection from different authorities.

Hill (1992) describes the challenges of adapting this new literacy. With prices decreasing for computers, videodisks, modems, and network usage, more and more preservice and inservice teachers are being trained to meet the challenge of presenting reading as a technological process (Mountain, 1993).

For research in the content areas, electronic aids further alter the reading process. Suppose a reader brings little background, little prior knowledge, to an encyclopedia article about George Washington. Help is built in. Most electronic encyclopedias can handle cross-referencing with a keystroke, so the reader can instantly access background information about any unfamiliar material in the article.

Instructional software that presents math word problems just won't allow the reader to make a mistake. Each response from the reader brings forth either praise or hints or guidance or correction. There is little or no motivation for metacognitive self-monitoring on the part of the reader, since the computer is doing such a thorough job of electronic monitoring.

The reading process may be altered technologically when a driver education student puts on a virtual-reality helmet. The viewing area of such a helmet makes the student feel that she is passing signs on a freeway at 50 miles an hour. The reader must get enough information from the signs to keep on route.

Such technological advances encourage students to think of reading as a highly interactive process. Anita Best (1992) suggests that electronic equipment, along with supportive teachers, can help empower students as interactive learners. Electronic literacy builds on Frank Smith's (1988) explanation of reading as mentally asking questions and finding answers. With technology, however, the process is mechanical as well as mental, and some of the answers come from the computer when the reader asks direct questions.

CONCLUSION

Reading is a complicated act that involves much more than decoding symbols. It also involves the following processes: visual, thinking, psycholinguistic, metacognitive, and technological. Merely sounding out words is not reading.

We learn about reading as a visual process from photographing eye movements. The reader's eyes make fixations and jump from fixation to fixation in saccadic movement. During a regression, readers look back at the word or words just read.

As a thinking process, reading involves word recognition, literal comprehension, interpretation, and critical/creative reading. Word recognition involves being able to read a word instantly and perfectly without use of a dictionary. Literal comprehension involves being able to recognize words and to understand their meaningful grouping into phrases, clauses, sentences, and paragraphs. Your mind stores the author's material and you give back exactly what is written in the textbook during literal comprehension. At the interpretation level you stop to think about what you have comprehended. Your mind produces opinions, reactions, and conclusions about the material read. At the critical/creative level you produce original ideas.

The psycholinguistic process is the interaction between thought and language. During the psycholinguistic process schemata help us construct meaning. The phonological, semantic, and syntactic features of our language help us communicate and interpret messages. The redundancies in our language allow us to read using minimal cues. We do not have to look at every letter or read every word on the page in order to obtain meaning.

The metacognitive process involves planning, forming a strategy, monitoring, and evaluating. Metareaders identify the reading task, form a strategy for reading the material, monitor their comprehension, and evaluate their learning.

The technological process involves interacting with computers. Computers can provide information not in the student's background, they can "pronounce" words for the student, and they can "read" the text through one or a variety of voices. Computers can assist the student who does not have the necessary skills.

From our discussion of the reading process, you were able to gain insight into the complexity of the reading process. You learned six ways of viewing reading—as a decoding process, as a visual process, as a thinking process, as a psycholinguistic process, as a metacognitive process, and as a technological process. Most people don't know that much about the reading process.

Your students, in their content area reading assignments, often are unable to cope with this complexity of the reading process. As a teacher you are faced with curriculum pressures, difficult and boring content materials, and students' incompetence; these factors will necessitate your helping students cope with their reading assignments. It can be done. It is a challenge teachers accept in order to make a difference.

POSTREADING

INTEGRATING WRITING

In your journal, describe your reactions to the view of the reading process presented in Chapter 1. Observe a young child who is learning to read, and describe your observations in terms of the reading process.

REVIEW

The following is a list of words and concepts related to Chapter 1. Organize these into categories, and be able to explain why you organized them as you did.

suprasegmental phoneme	psycholinguistic	reading process
bound morpheme	decoding	stress
symbol	miscue	morphological
fixation	morpheme	visual
literal comprehension	phonological knowledge	eye span
semantic knowledge	interpretation	saccadic
application	computers	word recognition
pitch	schemata	juncture
return sweep	graphic cues	syntactic knowledge
technological	regression	free morpheme

2

TEXTBOOK EVALUATION

"Hey, gang, I've been asked to serve on the textbook selection committee," Joe announced.

"The textbooks in my field are all alike," said Candy. "If you've seen one, you've seen 'em all. You can finish your committee work in a hurry, Joe, if you just flip a coin."

"I wouldn't say that," objected Michael. "I like to look through the table of contents and index before I select a textbook."

"Textbook publishers are a good source of information," said Roxie. "I'm sure they're capable of giving unbiased presentations of their materials."

"I've been doing a lot of reading about textbook selection and evaluation. I want to be well prepared when the committee meets." Joe pulled some forms from his briefcase. "There are a lot of factors to consider."

"Maybe you'd better tell us about some of them," said Michael. "We're going to have to teach from the textbooks your committee selects."

DISCUSS

Do textbooks in your content area meet the needs of your students? What features do you think are important when selecting a textbook for your content area?

PREORGANIZE

Go through the chapter and make a skeletal outline of the major headings and subheadings. This will provide you with a chapter organizer. Predict the contents of the text under one of these subheadings.

OBJECTIVES

After reading this chapter, you should be able to

1. discuss questions to consider when evaluating instructional materials.
2. define the terms *readability* and *readability formula*.

3. calculate the readability of textbooks using the SMOG formula, Fry graph, and Rix formula.
4. discuss the use of computers in calculating readability.
5. identify the limitations and uses of readability formulas.

GUIDELINES FOR SELECTING TEXTBOOKS

When selecting textbooks, many people look at the cover and illustrations for eye appeal, examine the durability, and check the copyright date and names of the major authors. Yet these are only minor points. Textbook publishers do market studies to determine what colors your eyes will be attracted to. Many states already have standards set for durability and page quality, standards followed by most publishers. And the textbook series probably was written by a team of people, not just the major authors listed on the title page.

Here are some of the more important questions for textbook evaluation, recommended by such authorities as Muther (1984–1985), McAndrew (1986), and Armbruster, Osborn, and Davison (1985):

1. Are students told what they are going to learn?
2. Are the concepts and vocabulary appropriate for your students?
3. What skills are taught in the textbook and how often are they reinforced?
4. Do the reinforcement activities include different teaching techniques and strategies?
5. Do the enrichment activities have students use new and different materials at the higher cognitive levels of analyzing, synthesizing, and evaluating?
6. Do the graphics clarify the concepts and ideas presented in the selection?
7. Are appropriate examples used?
8. Does the textbook have the characteristics of a good program in your content area? (You might need to look at some of the research about your subject area to answer this.)
9. Are your students moved to higher levels of concept and vocabulary development?
10. Has the program been used successfully in schools similar to yours?

TEXTBOOK EVALUATION CHECKLISTS

Understandability and learnability were identified by Davis and Irwin (1980) as two major factors to consider when evaluating textbooks. Their checklist is shown in Figure 2–1.

You can see from the Davis and Irwin checklist that examination of a text's concepts and vocabulary in relation to students' backgrounds (understandability) is imperative. Other factors include the text's organization, reinforcement, and motivation. The contents of the textbook must also be checked against the curriculum guide for your specific grade and subject.

FIGURE 2–1 • Readability Checklist

This checklist is designed to help you evaluate the readability of your classroom texts. It can best be used if you rate your text while you are thinking of a specific class. Be sure to compare the textbook to a fictional ideal rather than to another text. Your goal is to find out what aspects of the text are or are not less than ideal. Finally, consider supplementary workbooks as part of the textbook and rate them together. Have fun!

Rate the questions below using the following rating system:

5 = Excellent   2 = Poor
4 = Good   1 = Unacceptable
3 = Adequate   NA = Not applicable

Further comments may be written in the space provided at the end of the instrument.

Textbook title: _____

Publisher: _____

Copyright date: _____

UNDERSTANDABILITY

A. _____ Are the assumptions about students' vocabulary knowledge appropriate?

B. _____ Are the assumptions about students' prior knowledge of this content area appropriate?

C. _____ Are the assumptions about students' general experiential backgrounds appropriate?

D. _____ Does the teacher's manual provide the teacher with ways to develop and review the students' conceptual and experiential backgrounds?

E. _____ Are new concepts explicitly linked to the students' prior knowledge or to their experiential backgrounds?

F. _____ Does the text introduce abstract concepts by accompanying them with many concrete examples?

G. _____ Does the text introduce new concepts one at a time with a sufficient number of examples for each one?

H. _____ Are definitions understandable and at a lower level of abstraction than the concept being defined?

I. _____ Is the level of sentence complexity appropriate for the students?

J. _____ Are the main ideas of paragraphs, chapters, and subsections clearly stated?

K. _____ Does the text avoid irrelevant details?

L. _____ Does the text explicitly state important complex relationships (e.g., causality, conditionality, etc.) rather than always expecting the reader to infer them from the context?

M. _____ Does the teacher's manual provide lists of accessible resources containing alternative readings for the very poor or very advanced readers?

N. _____ Is the readability level appropriate (according to a readability formula)?

LEARNABILITY

Organization

A. _____ Is an introduction provided for in each chapter?

B. _____ Is there a clear and simple organizational pattern relating the chapters to each other?

C. _____ Does each chapter have a clear, explicit, and simple organizational structure?

Continued

FIGURE 2–1 • *Continued*

D. _____ Does the text include resources such as an index, glossary, and table of contents?

E. _____ Do questions and activities draw attention to the organizational pattern of the material (e.g., chronological, cause and effect, spatial, topical, etc.)?

F. _____ Do consumable materials interrelate well with the textbook?

Reinforcement

A. _____ Does the text provide opportunities for students to practice using new concepts?

B. _____ Are there summaries at appropriate intervals in the text?

C. _____ Does the text provide adequate iconic aids such as maps, graphs, illustrations, etc., to reinforce concepts?

D. _____ Are there adequate suggestions for useable supplementary activities?

E. _____ Do these activities provide for a broad range of ability levels?

F. _____ Are there literal recall questions provided for the students' self-review?

G. _____ Do some of the questions encourage the students to draw inferences?

H. _____ Are there discussion questions which encourage creative thinking?

I. _____ Are questions clearly worded?

Motivation

A. _____ Does the teacher's manual provide introductory activities that will capture students' interest?

B. _____ Are chapter titles and subheadings concrete, meaningful, or interesting?

C. _____ Is the writing style of the text appealing to the students?

D. _____ Are the activities motivating? Will they make the student want to pursue the topic further?

E. _____ Does the book clearly show how the knowledge being learned might be used by the learner in the future?

F. _____ Are the cover, format, print size, and pictures appealing to the students?

G. _____ Does the text provide positive and motivating models for both sexes as well as for other racial, ethnic, and socioeconomic groups?

READABILITY ANALYSIS

Weaknesses

1. On which items was the book rated the lowest?
2. Did these items tend to fall in certain categories?
3. Summarize the weaknesses of this text.
4. What can you do in class to compensate for the weaknesses of this text?

Assets

1. On which items was the book rated the highest?
2. Did these items fall in certain categories?
3. Summarize the assets of this text.
4. What can you do in class to take advantage of the assets of this text?

Source: C. S. Davis and J. W. Irwin (1980). Assessing readability: The checklist approach. *Journal of Reading, 24,* 129–130. Reprinted with permission of the International Reading Association.

Other authorities have identified various sets of criteria for use in textbook evaluation. Harker's (1977) five criteria are format and style, concept load, organization, background information, and readability. Strange and Allington (1977) identified decoding ease and conceptual difficulty as primary elements to consider when evaluating reading assignments for students. Jevitz and Meints (1979) suggested that freedom from cultural and sexual bias was important. They also recommended evaluating supplementary materials that might accompany the textbook, such as visual aids, workbooks, and teacher's manuals.

Taking a different perspective, Clary and Smith (1986) provide an appraisal sheet for readers and discuss seven points of view to take into account when selecting materials. These points of view include the concerns of students, local boards of education, district selection committees, reading educators, parents, local reading specialists, and teachers.

Blanchard and Mason (1985) suggest that computerized connections to data bases may extend the contents of textbooks. Many teachers use modems with their computers and thereby secure supplementary information. Some teachers are discovering that they need to help their students read the information (in text format) that they get from the data bases. As computers become standard classroom equipment, we will need to add computer-oriented criteria to textbook evaluation checklists. Such a checklist might include a separate category for rating the software that accompanies the text.

In selecting computer software and developing your software checklist, keep the following evaluation items in mind:

1. Be sure the software allows students enough time to respond. In fact, students should be allowed to control their own response time.
2. Be sure the vocabulary and sentence complexity are appropriate for your students.
3. The program should provide positive and immediate feedback.
4. The monitor or visual presentation should be clear and uncluttered.
5. The program should be "user friendly."
6. The software program should meet your instructional objectives.

Sirotnik (1985) suggests you consider the following questions:

1. Is the software biased or stereotyped?
2. Can the software be related to the real-life experiences of students?
3. Does the software engage students in higher-level cognitive activities?
4. Does the software encourage discovery learning, exploration, and invention?
5. Is the software integrated into the larger curriculum?
6. Does the software have provisions for individual differences in ability, learning styles, and so forth?
7. How does the software mesh with the role of teachers, peers, resource materials (pencil, paper, manipulatives), learning center activities, and so on?
8. Does the software provide for active learning on the part of the student?

READABILITY FORMULAS

Readability refers to the reading difficulty of printed materials. A book with a low readability is considered easy to read. A book with a high readability is considered difficult to read.

A readability formula is a mathematical calculation of a textbook's readability. Generally, readability is measured by using word and sentence difficulty.

After narrowing your choice of textbooks down to two or three that would do equally well in your subject, you might analyze each textbook's readability. This readability could be used as the final determining factor in your selection. Because of their ease of use, the SMOG and Rix formulas and the Fry graph will be presented in this chapter.

SMOG Formula

The SMOG formula was developed by McLaughlin (1969). Students reading at the level obtained using the SMOG formula can read the book without difficulty. For example, if your textbook's readability is grade 9 using the SMOG formula, this means that your students can read the book without help from you if their reading levels are at grade 9 or higher. If the reading levels of your students are lower than grade 9, they probably will need help from you when reading the textbook.

The SMOG formula analyzes thirty sentences from the book in question, as well as the polysyllabic words in these sentences. More specifically, the following procedure is utilized:

1. Count ten consecutive sentences from the beginning, ten from the middle, and ten from the end of the textbook. A sentence ends with a period, question mark, or exclamation point.
2. Count the number of polysyllabic words (words of three or more syllables) in each ten-sentence sample. If a word appears more than one time, it should be counted as many times as it appears.
3. Estimate the square root of the number of polysyllabic words to the nearest perfect square. For example, if you count 83 polysyllabic words, the nearest perfect square is 81. The square root of 81 is 9.
4. Add 3 to the estimated square root to arrive at the reading level.

The following list of perfect squares will aid you in using the SMOG formula:

$$\sqrt{1} = 1 \qquad \sqrt{25} = 4 \qquad \sqrt{81} = 9 \qquad \sqrt{144} = 12$$
$$\sqrt{4} = 2 \qquad \sqrt{36} = 6 \qquad \sqrt{100} = 10 \qquad \sqrt{169} = 13$$
$$\sqrt{9} = 3 \qquad \sqrt{49} = 7 \qquad \sqrt{121} = 11 \qquad \sqrt{196} = 14$$
$$\sqrt{16} = 4 \qquad \sqrt{64} = 8$$

Examples 2.1 and 2.2 will clarify the SMOG formula for you.

Example 2.1   SMOG Formula Calculations

	Number of Polysyllabic Words
First ten sentences	11
Second ten sentences	14
Third ten sentences	10
Total polysyllabic words	35
Nearest perfect square	36
Square root of 36	6
Square root + 3	9
Readability	grade 9

Example 2.2   SMOG Formula Calculations

	Number of Polysyllabic Words
First ten sentences	22
Second ten sentences	20
Third ten sentences	18
Total polysyllabic words	60
Nearest perfect square	64
Square root of 64	8
Square root + 3	11
Readability	grade 11

Fry Graph

The Fry graph originally was published in 1968 and has since been revised (Fry, 1977). If your students are reading at the level obtained using the Fry graph, they can read the book with help from you. For example, if your students are reading at the grade 6 level and you obtain a readability of grade 6 on a book when using the Fry graph this means that the students can read the book with help or instruction from you. Students reading above the readability level obtained using the Fry graph probably wouldn't need help from you.

The Fry readability graph (Figure 2–2) uses the average number of sentences and average number of syllables in three 100-word samples. Specifically, the following procedure is utilized:

FIGURE 2–2   •   Graph for Estimating Readability—Extended

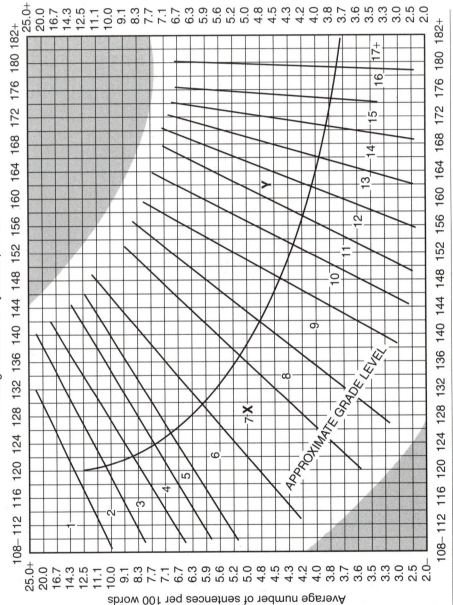

Average number of syllables per 100 words

Average number of sentences per 100 words

APPROXIMATE GRADE LEVEL

Source: E. Fry (1977). Fry's readability graph: Clarification, validity, and extension to level 17. *Journal of Reading, 21(3),* 249. This figure may be reproduced for educational purposes with the usual acknowledgment of source.

Note: Points X and Y refer to Examples 2.3 and 2.4.

1. Select a 100-word passage from the beginning, a 100-word passage from the middle, and a 100-word passage from the end of the book. "A word is defined as a group of symbols with a space on either side; thus Joe, IRA, 1945 and & are each one word" (Fry, 1977).
2. Count the number of sentences in each of the 100-word samples. A sentence ends with a period, question mark, or exclamation point. Use a decimal for partial sentences.
3. Calculate the average number of sentences in the three samples.
4. Count the number of syllables in each of the 100-word samples. A syllable is defined as a phonetic syllable. "When counting syllables for numerals and initializations, count one syllable for each symbol. For example, 1945 is 4 syllables and IRA is 3 syllables, and & is one syllable" (Fry, 1977).
5. Calculate the average number of syllables in the three samples.
6. Round off all calculations to the nearest tenth.
7. Plot the average number of syllables and the average number of sentences on the graph. The readability is found at the point of intersection.

Examples 2.3 and 2.4 will aid you in understanding the Fry graph.

Example 2.3   Fry Readability Calculations

	Sentences	Syllables per 100 Words
Sample 1	5.6	124
Sample 2	4.9	130
Sample 3	4.6	134
Total	15.1	388
Average (divide by 3)	5.0	129.3

Plot 5.0 sentences and 129 syllables on the graph in Figure 2–2. (See point **X** on the graph.)

Readability = grade 7

Example 2.4   Fry Readability Calculations

	Sentences	Syllables per 100 Words
Sample 1	4.6	156
Sample 2	5.1	161
Sample 3	4.3	170
Total	14.0	487
Average (divide by 3)	4.7	162.3

Plot 4.7 sentences and 162 syllables on the graph in Figure 2–2. (See point **Y** on graph.)

Readability = grade 12

Rix Formula

Rix (Anderson, 1983) is the third of many available readability formulas that you may utilize. Students should be reading at the readability level of the textbook analyzed using the Rix formula to read it with help from the teacher.

The Rix readability is calculated this way: (1) count a number of sentences randomly selected from throughout the book and the number of long words (seven or more characters) they contain; then (2) divide the number of long words by the number of sentences. Using this score, you can obtain the readability of your textbook. Unlike the Fry, the Rix does not involve counting syllables; and unlike the SMOG, it does not require calculating nearest perfect squares. The Rix formula is shown in Figure 2–3. Examples 2.5 and 2.6 illustrate the use of the Rix formula.

Example 2.5   Rix for Shorter Text

Number of sentences used	10
Number of long words	5
Rix score (5 ÷ 10)	.5

Locate the Rix score on the chart in Figure 2–3.

Readability = grade 3

FIGURE 2–3 • **Rix: A Simpler Version of Lix for Estimating Reading Difficulty of English Texts by Grade Level**

DIRECTIONS

1. Select a sample of sentences from the book to be analyzed. The number of samples depends in part on the size of the book and in part on the consistency of writing. As a guide: for short texts, ten samples of ten sentences each, taken regularly through the book, may be sufficient; for longer works, samples of at least twice this size will probably be required. Very short texts may be analyzed in their entirety.
2. For each total sample (excluding headings, captions, etc.):
   a. Count the number of sentences.
      A sentence is defined as a sequence of words terminated by a full-stop (period), question or exclamation mark, colon, or semicolon. However, in direct speech, sequences like "Where?" he asked, and "Go!" he ordered, count as single sentences.
   b. Count the number of long words (i.e., words of seven or more characters after excluding hyphens, punctuation marks, and brackets).
      A word is defined as a sequence of characters bounded by white spaces. Thus numbers like 1,461 and 10.2, hyphenated sequences, abbreviations (e.g., IRA, a.m.), dates such as (1981–1982), and symbols like % count as single words.
3. Determine Rix by dividing the number of long words by the number of sentences (work to two decimal places).

INTERPRETATION

To find the equivalent grade level of difficulty for Rix, locate the Rix score in the left-hand column and the corresponding grade in the right-hand column.

Rix Score	Equivalent Grade Level
7.2 and above	College
6.2 and above	12
5.3 and above	11
4.5 and above	10
3.7 and above	9
3.0 and above	8
2.4 and above	7
1.8 and above	6
1.3 and above	5
0.8 and above	4
0.5 and above	3
0.2 and above	2
Below 0.2	1

Source: J. Anderson (1983). Lix and Rix: Variations on a little-known readability index. *Journal of Reading, 26,* 495. This figure may be reproduced for educational purposes with the usual acknowledgment of source.

Example 2.6   Rix for Longer Text

Number of sentences used   50

Number of long words   150

Rix score (150 ÷ 50)   3

Locate the Rix score on the chart in Figure 2–3.

Readability = grade 8

If you have access to a computer, and readability software, the work involved in calculating readability can be greatly reduced. Basically, you "type" the text material into the computer and follow the directions on the computer program.

LIMITATIONS AND USES OF READABILITY FORMULAS

Although readability formulas serve as an aid in selecting reading materials, they do not measure the number of different concepts presented in a reading selection; the abstractness or concreteness of ideas; the organizational format of the material; the style or sentence complexity of the material; the size or style of type in the material; the experiential background of students who will read the material; or student interest in the material. Readability levels may differ significantly within textbooks (Armbruster, Osborn, & Davison, 1985). Different formulas also yield different readabilities. The Fry graph and Rix measure instructional level readability, whereas the SMOG formula measures independent reading level readability (Ball, 1976).

Despite such limitations, readability formulas are valuable for specific purposes. They can provide the teacher with a basis for selecting one of several texts being considered for a course. They provide an objective measure of a textbook's difficulty. They may help a teacher analyze the difficulty of a specific selection in a textbook. And they may be utilized as an aid in selecting materials on a variety of reading levels (Noe & Standal, 1985).

CONCLUSION

The textbook is still the major instructional tool for teaching content area subjects, so you must decide what criteria you will use in selecting textbooks. Further, you need to exercise much caution throughout the textbook selection process.

A number of factors should be considered in textbook selection. Many of these are related to the concepts and ideas presented in the textbook, reinforcement and extension of skills, and your students' backgrounds.

Another important factor is readability. Readability refers to the reading difficulty of printed materials. A readability formula is used to make mathematical calculations of a textbook's readability. In this chapter you learned how to calculate readability using the SMOG formula, which uses the number of polysyllabic words in thirty sentences, the Fry graph, which uses average sentence length and average number of syllables, and the Rix formula, which uses the number of sentences and the number of long words.

The use of computers has lessened the difficulty of calculating readability as many software programs are now available.

Readability formulas have limitations, such as not measuring the abstractness or concreteness of concepts, the number of different concepts presented, or the visual comfort of the size and style of print. As a result of these limitations, additional textbook evaluation instruments should include such items as understandability, organization, reinforcement, and motivation.

As you increase your use of computer software in the classroom, you will need to establish guidelines for selecting software programs. Response time, vocabulary and sentence complexity, positive and immediate feedback, and visual presentation are items to consider when evaluating your computer software programs.

POSTREADING

INTEGRATING WRITING

In your journal, describe your view of using both subjective and objective evaluation procedures when you select a textbook for your content area. Describe a time when you had difficulty reading a textbook. Why do you think you experienced this difficulty?

REVIEW

The following is a list of words and concepts related to Chapter 2. Organize these into categories, and be able to explain why you organized them as you did.

readability	understandability	Fry graph
formulas	SMOG	learnability
objective	subjective	Rix

PRACTICE

Do Enabling Activities 1, 2, 3, 4, and 5 in Appendix A.

3

INFORMAL READING ASSESSMENT

"Fred, I'd like to see you after class," said Mr. Luke.

"Now what did I do wrong?" wondered Fred under his breath. "I haven't been doing anything."

"Fred, you've been in my class for three weeks, and you haven't completed one assignment. What seems to be the problem?" asked Mr. Luke.

"I'm not causing any trouble in class, Mr. Luke," replied Fred.

"I know you're not disruptive, Fred," responded Mr. Luke. "You're very courteous and I appreciate that. But you'll never be able to pass this course if you don't complete your assignments."

"I would do the assignments, Mr. Luke," Fred started, "but when I just look at the material in the book, I don't understand it."

"I have an idea, Fred. I have a test I'd like you to take, but you won't receive a grade on it. Just do your very best," directed Mr. Luke. "From this test, I'll be able to find out how I might be able to help you. How about giving it a try?"

"Well, OK," Fred responded cautiously.

DISCUSS

What reasons might students have for not completing reading assignments? What questions might you ask students to determine what "reading" means to them?

PREORGANIZE

Go through the chapter and make a skeletal outline of the major headings and subheadings. This will provide you with a chapter organizer. Predict the contents of the text under one of these subheadings.

OBJECTIVES

After reading this chapter, you should be able to

1. define these four reading levels:

    independent level
    instructional level
    frustration level
    capacity (listening comprehension) level

2. construct, administer, score, and interpret the results of a cloze procedure and a maze test.
3. identify the metacognitive differences between good and poor readers.
4. identify questions that can be used to identify students' metacognitive abilities.
5. identify possibilities for motivating your students.
6. use interest inventories to identify the interests of students in your classes.
7. describe what a portfolio is and how you can use portfolio assessment in your content area.

INFORMAL READING ASSESSMENT: DEFINITIONS

Informal assessment may take the form of observation of students' daily performance (Blanton, Farr, & Tuinman, 1972), or it may take the form of a test, either a teacher-constructed test or a purchased informal instrument. (An informal test does not have established norms and has not been standardized.)

Before reading about the various informal reading procedures presented in this chapter, you should be familiar with the definitions of several terms used in informal assessment. These include the following "levels" of reading:

*   *Independent level:* The independent reading level is the level at which students may read material without previous instruction by the teacher. Students have little or no difficulty reading the words or understanding the vocabulary, and they have excellent comprehension of the material they read. This is the level at which supplementary and recreational reading materials should be assigned to students.
*   *Instructional level:* The instructional reading level is the level at which students may read material with aid from the teacher. Students may have some difficulty reading some of the words, knowing the meanings of words, and/or comprehending the material.
*   *Frustration level:* The frustration level is the level at which students cannot benefit from instruction with a particular material. Students are unable to pronounce many of the words; they may not know the meaning of many of the words; and/or they may be unable to comprehend the material they read.
*   *Capacity level:* The capacity level is often referred to as the listening comprehension level or reading potential level. It is the highest level at

which students can comprehend material which is read *to* them. It is the level at which listeners achieve at least 70 percent comprehension. Students understand words, their relationships, and concepts when listening to material read orally, but may be unable to recognize or comprehend them in print.

INFORMAL ASSESSMENT TECHNIQUES

You're faced with 120 new students on the first day of the school year. How will you ever get to know these students? How long will it take you to learn which students can read your textbook easily and which students struggle with every other word? The following informal procedures will help you identify the reading levels of these students during the first few days of the term.

Cloze Procedure

One informal testing procedure is the cloze procedure. Wilson Taylor is credited with developing this procedure, which he first presented at an Association for Education in Journalism convention workshop in 1953. Soon after, a description of the technique appeared in the *Journalism Quarterly* (Taylor,1953).

Originally, cloze was intended as a new approach to readability. It derived its name from the term *closure,* which refers to the tendency of human beings to complete a pattern that is familiar but not quite finished. In language, people will complete an incomplete sentence. For example, most people reading or hearing the sentence, "Don't make a mountain out of a _____" would fill in the blank with the word *molehill.*

Taylor (1953, 1956) and Bormuth (1968) describe the cloze readability procedure. Basically, the procedure involves selecting passages whose difficulty is to be determined, replacing every fifth word in the passage with blanks of equal length, administering the tests to students who have not read them before by having them fill in the blanks with the word they think was deleted, and scoring the responses. Students have made a successful "cloze" if they complete the blank with the correct word.

To construct a cloze test follow these steps (Rankin & Culhane, 1969):

1. Select a passage of about 250–300 words that is representative of the text's difficulty. Use entire paragraphs, not portions of paragraphs.
2. Be sure the passage is from the front of the book and one the students have not seen before. A passage from the middle or end of the book might contain information requiring knowledge from the beginning of the book.
3. Beginning with the second full sentence, delete every fifth word.
4. Do not delete words from the first or last sentence in the selection.
5. Retype the passage leaving blanks of equal length (fifteen or twenty spaces) in place of the deleted words.

6. Have students read the passage themselves and fill in the words they think belong in the blank spaces.

7. Count the number of correct responses. A correct response is a word that is the same as the original word. Ekwall and Shanker (1983) recommend using a plastic overlay to aid in scoring cloze tests.

8. Determine the percentage of correct responses.

9. Ascertain the difficulty of the selection for students.
   Independent level: 61–100% correct
   Instructional level: 41–60% correct
   Frustration level: 0–40% correct

To determine the student's percentage of correct responses, divide the number of correct responses by the total number of blanks. For example, if there were 46 blanks and the student completed 24 correctly, the percentage of correct responses would be 52 (24 ÷ 46 = .52).

If a student scores poorly on a cloze test, you don't know whether it's because the student doesn't comprehend the material or doesn't know how to decode the words. A simple way to check for this is to have students who score poorly read the passage aloud. Students who make many oral reading errors are having difficulty decoding the words.

On the surface the cloze procedure may appear to be the same as a sentence completion or fill-in-the-blank test; however, if you look more critically, you will notice differences. In sentence completion tests, the words are omitted after being pre-evaluated. In cloze, words are deleted systematically; there is no pre-evaluation involved. In sentence completion, whole phrases or clauses may be deleted. In cloze, only one word is deleted at a time. Example 3.1 presents a cloze test with the correct answers included.

Taking a cloze test probably will be a new experience for your students. Let your students practice on a couple of paragraphs before taking the actual cloze test. Remind your students to read the entire passage before they try to fill in the blanks; the remainder of the passage might give them clues to some of the word deletions. Review the correct answers with your students. Ask students who correctly replaced the word to tell the rest of the class how they arrived at the answer.

Note that there is no time limit on taking a cloze test. You should therefore provide additional activities for students who finish early.

Teachers often ask why only exact replacements are accepted as correct answers. First, it would take a very long time to score tests if you tried to identify correct synonyms on each student's paper. Second, McKenna (1976) found no significant difference in the reading level placements of students whether exact replacements or synonyms were counted as correct.

Readence, Bean, and Baldwin (1981) identified another use of the cloze procedure for readability purposes. Select your textbook on the basis of how well students can read it. A textbook at a majority of your students' independent level is too easy for your class. A textbook at a majority of your students' frustration level will be too difficult.

Example 3.1   Cloze Test with Correct Answers

In June of 1702, I, Lemuel Gulliver, ship's surgeon, went on board the ship *Adventure*, bound for the Cape of Good Hope. In a storm that _*lasted*_ for twenty days, we _*were*_ blown so far off _*course*_ that the oldest sailor _*aboard*_ could not tell in _*what*_ part of the world _*we*_ were.

But our food _*held*_ out well, and our _*ship*_ was strong, so the _*main*_ thing we needed was _*fresh*_ water. When we spotted _*land*_ , the captain sent out _*a*_ dozen men in a _*longboat*_ , with buckets of water. _*I*_ went with them so _*that*_ I could see the _*country*_ .

On the shore we _*spread*_ out and went exploring. _*I*_ hoped to find some _*fresh*_ water near the sea, _*but*_ there was no sign _*of*_ a river or spring. _*I*_ walked alone to a _*part*_ of the shoreline that _*was*_ bare and rocky. There _*I*_ climbed a hill from _*which*_ I could see most _*of*_ the beach.

And what should _*meet*_ my eyes, but the _*sight*_ of my shipmates rowing _*back*_ to the *Adventure* without _*me!*_ I was about to _*shout*_ to them when I _*saw*_ a huge creature walking _*after*_ them in the sea. _*The*_ water was barely up _*to*_ his knees! He was _*taller*_ than a church steeple!

*But* the men were almost _*back*_ to the ship. I _*could*_ see that they would _*get*_ away, but I dared _*not*_ think what this meant _*for*_ me. Suppose this giant turned back and spotted me.

Source: From "Gulliver in the Land of the Giants," in *Jamestown Heritage Readers, Book F,* pp. 204–205, by L. Mountain, S. Crawley, & E. Fry. Copyright 1991 by Jamestown Publishers, Providence, Rhode Island. Reprinted by permission.

Suppose you use a readability formula on six textbooks and also examine them for motivation, understandability, learnability and reinforcement (Davis & Irwin, 1980). You are able to eliminate three texts, but three still remain. Which text would you choose?

Your next step is to develop cloze tests for the three texts still remaining. Then administer these cloze tests to the classes who will use the text. Suppose the students in these classes have the following scores on the cloze tests for the three textbooks (you will have more scores using actual classes).

Book 1: 21, 58, 33, 19, 68, 25, 11, 61, 40, 18
Book 2: 71, 49, 83, 65, 37, 69, 77, 29, 73, 84
Book 3: 43, 56, 88, 21, 49, 76, 33, 54, 61, 42

Which textbook would you select? The average percentage of comprehension for students in Book 1 is 35.4. Two students are at the independent level, seven at the frustration level, and one at the instructional level. The average percentage of comprehension for students in Book 2 is 63.7. Seven students are at the independent level, two at the frustration level, and one at the instructional level. The average percentage of comprehension for students in Book 3 is 52.3. Three students are at the independent level, two at the frustration level, and five at the instructional level.

Clearly, Book 3 is the best choice. The average percentage of comprehension is at the instructional level using cloze procedure criteria. Book 1 is too difficult, and Book 2 is too easy.

Maze Technique

The maze technique is an offshoot of the cloze procedure. It was originally developed by Guthrie (1973) to study sentence comprehension and the use of syntactic cues during silent reading. During this study Guthrie found a correlation of .85 between the maze test and the Gates-MacGinitie Vocabulary Test, and a correlation of .82 between the maze test and the Gates-MacGinitie Comprehension Test. The maze test also had a high reliability (.90 to .93).

In a later study, Guthrie and others (1974) described the construction of, and guidelines for using, the maze technique. The following steps should be followed in the construction of a maze test:

1. Select a passage of about 120 words that represents the text's difficulty.
2. Beginning with the second sentence, delete every fifth word. The first sentence in the passage should remain intact.
3. Replace each deleted word with a multiple choice.
   a. One choice should be the correct word.
   b. Another choice should be an incorrect word that is the same part of speech (noun, verb, modifier, function word).
   c. A final choice should be an incorrect word that is a different part of speech.
4. Retype the passage and replace each deleted word with its three multiple choice options.
5. Have students read the passage silently and circle the word they think belongs in place of the deleted word.
6. Count the number of correct responses. A correct response is the original word that was deleted.
7. Determine the percentage of correct responses.
8. Ascertain the difficulty of the selection for students.

Independent level:	85–100% correct
Instructional level:	60–84% correct
	60–70% correct (optimal level)
Frustration level:	below 60% correct

Example 3.2 shows a maze test with correct answers indicated.

There are 25 possible correct answers in the following maze test. Divide 25 into the number of correct responses to get the percentage of correct responses. If a student had 16 correct answers, the student's score would be 64 percent (16 ÷ 25 = .64). This student would be at the optimal instructional level using maze scoring criteria.

Any students who perform poorly on the maze test should read the passage, or a list of words contained in the passage, to the teacher, who can then compare the maze test percentage with the oral reading or word recognition percentage. If the maze percentage is 20 percentage points or more lower than the oral reading or word recognition score, comprehension is a major problem for the student (Guthrie, 1974).

As with the cloze test, remember to provide additional activities for those student who finish early, so that those students will not be sitting idly while waiting for other students to complete the test.

METACOGNITION AND INFORMAL DIAGNOSIS

In an extensive review of literature on metacognition, Wong (1986) found that poor readers were similar to young readers in their views of reading. Both young readers and poor readers viewed reading as a decoding rather than a metacognitive task. Both groups failed to see reading as a process of developing understanding. Garner and Kraus (1981–1982) provide us with further insights into how good and poor comprehenders approach reading. Good and poor comprehenders in grade 7 were interviewed about how they approached reading. These three key questions were used in the interviews:

1. What things does a person have to do to be a good reader?
2. If I gave you something to read right now, how would you know if you were reading it well?
3. What makes something difficult to read?

There were marked differences between the answers of good comprehenders and poor comprehenders to these questions. Good readers' responses to things a person must do to be a good reader included get the ideas, picture things in your mind, understand what you're reading, comprehend the important stuff. Poor readers, on the other hand, responded to the same question with work hard, know all the words, learn new words, and pronounce the words right. It is apparent that good readers view reading as a process of comprehension; poor readers view reading as word identification.

In response to knowing if they were reading well, good comprehenders viewed reading as a process of understanding whereas poor readers viewed reading in a mechanical way. The responses of good readers included getting the big ideas,

Example 3.2   Maze Test with Correct Answers

Student's Name _____   **Date** _____

A nurse came in with a baby about a year old in her arms.

(me)   I'm
When the baby spied I'm , he yelled to have (me) for a plaything.

        they   they
uncle   it   it's
The swift , being very foolish, put (me) toward the baby, within (his) reach.
(mother)   last   shoe

        I   (into)   threw
Suddenly he seized dog and put my head outside his mouth. But I (screamed) so
    (me)   last   now

    went   fly   boat
loudly that he (got) frightened and let me (drop.) I should certainly have lost
        hat   net   (broken)

        it   (nurse)   in
all my bones in (the) fall had not the nanny put out her apron (to) catch me.
        one   float   hat

        we   (in)   lights
The one (I) grew to like best related the family was the next daughter. She
            horse   by   (older)
        (bed)   post   (called)
made a box for me from the (cradle) in her dollhouse. I yelled her
    wishing   barking   light
            (nurse)   farms   saw
Glumdalclitch, or little doll , and she took very bad care of me. She (was) very
                wept   (good)   hand
            (and)   blue
good with needle in thread and made me one new shirts.
                a   (seven)

Source: From "Gulliver in the Land of the Giants," in *Jamestown Heritage Readers, Book F,* p. 207, by L. Mountain, S. Crawley, & E. Fry. Copyright 1991 by Jamestown Publishers, Providence, Rhode Island. Reprinted by permission.

understanding what is said, understanding without reading the material over and over again, and not having trouble getting the main point. Poor comprehenders responded with knowing all the words, reading fluently out loud, not pausing too much, and pronouncing all the words correctly.

The elements that make something difficult to read were also viewed differently by good and poor comprehenders. Good comprehenders identified being unfamiliar with the material, technical terms that don't have meaning to them, subjects that are hard to understand, and badly written material in which the ideas are hard to identify, as making material difficult to read. Poor comprehenders identified characteristics related to individual words, such as small print, long words, a lot of big words, and "weird," intellectual words as making material difficult to read. Asking students these three questions,

1. What things does a person have to do to be a good reader?
2. If I gave you something to read right now, how would you know if you were reading it well?
3. What makes something difficult to read?

can provide you with insight into whether students regard reading as a metacognitive process.

Wong's (1986) review also highlighted the poor reader's inability to identify inconsistencies within written materials. When asked if passages containing conflicting information needed to be rewritten, poor readers indicated there was no need for rewriting. Good readers, on the other hand, recognized the need for rewriting.

Wong and Jones (1982) provide us with a five-part procedure for self-monitoring. You can use this method to assess students' self-monitoring behavior:

1. Why are you studying this passage?
2. Find the main idea or main ideas in the paragraph and underline it (them).
3. Think of a question on the main idea you have underlined. (A good question targets the main idea and paraphrases it.)
4. Learn the answer to your question.
5. Always look back at the questions and answers to see how each successive question and answer adds more information for you.

The summarizing ability of good and poor readers in grade 8 was studied by Winograd (1984). Winograd found that both good and poor readers understood what *summary* meant. Both groups of students understood that a summary contained the most important ideas in the original passage.

Winograd (1984) found that good readers, beyond knowing the basic definition of *summary,* were better judges of important information than poor readers. Good readers used textual importance in identifying important information. Poor readers' selections of important information were based on details that they could visualize and that were of interest to them. Another interesting finding was that there was no strong relationship between what poor readers thought was important and what they wrote in their summaries.

In addition to surveying how students approach reading by having them apply a self-monitoring procedure and by observing their summary-writing ability, you also can observe students' nonverbal and verbal signals. Garner and Reis (1981) highlight the following verbal and nonverbal expressions that signify a lack of comprehension: making faces, shrugging shoulders, rolling eyes, shaking the head, and making verbal comments such as, "That's a hard one; can we skip it?"

MOTIVATION AND INTERESTS

Motivation is a person's incentive or drive to learn or engage in an activity. Students' motivation to learn will affect their interests and achievement. Frymier (1985) identified these five characteristics of motivated learners that a teacher can observe:

1. *Perception of time*—Motivated students use time in realistic ways. They are aware of the present, past, and future; but they are not fearful or preoccupied with time.
2. *Openness to experiences*—Motivated students reach out for, and are open to, new experiences.
3. *Self-concept*—Motivated students seem to feel that they are important and worthwhile. They have a clearer conception of who they are than unmotivated students.
4. *Values*—Motivated students tend to value abstract and theoretical ideas.
5. *Tolerance of ambiguity*—Motivated students often are attracted to things that lack clarity or that are unknown or novel.

Seven factors that affect the development of interests were also identified by Frymier (1985). As a teacher, you can control many of these factors.

1. *Previous experience*—Students won't develop interest in something if they have never experienced it.
2. *Self-concept*—If students feel threatened by information, they will reject it. If they see information as useful or helpful, however, they will accept it as improving the self.
3. *Values*—Students' interests are aroused if they feel the subject matter is presented by people they think are "authorities."

4. *Meaningfulness of the subject matter*—If students see information as making sense, rather than as bits and pieces of meaningless information, it will interest them more.
5. *Sequencing, pacing, spacing, and repeating*—Teachers need to recognize the individual differences of their students. What's good for one student isn't necessarily good for another.
6. *Degree of compulsion involved*—If students feel that they have some degree of choice, and less compulsion, their interest probably will be higher.
7. *Complexity of subject matter*—Students who are more intellectually able and psychologically flexible are more attracted to complexity than simplicity.

Curriculum materials also affect students' interests. Frymier (1985, p. 16) lists nine questions you should consider when selecting curriculum materials.

1. Is the . . . material attractive or plain?
2. Is the material stimulating . . . or calming?
3. Does the . . . material evoke reaction and response . . . or is it routine?
4. Are the examples . . . provocative? Do the examples stimulate thought or reaction or response of some kind?
5. Is there marked contrast in color, sound, organization, or conceptualization?
6. Is the . . . material unique or is it ordinary?
7. Is the material complex, intricate, and involved or is it simple and uniform?
8. Does the material provide immediate feedback to the learner, or is feedback not available?
9. Is the curriculum material activity-oriented or is it passivity-oriented?

If students are reading motivating materials centered around their interests, they will be more inclined to pursue topics in greater depth and contribute to class activities. Of course, getting a true reading of students' interests is not easy. You may use daily observation or administer an interest inventory to aid in the selection of materials and to capitalize on student interests. If you use an interest inventory, you should be alert to students possibly writing what they think you want to read rather than their true feelings. Examples 3.3 through 3.7 are samples of interest inventories you can develop for your class.

You might administer an interest inventory at the beginning of the school year to identify your students' interests. You can then draw on these interests in developing examples to use with your content area and in guiding students to books and other materials for additional reading or reports.

Example 3.3   General Interest Inventory

1. What video games do you like to play?
2. What pets do you have?
3. What clubs or organizations do you belong to?
4. What hobbies do you have?
5. How much time do you spend watching TV each day?
6. What are your favorite TV programs?
7. Do you listen to the radio? What radio programs do you enjoy listening to?
8. What magazines do you enjoy reading?
9. What job or career are you interested in?
10. Where would you like to travel?
11. What sports do you like?
12. Do you like to see plays performed on stage?
13. What sections of the newspaper do you read?
14. Do you enjoy reading books for pleasure? What book(s) have you recently read?
15. What kinds of books do you like to read?
16. What school subjects do you like?

Example 3.4   Literature Interest Inventory

1. Do you read comic books? Which ones?
2. What magazines do you read?
3. Which newspaper sections do you like best? Which sections do you like least?
4. Check the topics you would like to read about.

adventure	entertainment	music
animals	fairy tales	mystery
arts and crafts	fashion	plays
aviation	financial news	poetry
biographies	folktales	political news
comics	government	radio
computers	headlines	space
cooking	history	sports
crime	homemaking	store advertisements
detective stories	humor	travel
drama	jobs or employment	war
editorials	love stories or romance	westerns

5. List other topics of interest to you:

Example 3.5   Science Interest Inventory

1. Do you watch science programs on TV? Which ones?
2. Do you like to do experiments in science?
3. Do you like to listen to guest speakers in science?
4. Do you like to see films and filmstrips in science?
5. Do you like to view videotapes in science?
6. Do you like to listen to lectures in science?
7. Do you like to make models in science?
8. Which of the following do you like to read about in science? Put a check beside those you like.

aeronautics	conservation and ecology	nuclear power
animals	geography	nutrition
anthropology	geology	oceans
astronomy	genetics	planes
automation	insects	planetariums
biology	light and sound	plants
birds	lives of scientists	scientific equipment
birth	machines	space
careers in science	medicine and disease	weather
chemistry	meteorology	zoos

9. Other topics you like to read about:

Example 3.6   Social Studies Interest Inventory

1. What news magazines (like, Time) do you enjoy reading?
2. What news-related television programs do you enjoy watching?
3. Do you like to listen to guest speakers in social studies?
4. Do you like to make reports in social studies?
5. Do you like to see films and filmstrips in social studies?
6. Do you like to view videotapes in social studies?
7. Do you like to listen to lectures in social studies?
8. Do you like to work on group projects in social studies?
9. Do you like to make models in social studies?
10. Do you like to make maps in social studies?

11.   Which of the following topics in social studies do you like to read about? Put a check beside those you like.

Australia and New Zealand
biographies
Canada
careers
China
cities
colonial life
communication
community services
comparative community
    studies
conservation
contributions of ethnic
    groups
desert regions
Eastern Europe and
    Russia
economics
education
energy

equal rights
Europe
exploration and
    colonization
families
first Americans
future
geography
government
Greece and Rome
holidays
India and Pakistan
interdependence
Latin America
law
medical advances
Mexico
middle ages
Middle East
North Africa

nuclear war
Old World
Orient
pioneer life
producing food,
    shelter, clothing
recreation
regions of the United States
religions
rural and urban communities
South Africa
South America
state histories
Third World countries
transportation
war
Western Europe
westward movement
world hunger

12.   List other topics of interest to you:

_____

Example 3.7   **Math Interest Inventory**

1.   Place a check beside the following things you like to do.

count
add
subtract
multiply
divide
work with geometric shapes
compute probability

calculate area and perimeter
work with fractions
measure objects
read and write Roman
    numerals
measure rays and angles

2.   Place a check beside the activities you enjoy.

measuring a room for a new carpet
playing Monopoly
developing computer programs
reading about mathematicians
estimating a budget

balancing a checkbook
playing Blackjack
playing cribbage
running computer programs
calculating the distance for a trip

3.   Check the math-related things in which you're interested.

income tax	basketball standings
sales	weather charts
budgets	maps and globes
stock market	measuring ingredients
football standings	building scale models
baseball standings	drafting
geoboards	computers
solving problems	

4.   List other math-related activities in which you are interested:

PORTFOLIO ASSESSMENT

Maybe you have heard about portfolio assessment; perhaps your school district is using or considering using it. You may have wondered what it is, asking yourself, "What is a portfolio? What is portfolio assessment?"

Think of an artist. An artist puts together a collection of her best work and presents it when seeking a job. She has put together a portfolio. Think of yourself applying for a job. You may put together a collection of materials that includes transcripts, letters of recommendation, the program of a conference at which you made a presentation (McDaniel & Mountain, 1993), the school newspaper on which you served as editor or reporter, pretest/posttest results of students you have tutored, and a unit you developed and taught along with pictures of students engaging in activities from your unit. You have put together a portfolio of your accomplishments.

Portfolio assessment is a systematic process of collecting a student's work for the purpose of showing progress over an extended period of time, not just the immediate moment. Coffman and Sharpe (1993) identify the following characteristics of portfolios:

1.   A portfolio is a collection of student's work over a period of time.
2.   Physically, portfolios are larger than a report card, but smaller than a steamer trunk.
3.   Portfolios are more closely tied to instruction than traditional forms of assessment.
4.   Portfolios foster a collaborative partnership between teachers and students.
5.   Portfolios should be graded (through use of descriptions that illustrate strengths and needs, or a combination of a grade and description).

Portfolios contain a variety of items to sample students' daily work over an extended period of time. These items might include, but are not limited to, written reports, essays, artistic work (music, photographs, illustrations, video and audio

TABLE 3–1 • Portfolio Assessment versus Standardized Testing

Portfolio Assessment	*Standardized Testing*
Occurs in the child's natural environment	Is an unnatural event
Provides an opportunity for student to demonstrate strengths as well as weaknesses	Provides a summary of child's failures on certain tasks
Gives hands-on information to the teacher on the spot	Provides little diagnostic information
Allows the child, parent, teacher, staff to evaluate the child's strengths and weaknesses	Provides ranking information
Is ongoing, providing multiple opportunities for observation and assessment	Is a one-time "snapshot" of a student's abilities on a particular task
Assesses realistic and meaningful daily literacy tasks	Assesses artificial tasks that may not be meaningful to the child
Invites the child to be reflective (metacognitive) about work and knowledge	Asks child to provide a singular, desired response
Invites the parent to be reflective of child's work and knowledge	Provides parent with essentially meaningless and often frightening numerical data
Encourages teacher-student conferencing	Forces teacher-administration conferences
Informs instruction and curriculum; places child at center of the educational process	Reinforces idea that the curriculum is the center of the educational process

Source: From *Portfolio Assessment: Getting Started* by A. A. DeFina, p. 39. Copyright © 1992, Scholastic. Reprinted by permission of Scholastic Inc.

productions, and so on), lab experiment results, workbook pages, journal entries, interest surveys, reading lists, book reviews, and tests and quizzes.

DeFina's (1992) comparison between portfolio assessment and standardized testing is shown in Table 3–1.

Portfolios can give students a purpose for doing assignments. As they review their portfolios, they see growth in their performance and skill acquisition. They can thus see reasons for doing particular assignments. Students and teachers can ascertain whether previously learned material is being integrated with new learning.

Utilizing portfolios helps establish rapport between students and teachers. Through conferencing, students' progress can be discussed, suggestions for further growth through application to different situations can be made. Further, teachers can gain better insight into students' use of higher-level thinking skills.

Using portfolios can result in more creative grading structures, grading structures that move away from the strict A, B, C system. Report cards can be narrative or a combination of narrative and grade. Criteria such as rating scales can be established, rather than strict 0 to 100 test percentages. If students merely give back dates and events on a social studies assignment, they might receive a 1; if they give evidence of new insights or application to different situations, they might receive a 10.

DeFina (1992) cautions that you should know your goals and understand your purpose prior to incorporating portfolio assessment into your classroom. You should be able to explain why and how portfolios provide you and your students with a better system of purpose setting and evaluation.

CONCLUSION

There are four terms with which you should be familiar in informal reading assessment. The independent reading level is the level at which students can read material without assistance from the teacher. The instructional level is the level at which students should be taught. The frustration level is the level at which students will not benefit from instruction. The capacity level is a student's listening comprehension or potential level.

Two informal assessment techniques help identify reading level. The cloze procedure involves deleting every fifth word from a 250-word passage and having students supply the correct word. The maze technique is similar to cloze except it is shorter and multiple choices are used instead of blank spaces.

Students' metacognitive abilities can be assessed through questioning. Generally, poor readers view reading as a decoding process whereas good comprehenders emphasize looking for meaning.

Motivation and interests play an important part in students' achievement. You can identify motivated students and control some of the factors that affect the development of interests. You can administer interest inventories to identify the specific interests of your students.

The portfolio is a means of assessment that involves more than grading using an A, B, C system. A portfolio is a collection of a student's work over a broad spectrum of areas. Using portfolios involves assessing student progress over a long period of time.

POSTREADING

INTEGRATING WRITING

In your journal, describe which assessment procedure would be most effective in your content area. How might you use portfolio assessment?

REVIEW

The following is a list of words and concepts related to Chapter 3. Organize these into categories, and be able to explain why you organized them as you did.

informal assessment	instructional	cloze procedure
independent	portfolio	motivation
informal techniques	frustration	metacognition
interest inventory	maze test	functional reading levels

PRACTICE

Do Enabling Activity 6 in Appendix A.

4

VOCABULARY DEVELOPMENT

Joyce strode into the teachers' lounge, muttering, "Words, words, words."

"Are you quoting Shakespeare?" Stephanie asked innocently. "Or are you reacting to our students' vocabulary scores on the standardized tests?"

Ann moaned, "I'm tired of hearing about those test scores. I don't have to be concerned with vocabulary. I teach music."

"Don't underrate yourself, Ann," said Joyce, "You teach vocabulary every day—the vocabulary of music. You teach your students notes and time signatures; and your students need to read and understand the meanings of words in songs."

"I'm going to stop worrying about teaching to those tests," said Stephanie. "From now on I'm going to concentrate on teaching the important words and concepts in each chapter. I'll be under a lot less stress; and I don't think it will have a negative impact on any test results."

"I think you have a good point," said Joyce. "We'll all be a lot better off if we forget about these tests and teach what's important in our own classes. I bet it will be a lot more relevant for students also."

DISCUSS

How does knowing the meanings of words influence comprehension? In what ways might the vocabulary in your content area pose a problem to students? What do you think is the best way to learn vocabulary?

PREORGANIZE

Go through the chapter and make a skeletal outline of the major headings and subheadings. This will provide you with a chapter organizer. Predict the contents of the text under one of these subheadings.

OBJECTIVES

After reading this chapter, you should be able to:

1. formulate a rationale for teaching vocabulary in content areas.
2. describe principles of vocabulary instruction.
3. identify and give examples of eight ways in which words change meanings or are added to our language.
4. identify examples of figures of speech.
5. define and give examples of the various word relations.
6. develop a deductive and an inductive lesson for teaching a concept in your content area.
7. describe and demonstrate the use of vocabulary strategies that promote visual images.
8. develop and demonstrate strategies for teaching vocabulary using categorization.
9. identify and write an example of each of the nine types of semantic context clues.
10. describe and present lessons using at least one strategy for teaching context clues.
11. develop a lesson for teaching structural analysis.
12. define the following terms:

amelioration	specialization	acronym
pejoration	euphemism	borrowing
generalization	coining	contextual analysis
synonym	homonym (homophone)	multiple meanings
antonym	homograph	denotative
association	analogy	connotative
classification	concept	hyperbole
irony	metaphor	onomatopoeia
oxymoron	personification	simile

VOCABULARY GROWTH

Vocabulary development is essential for success in content area subjects. Comprehension is largely dependent on your students' understandings of the many concepts and words they will encounter while reading content area materials. This section of the chapter provides some background on the size of students' vocabularies versus the requirements of content area materials, and presents guidelines for vocabulary development.

Vocabulary Size

Have you ever wondered how large your vocabulary is? You might think that it would be easy to calculate. Yet it is quite complex. Are you talking about expressive vocabulary (speaking and writing), or are you talking about receptive vocabulary (listening and reading)? How are you going to count or measure vocabulary? Will you tape-record people talking and count the different words they say? Maybe you will count all the words people write. Or, perhaps you will count all the words on a vocabulary test. Will you count only basic vocabulary (*lock*) or will you count total vocabulary, which includes all forms of the basic word (e.g., *locks, locking, unlock, relock, lockjaw, lockmaker, locknut, locksmith, lockout, lockup*).

A number of studies have been conducted estimating the number of words students know. Smith (1941) estimated the basic vocabulary of students in grades 1, 6, and 12 to be 17,000, 32,000, and 47,000, respectively. Dale (1965) estimated the basic vocabulary of students in grades 1, 6, and 12 to be 2,500–3,000, 8,000, and 14,000–15,000, respectively. In a later study, Graves (1986) estimated that entering grade 1 students have listening vocabularies of 10,000 words.

Several recent studies have estimated the number of different words students read. You will notice the very rapid increase from grades 1 through 12. At the end of grades 1 and 4, students read about 4,000 and 14,000 words, respectively (White, Graves, & Slater, 1990). By the time students are in grade 7 and toward the end of grade 12, they read approximately 25,000–50,000 and 40,000–80,000 words, respectively (Miller & Gildea, 1987). However, materials read by students in high school contain over 100,000 different words (Nagy, Herman, & Anderson, 1984).

Herein is a rationale for teaching vocabulary in your content area. You easily can observe the large discrepancy between students' reading vocabularies and the number of different words found in materials read by those students.

Guidelines for Vocabulary Development

Vaughan, Crawley, and Mountain (1979) reviewed research on vocabulary teaching and arrived at three guidelines: (1) teach directly, not incidentally; (2) categorize words; and (3) use strategies to promote mental imagery.

In an extensive review of literature, Tomas (1977) concluded that any direct teaching of vocabulary appeared to produce better results than assuming that students will learn vocabulary on their own. Studies by Traxler (1938) and Eichholz and Barbe (1961) support the view that direct vocabulary teaching is better than incidental learning.

The categorization of words as an aid to memory is supported by the research of organizational memory theorists. Manis (1966), Asch (1969), Rundus (1971), and Reynolds and Flagg (1977) are only a few of the psychologists whose research supports the categorization of words as a teaching aid.

Promoting mental images has been supported by the research of Paivio (1971), Reynolds and Flagg (1977), and Jiganti and Tindall (1986). Words that produce high mental images *(elephant, car)* were found by Wolpert (1972) to be easier to retain than those that produce either low images or no images *(the, there)*.

Nelson-Herber (1986) provides us with these additional generalizations about vocabulary instruction:

1. Students' vocabularies have strong relationships to their reading comprehension.
2. Learning vocabulary through context may be more effective than teaching using definitions.
3. Using students' backgrounds of knowledge is more effective than using definitions.
4. Involving learners in the learning process is more effective than memorizing definitions.

In a review of research on teaching vocabulary, Blanchowicz (1985) presented the following guidelines for vocabulary instruction:

1. Introduce vocabulary in related sets to build a schema or structure for teaching and learning new words. (In other words, categorize vocabulary.)
2. Involve the learner in the learning process. Don't just tell the student the definition.
3. Teach the most usable vocabulary. Use these questions as a guide: "Is it important for the students to know this word five years from now? Will knowing this word help them figure out other words related to it? Is the word's meaning essential to understanding the selection?" (Blanchowicz, 1985, p. 879)
4. Provide many opportunities for students to use the new vocabulary.
5. Provide opportunities for follow-up. Be sure vocabulary development is ongoing.
6. Introduce your students to books on word study.
7. Teach students how to learn word meanings on their own—how to transfer skills such as dictionary and thesaurus usage and use of context to other situations.

Before making a reading assignment, prepare students for new words and concepts they will encounter. Select for special attention those words students will use most often throughout their lives and those most pertinent to understanding the content of the reading assignment.

DEVELOPING BACKGROUND KNOWLEDGE FOR VOCABULARY GROWTH

One of the basic comprehension failures of students is their failure to understand the meanings of the vocabulary in a selection. A metareader will search out meanings to unknown words that hinder comprehension. But poor readers are concerned only with pronouncing the words; and many of these students don't know how to find the meanings of unknown words.

In this section you will learn several strategies for helping students learn words and relate words to their personal experiences (a goal of reading instruction recommended in *Becoming a Nation of Readers).* Background will be provided through a discussion of word histories, figurative language, and word relations. More specific strategies that promote mental imagery, categorizing, use of context clues, and morphemic analysis will also be presented.

Word Histories

How do words change meanings? How do words come into our language? Words change meanings through generalization, specialization, amelioration, pejoration, and creating euphemisms. They come into our language through coining, borrowing or loanwords, eponomy, and developing acronyms. Let's look at some examples of these word histories.

- **Generalization** brings about the broadening of a word's meaning. *Shipped* once meant sent by boat. Today it may mean sent by boat, airplane, bus, train, or spacecraft. *Kleenex* originated as a brand name. People now use it as a general term meaning any facial tissue.
- **Specialization** is the opposite of generalization. Through specialization a word's meaning becomes narrowed. *Malaria* once meant bad air. It is now a specific disease.
- **Amelioration** involves elevating the meaning of a word. The word *minister* once meant a common servant. A minister is now a servant of God or a high governmental official. The word *nice* once meant ignorant, but now means pleasing or agreeable.
- **Pejoration** is the process by which the meaning of a word is lowered or degraded. A *villain* was once a person from a villa. Now a villain is a scoundrel. A *diaper* was an ornamental cloth. It now covers a baby's posterior. *Grass* once was used for grazing animals. It's now used as a synonym for marijuana, which is illegally smoked.
- **Euphemisms** are pleasant sounding terms we develop to take the sting out of unpleasant ideas. People no longer die; they pass away. They are not buried but put to rest. We no longer send replacements in for the dead, injured, or tired during war; we now send reinforcements. A person is no longer average but is now competent. People don't put their false teeth in to eat; they wear dentures. One's skin no longer has pimples but blemishes on it. And we no longer have tax increases; we have revenue enhancements.
- **Coining** is making new words up from existing words. If smoke mixes with fog it creates *smog.* If it's too late to eat breakfast and too early for lunch, you might eat *brunch.* A room which is used as a cafeteria and an auditorium is called a *cafetorium.*

- **Borrowing** words from other languages is an American custom. You can watch a *raccoon* (American Indian) in the morning, have the *chauffeur* (French) drive Shawna to *kindergarten* (German), cook lunch on a *hibachi* (Japanese), have *pizza* (Italian) for dinner, and read about *sputniks* (Russian) in the *encyclopedia* (Greek) during the evening.
- **Eponyms** are derived from people's names. *Watt,* a term that describes a measure of electricity, came from James Watt. *Melba* was derived from Nellie Melba, who sang at the Metropolitan Opera in New York. The toast she asked for one day was burned; she liked it; and "melba toast" was invented.
- **Acronyms** are words formed from the first (or first few) letter(s) of several words. They are pronounceable units. Will AWAC (Airborne Warning And Control System) aircraft be sent to OPEC (Organization of Petroleum Exporting Countries)?

Piercey (1982) recommends telling an unusual story about the origin of a new word's meaning. For example, we use a centigrade or Celsius thermometer in metric measurement. This thermometer was invented by the Swedish astronomer, Anders Celsius. The step ladder was invented by Jonathan Step to help him pick apples.

The following books offer unusual stories or word histories:

Asimov, I. (1968). *Words from history.* Houghton Mifflin.
——— (1961). *Words from the myths.* Houghton Mifflin.
——— (1959). *Words from science.* Houghton Mifflin.
Funk, W. J. (1950). *Word origins and their romantic stories.* New York: Funk and Wagnall's.

Figurative Language and Idioms

We were all ears, our hair stood on end, and our blood ran cold as we watched the horror movie.

Figurative language and idioms contain meanings that are different from their literal meanings. Just picture yourself with ears all over your body, your hair standing on end, and cold blood running all through your veins. In reality this literally does not happen, but the effect of the idea we want to convey is heightened when we use figurative language and idioms.

Figurative Language

Students' difficulty with figurative language was highlighted in a study by Carter (1977). Grade 7 students were unable to understand the figurative language in their social studies textbook. The students' interpretation of the figures of speech were at the literal level. They thought, for example, that the "dark horse candidate," Warren Harding, was the first African-American president of the United States.

As teachers, you should identify metaphors and similes your students will read. Then you should isolate and teach vocabulary that is important to identifying the meanings of these figures of speech (Readence, Baldwin & Richelman, 1983).

In order to read figurative language, students first must recognize nonliteral language. They must understand that comparisons are being made. Students then must understand the denotative and connotative meanings of the words being used. And, finally, students must know why the author is making comparisons and understand the similarities between the things being compared (Sherer, 1977).

Figurative language expressions are called figures of speech. Let's take a look at some of the specific types of figures of speech.

- A **hyperbole** is an exaggeration or overstatement. Example: I am so hungry, I could eat a horse.
- **Irony** is used to express the opposite of its literal meaning. It's humorous, light sarcasm. Example: Your performance was magnificent. You bombed out.
- A **metaphor** is an analogy or comparison between two different things, but the words *like* and *as* are not used. Example: Philip is a sly fox.
- **Onomatopoeia** is the use of words whose sounds suggest their meaning or sense. Examples: Hiss went the snake. Bang went the gun.
- **Oxymorons** are words used together as a unit but that are opposite in meaning. Example: Stephen Douglas was called a little giant.
- **Personification** involves giving human qualities to a thing or an abstraction. Example: The fox spoke in a soft, inviting manner.
- A **simile** is a direct comparison between two different things using the words *like* or *as*. Example: A teacher with a hundred students is as busy as a beaver.

Turner (1976) outlines many strategies for teaching figurative language. Several ideas are highlighted below.

1. Have students complete unfinished similes. Quick as a what?
2. Have students discuss the meanings of nicknames.
3. Cut examples of figurative language from the newspaper or magazines.
4. Have students write figurative expressions to describe their moods or feelings.
5. Have students look for examples of figurative language in prose or poetry (or their content area textbooks). Discuss the meanings of these figures of speech.

Piercey (1982) outlines two additional strategies for teaching figurative language.

1. Look through the sports section of the newspaper and find out how many different ways sports writers describe an event. What words do they use in place of *win?* "The Longhorns stampeded the Owls" is another way of saying that the Longhorns beat the Owls. The word *stampeded* adds color to the description of the game. Have students clip twenty to twenty-five words that mean "win." Mount these

on 8 1/2-by-11-inch paper and include the name of the sport, the score, and the victory margin or what the score means ("won by three touchdowns").

2. Have students listen to popular music for a week and write down all the metaphors and similes they hear. Then have students read their findings to the class and discuss these findings. This can be expanded to listening to commercials, reading advertisements, and reading the editorial and sports sections of the newspaper. Extend this activity further by having students identify metaphors and similes that are used in their textbooks.

Idioms

Idioms are expressions in language whose meanings cannot be determined by the meanings of the specific elements of the expression. Idioms are specific expressions of a culture or group of people. Many figures of speech are also idioms, as you can see from the list in Table 4–1.

TABLE 4–1 • Selected Idioms

to dream up	bring the aircraft out of its fatal dive
a trick up his sleeve	eat your heart out
the cat got her tongue	take the bull by the horns
cut it out	quick as a wink
flying downstairs	strong as an ox
eats like a bird	stole the show
with heavy heart	come off it
to be on Easy Street	to be in the doghouse
dark horse candidate	leaping into one's mouth
a pain in the neck	henpecked
bum rap	double header
cool as a cucumber	runs like a deer
keep a sharp eye out	full of beans
he's spaced out	pocket veto
for crying out loud	jumping out of my skin
icy stare	lame duck president
stiff as a board	skinny as a rail
green as grass	soldier of fortune
the fair-haired boy	make a mountain out of a molehill
the land of milk and honey	our ship is sinking
boggles the mind	flat as a pancake
catch a cold	I'm all tied up
dipping into the till	glassy eyes
rules with a heavy hand	sour as a pickle
caught red-handed	raining cats and dogs
stubborn oil must be forced out	slow as molasses
lame duck session	before night falls
fruitless bargaining session	chew the fat
blow off steam	hot bed of turmoil
backbone of a jelly fish	it's a rat's nest
hard as a rock	slept like a log
exercise in nuclear war	framer of the Constitution
shattered economy	the week of flashing knives in Congress
satisfy back taxes	

Word Relations

Words have many relations to each other that students should be aware of in order to understand differences in meanings. Understanding these differences in meanings helps students use the dictionary and comprehend materials they read. Pearson and Johnson (1972) suggest nine relations words have to each other. Words may be

- **Synonyms**—words having same or similar meanings; *fast-rapid.*
- **Antonyms**—words with opposite meanings; *fast-slow.*
- **Associations**—words THAT often occur together in our language; *pita-pocket, rye bread.*
- **Homonyms** or **homophones**—words that sound alike but have different spellings and meanings; *fur-fir, raise-raze.*
- **Homographs**—words spelled alike but pronounced differently and having different meanings; *wind-wind.*
- **Analogies**—two pairs of words related in a similar way; *boat-cargo:: glass-water.*
- **Classifications**—words belonging to the same class; *tree-oak, maple, dogwood.*
- Words with **multiple meanings**—*shower* given before a wedding, rain, something in the bathtub.
- Words with **denotative-connotative meanings**—words having literal meanings different from their emotional or interpretive meanings; *yellow*-a color, *yellow*-without courage.

Several activities follow for teaching word relations.

1. In headline writing, journalists must fit their headlines into a small space and use short words to convey a story's main idea accurately. Give students the opportunity to work with selecting synonyms by providing them with headlines with major words blocked out. Synonyms and the original word are listed on cards. Students go through the list of synonyms and select the one they think appeared in print. The students' choices can be checked against the original headlines (Piercey, 1972, p. 95).

2. In math we use synonyms. "Math synonyms are quantitatively equivalent but linguistically varied" (Mountain, 1993). For example, 20 nickels, 10 dimes, 4 quarters, and 1 dollar are math synonyms. Here are other math synonyms: 365 days, 12 months, and 1 year; 4 quarts, 8 pints, and 128 ounces; and 25%, .25, 1/4, and quarter. Develop stories into which the students place appropriate synonyms. For example, ask students to use 25%, .25, 1/4, or *quarter* in each blank space in the story.

Sally didn't want to go to the picnic. There was a _____ chance of rain. She was already a _____ of an hour late. More than 3/4 of her pals had cancelled, so less than _____ would be there. From a phone booth, it would cost only $ _____ to call and say she couldn't make it. (Mountain, 1993)

3. Have students read stories and articles to determine the different words writers use instead of *say*. Students should then make a list of the different words used and their meanings. How would the use of these different words change the meaning of the article or headline (Piercey, 1972, p. 88)?

4. Give students copies of paragraphs or poems in which homonyms (see Table 4–2) or homophones are incorrectly used, and have students correct them. The following poem is an example of one in which homonyms need to be corrected.

Homophones*

Wood you believe that I didn't no
About homophones until too daze ago!
That day in hour class in groups of for,
We had to come up with won or more.

Mary new six; enough to pass.
But my ate homophones lead the class.
Then a thought ran threw my head.
"Urn a living from homophones," it said.

I guess I just sat and staired into space.
My hole life seamed to fall into place.
Our school's principle happened to come buy,
And asked about the look in my I.

"Sir," said I as bowled as could bee,
"My future rode I clearly sea."
"Sun," said he, "move write ahead.
Set sale on your coarse. Don't be mislead."

I herd that gnus with grate delight.
I will study homophones both day and knight.
For weaks and months, through thick oar thin.
I'll pursue my goal. Eye no aisle win.

Mental Imagery

Concept learning, the vocabulary overview guide, word maps, and motor imaging strategies help students learn and retain word meanings by developing clues for retention. In the vocabulary overview guide the clue is a word. In the motor imaging strategy the clue is a psychomotor association.

Learning Concepts

Imagine yourself faced with the task of recalling the specific names of every tree, every dog, every car, and every flower. Further, imagine that you had never heard of the general words *tree, dog, car,* or *flower* before. Suppose that, in order to communicate with people, you always had to use the specific names for each tree, dog, car, and flower. How would you cope with such a task?

*G. E. Coon (1976). Homophones. *The Reading Teacher, 29,* 652. Reprinted with permission of the International Reading Association.

TABLE 4–2 • Selected Homonyms

aid, aide	great, grate	pail, pale
air, heir	grown, groan	peace, piece
all, awl	hale, hail	peal, peel
alter, altar	hair, hare	plane, plain
assent, ascent	hear, here	pray, prey
basis, bases	heel, heal	principal, principle
be, bee	heroine, heroin	raise, raze
beach, beech	hole, whole	red, read
bear, bare	horse, hoarse	right, write, rite
beat, beet	I, eye	road, rode
blue, blew	idle, idol	seen, scene
bore, boar	I'll, aisle	see, sea
bow, bough	in, inn	seem, seam
bowl, bole	insight, incite	sell, cell
brake, break	its, it's	sail, sale
bury, berry	knows, nose	sore, soar
by, buy, bye	led, lead	sole, soul
capital, capitol	lone, loan	some, sum
cent, sent, scent	low, lo	sun, son
cereal, serial	made, maid	so, sew, sow
choir, quire	mail, male	stake, steak
compliment, complement	medal, metal	steal, steel
counsel, council	meat, meet,	there, their, they're
days, daze	minor, miner	through, threw
dear, deer	morning, mourning	to, two, too
desert, dessert	need, knead	toe, tow
die, dye	new, knew, gnu	vain, vane, vein
earn, urn	night, knight	wait, weight
eight, ate	no, know	waste, waist
fair, fare	none, nun	way, weigh
feet, feat, fete	not, knot	where, wear
fir, fur	one, won	whose, who's
flower, flour	or, oar	wood, would
forth, fourth	our, hour	you, ewe, yew
gorilla, guerrilla	pain, pane	

Undoubtedly, unless you are a very unusual person, you would become frustrated with learning all the specific names. You might never be able to remember all of the specific names for the trees, dogs, cars, and flowers. Your memory system would become overburdened.

To cope with the problem of learning individual names or terms for everything we see, do, or feel, we develop *concepts,* or mental constructs of categories. We develop labels for these concepts, labels that allow us to categorize symbols, words, or phrases (not complete sentences) used to refer to groups of one or more objects, qualities, actions that have certain common characteristics. Concepts allow us to categorize things according to essential or criterial attributes. These essential attributes are the basic characteristics that, when present in a specific pattern, sequence, or relationship, create a category or concept.

For example, instead of remembering every type of dog by name (collie, poodle, boxer, terrier, etc.), we learn the concept *dog* because we have learned its essential attributes. These essential attributes are size, body parts, sound, color, body cover, and weight. Nonessential attributes might include collar, leash, and clothing.

The more visual and direct our experiences with concepts, the easier they are for us to learn. Dale (1969) placed learning experiences into hierarchal order for learning concepts (Figure 4–1). The easiest concepts to learn are those represented by direct, purposeful experiences. The most difficult concepts to learn are those at the top of the cone; these are those concepts represented only by verbal symbols.

Concepts serve several basic functions. They make communication easier. We can avoid long, detailed explanations by using concepts. We can organize pieces of information and treat them in a similar way rather than learning each piece of information as an entity in itself. Concepts make it easier for us to satisfy our immediate needs (Cooper et al., 1977). And concepts help readers recognize words when they are used in context (Stoodt, 1981).

Concept learning is basic to the development of vocabulary and comprehension in all areas of the curriculum. Teachers use concepts every day. *Mammal, democracy, prime number, media,* and *propaganda* represent only five of the numerous concepts commonly developed in content area classrooms.

There are two basic models for teaching concepts: the deductive concept attainment model and the inductive concept attainment model. You will recall from educational psychology or curriculum courses that a deductive approach is similar to a lecture approach. In deduction, the teacher tells students the important information and the students move from the general principle to specific examples. Using an inductive approach, students move from specific examples to formulate a definition. In induction, the teacher does not tell students the definition. On the next several pages are examples of each of deductive and inductive strategies for teaching concepts (Examples 4.1–4.4).

Deductive Concept Attainment.   DeCecco (1968) outlines a six-step procedure for deductive concept attainment.

Step 1:   Choose a concept. Be sure your students know all prerequisite concepts.

Step 2:   Tell your students what they should be able to do after they have learned the concept.

Step 3:   Tell your students the name of the concept. Define the concept for your students. Present a couple of examples so that students can see the relationships between the concept and its definition.

Step 4:   Show positive and negative (non-) examples to your students. Explain why each positive example is an example and why each negative example is not an example (is a nonexample).

Step 5:   Present additional positive and negative examples, and have your students classify each as being an example or nonexample of the concept. Have the students explain why they classified the examples as they did.

Step 6: Verify your students' learning. This evaluation can be similar to a posttest.

Example 4.1 will help you learn a concept using a deductive concept strategy. A nonsense concept has been used to engage your thinking rather than using a concept you already understand.

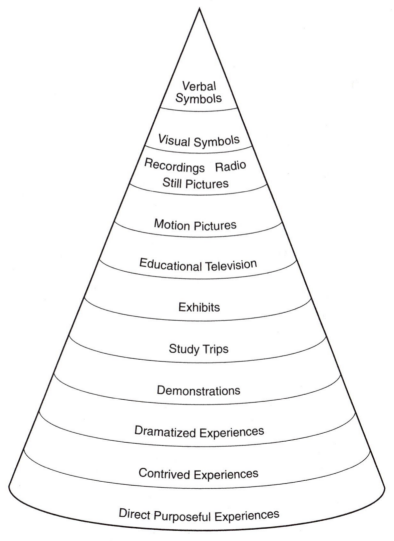

FIGURE 4–1 • Cone of Experiences

Source: E. Dale (1969). *Audiovisual Methods in Teaching.* 3rd ed. Holt, Rinehart & Winston, p. 107. Reprinted by permission of the publisher.

Example 4.1   Deductive Concept Attainment Lesson

1. At the end of this lesson you should be able to draw an example of a *zipple*.
2. A *zipple* is a car, a tree, and a house in that specific order.
3. This is a *zipple*. It is a car, a tree, and a house in that specific order.

This is another *zipple*. There is still a car, tree, and house in that order. It doesn't matter if the objects are upside down or on their sides.

This is another *zipple*. It is still a car, tree, and house in that order. It doesn't matter if the objects are upside down.

This is not a *zipple*. We don't have the car, tree, and house in the proper order.

This is not a *zipple* because the objects are not in the correct order.

4. Which of these are *zipples?* Which are not *zipples?* Give your reasons why as you label each example.

a.

b.

c.

5. Draw a zipple.

How might you use a deductive concept attainment lesson with an English class? Let's look at Example 4.2, which explains the concept of *alliteration.*

Example 4.2 Deductive Concept Attainment Lesson

1. Concept: *alliteration*
2. At the end of this lesson, you should be able to identify examples of *alliteration* and write your own sentence or jingle to show alliteration.
3. *Alliteration* is the repetition of initial consonant sounds in words in a line of poetry or in prose.
4. Here are several examples of *alliteration.* What initial consonant sound is repeated in each of these examples?

   a. The white-washed walls were stained by dirty hands.
      (Yes, the sound of *w* is repeated.)
   b. The sunburned sailor showed signs of dizziness.
      (Yes, the sound of *s* is repeated.)
   c. The double-dealing dealer made the players look dumb.
      (The sound of *d* is repeated in this sentence.)

   Here are several nonexamples of alliteration. None of the initial consonant sounds are repeated.

   a. He uttered about the clutter, but not a mutter was heard by others as they fluttered.
   b. The villagers' moans were heard as the ocean waves rolled on shore and increased the death toll.

5. Identify which of the following sentences contain *alliteration.* What consonant sound is repeated?

   a. Peter Piper picked a peck of pickled peppers.
   b. Life with all its dreams also holds sorrow.
   c. The slippery sidewalk slowed weary shoppers to a crawl.
   d. The drought ended with a dreary, damp, drizzly day.
   e. The beginning of a new day is near.

6. Write a sentence or jingle that clearly shows *alliteration*.

Inductive Concept Attainment. Now that we've seen how to use a deductive concept attainment lesson in a class, let's look at the inductive concept attainment model. This six-step procedure is based on Bruner's concept attainment model and adapted by Lyle Smith (unpublished).

Step 1:   Select a concept. Do not define the concept for the students. If the students would not be able to associate the concept with the concept name (that is, if students previously have not learned the concept), go to Step 2a. If some students would be able to associate the concept with its name, go to Step 2b.

Step 2a: Describe the performance expected of the students after they have learned the concept. Provide the students with clear verbal associations of the concept. Name the concept and (if appropriate) have students repeat the concept name.

Step 2b: Do not tell students the concept name. Tell students they are to review and learn more about a concept they have learned previously.

Step 3:   Remind students that, if they discover what the concept is, they are not to reveal the answer to other students.

Step 4:   Provide several positive and negative (non-) examples of the concept in close succession. Sequence the positive and negative examples so that each one reveals a new attribute that is relevant to the concept.

Step 5:   Seek evidence that the concept has been discovered by providing new positive and negative examples and asking students to identify the positive examples.

Step 6:   Verify student learning of the concept.

Now, let's see if you can learn a concept using the inductive approach. Today, you'll learn what a *gazbak* is. It's a nonsense concept, which we use to have you more fully engage in the thinking processes.

Example 4.3   Inductive Concept Attainment Lesson

1. Concept: *gazbak*
2. (Use step 2a.) Today you are going to learn what a *gazbak* is. After looking at examples of *gazbaks,* you should be able to define the concept *gazbak.*
3. If you figure out what a *gazbak* is before we finish, please don't say the answer aloud. Give others in the class a chance to figure it out.

4. This is a *gazbak*.

This is a *gazbak*.

This is a *gazbak*.

This is a *gazbak*.

This is not a *gazbak*.

This is not a *gazbak*.

This is not a *gazbak*.

5. Which of these are *gazbaks?*
   a.

   b.

   c.

d.

6. Define *gazbak*. (A *gazbak* is a star, duck, and ice cream cone in that specific order.) Students might also draw a *gazbak* or identify additional examples on individual worksheets.

Now, let's see how you might be able to use an inductive lesson to teach the concept *polygon* in a geometry class.

Example 4.4 Inductive Concept Lesson

1. Concept: *polygon*
2. (Use step 2b.) Today you are going to learn more about a concept you learned before. At the end of class you should be able to name and define the concept and identify examples of it.
3. If you discover what the concept is, don't give the answer away to others who have not discovered it.
4. This is an example.

This is an example.

This is an example.

This is not an example.

This is not an example.

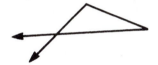

This is not an example.

5. Is this an example?

Is this an example?

Is this an example?

6. What concept did we study? What is a *polygon?* (A *polygon* is the union of three or more line segments in the same plane, each of which intersects

exactly two of the other segments, once at each point.) Which of these are *polygons*?

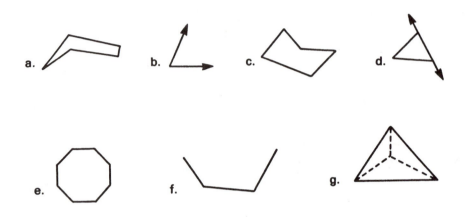

There are three possible errors students might make when they are trying to learn concepts: overgeneralization, undergeneralization, and misconception (Klaus-meier et. al., 1974; Smith, undated). If you answered a, c, and e in question 6 of the polygons lesson, you made none of these errors. Choices a, c, and e are polygons; the others are not.

- **Overgeneralization.** Students who overgeneralize identify some non-examples of the concept as being examples. Students who overgeneralize should be given the opportunity to examine more non-examples to elimi-nate overgeneralization errors.
- **Undergeneralization.** Students who undergeneralize identify some ex-amples of the concept as being nonexamples. Students who under-generalize need opportunities to examine a greater variety of examples.
- **Misconception.** These students identify some examples of the concept as being nonexamples and identify some nonexamples of the concept as being examples.

Duffelmeyer (1985) describes the positive and negative instances strategy as a way of using students' experiences to learn concepts. The strategy involves these steps:

1. Select a word you want to teach and determine its definition.
2. Identify a positive and negative instance of the word.

3. Display the word to your students, pronounce it, and have your students pronounce it.
4. Tell your students the meaning of the word.
5. Provide students with a positive or negative example in which the word is used. Ask students if it is used correctly and have them explain their answers.
6. Provide students with another example in which the word is used. Ask students if it is used correctly and have them explain their answers.
7. Have students give positive examples of the use of the word. In science, you might be studying the word *buoyant,* which means "having the capacity to float." A hollow plastic or rubber ball is an example of a buoyant object. On the other hand, a solid golf ball is a nonexample of a buoyant object.

To teach the word *buoyant,* display the word on the board, pronounce it, and have your students pronounce it. Tell your students that the word *buoyant* means "able to float." Next, tell your students to imagine themselves trying to push a beach ball down into the water. Would the beach ball be an example of a buoyant object? Yes—if you've ever tried to push a beach ball under water, you know that it pushes back up and floats. Now ask your students about pushing a golf ball under water. Is a golf ball an example of something buoyant? No, it isn't. If students put the golf ball into the water, it would sink. If students are unsure about what would happen, demonstrate buoyancy using various objects. Next, have students give examples of buoyant objects from their own experiences.

Vocabulary Overview Guide

The vocabulary overview guide (Carr, 1985) requires students to identify unknown words, ascertain their definitions from context if possible, and develop mnemonic or imagery clues to help themselves remember the definitions. Students can use the overview guide while engaging in independent study. The steps are as follows:

Step 1: Use Context to Define the Word

1. Direct students to survey the selection.
2. Have students skim the selection and underline words they don't understand.
3. Instruct students to try to figure out the words' meanings from context. Then have them check the meanings using the dictionary.
4. Write the definitions in the text next to the unfamiliar word or on a sheet of paper. Be sure the definition is handy.
5. Have students read the passage using their definitions.

Step 2: Complete the Vocabulary Overview Guide

1. Write the passage's title on the top line of the vocabulary overview guide. (See Example 4.5.)

2. Complete the category titles by selecting subcategories of words. Place this information on the second row of the vocabulary overview guide.
3. Write the vocabulary words under the appropriate category.
4. Write a synonym beneath the word to be used as a definition.
5. Have each student write a personal clue in the clue box that relates the word to his or her personal experience.

Step 3: Study the Vocabulary

1. Instruct students to read the title and categories and recall the vocabulary words under each.
2. Have students cover the synonym and clue word and try to recite each synonym and clue for each vocabulary word.
3. Have students uncover the synonym and clue words if they cannot remember.
4. Instruct students to review often.

In Example 4.5, the passage title was Weather. When we study weather, we study instruments and conditions. Two instruments discussed in the chapter were the thermometer and the barometer. A *thermometer* is used for measuring temperature. If we picture ourselves when we were sick, we will remember that a thermometer was used to measure our temperature. The word *frigid* means "very cold." We might picture an igloo as being in a very cold place and remaining frozen. Similar thought processes are used to remember *barometer* and *blizzard*.

Example 4.5   Vocabulary Overview Guide

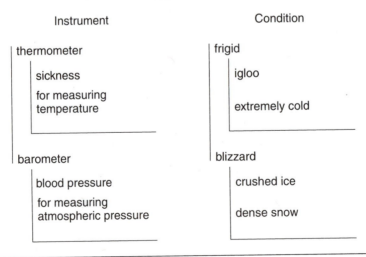

WEATHER

Instrument

thermometer
  sickness
  for measuring temperature

barometer
  blood pressure
  for measuring atmospheric pressure

Condition

frigid
  igloo
  extremely cold

blizzard
  crushed ice
  dense snow

Word Maps

Word maps are recommended by Schwartz and Raphael (1985) to help students form visual representations of definitions. Students work individually or in small groups to complete three categories developing the map: (1) What is it? (2) What is it like? and (3) What are some examples? This strategy is most appropriate when working with nouns, but it can be used with other parts of speech. A word map exploring the concept *pollution* is pictured in Example 4.6.

Example 4.6   Word Map

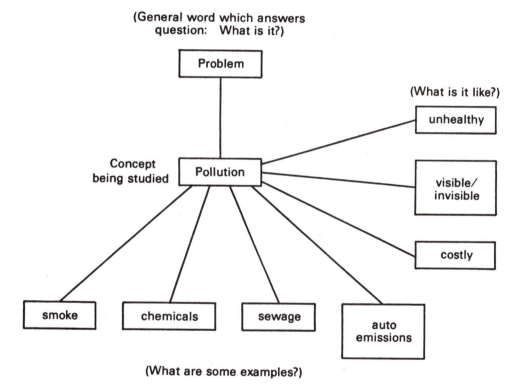

Definition: *Pollution* is an environmental problem that is costly, unhealthy, and may be visible or invisible. Some examples are smoke, chemicals, sewage, and auto emissions.

A group discussion might go like this:

Tim: Our job is to be able to tell Mr. Max the definition of *pollution*. How can we get started?

PAT: I know I can locate the definition in the dictionary. I'll find out how it's defined in my dictionary.

SUSAN: I've seen "pollution" as a topic in the encyclopedia. I'll look there.

JEAN: What do you call the list of words at the end of our book that has definitions.

TIM: It's called a glossary.

JEAN: I'll look in the glossary.

TIM: Yes, and the index in our science book lists pollution. I'll find out what our science book tells us about it.

    (Ten minutes later.)

What did everyone find out?

    (Students tell each other what they found out, but they don't write anything word for word.)

PAT: From everything we've said, I think that pollution is a big problem.

SUSAN: It sure is. And from what we've found out, it costs us a lot of money each year.

JEAN: It not only costs a lot but it can cause or aggravate a lot of health problems such as asthma, cancer, lung problems, and birth defects.

TIM: We can't always see pollution. Sometimes it's invisible.

PAT: We know of a lot of different examples of pollution in our own city.

JEAN: Yes, car exhaust, sewage, chemicals, and smoke are only a few types.

TIM: Then how can we define *pollution*?

SUSAN: What about this? Pollution is an environmental problem that is costly, unhealthy, and may be visible or invisible. Some examples are smoke, chemicals, sewage, and auto emissions.

ALL: That's good.

MR. MAX: How have you defined pollution?

TIM: *(Reads his group's definition.)*

MR. MAX: Good. You categorized the characteristics of pollution into one word problem. When you explained what pollution was like, you told us the information you found in the reference books you used. And then you did a very good thing. You went inside your own heads to give us examples of pollution.

Motor Imaging

Motor imaging (Casale, 1985) requires students to develop psychomotor associations for words. Students develop hand and body gestures to create an image of a word. The steps in the motor imaging strategy are as follows:

1. Write the word on the board. Pronounce the word. Define the word.
2. Have your students imagine a pantomime to show the word's meaning.
3. At a specified time, signal and have all students do their pantomimes together.
4. Demonstrate the most commonly used pantomime to the students. The students then say the word while doing the demonstrated pantomime.
5. Follow the same procedure for each new word.
6. The students then read the selection containing the new words.

You might want to introduce the word *succinct* to your students. Write the word on the board. Pronounce it. Then tell your students that *succinct* means "compact expression, without wasted words, concise." To pantomime this, students might cup their hands and move them back and forth toward each other as if they were trying to compress a snowball.

Categorizing Strategies

Vocabulary scavenger hunts, list-group-label, semantic feature analysis, and semantic mapping are examples of strategies that involve categorizing, pupil involvement and direct teaching. Let's look at each of these strategies.

Vocabulary Scavenger Hunts

Vocabulary scavenger hunts (Cunningham, Crawley, & Mountain, 1983; Vaughan, Crawley, & Mountain, 1979) not only involve categorizing, pupil involvement, and direct teaching; they also involve promoting mental images. The following steps are used in vocabulary scavenger hunt lessons:

1. Teams of three to five students are formed.
2. A copy of a vocabulary scavenger hunt worksheet is given to each student. (See Example 4.7.)
3. Each student, independently, tries to categorize the words (Step 1 in the example).
4. Students in a team compare their answers and arrive at a consensus for categorizing the words.
5. Now students must hunt for objects, pictures, or drawings of the items listed on the worksheet.

Scavenger hunts provide an excellent means of introducing students to the new vocabulary for units in science, social studies, art, and music. Give students a list of terms related to the topic. Have them locate the objects or pictures of the objects, and then use these objects or pictures for a display table or bulletin board.

Example 4.7   Vocabulary Scavenger Hunt Worksheet

Vehicles

1. Write the following words in three lists in the chart below.

jeep	plane	kayak	ambulance
jet	barge	rocket	helicopter
taxi	hearse	blimp	tugboat
canoe	sloop	tanker	convertible
yacht	glider	trolley	carriage

Land vehicles	Water vehicles	Air vehicles

2. Meet with your team. Discuss the words until your whole team can agree about which items belong under each heading. Write lists below that show the group's best thinking.

Land vehicles	Water vehicles	Air vehicles

3. Decide who will search for a picture, drawing, or tracing of each item. Write that person's initial beside the item. Now go find your items for this scavenger hunt.

4. After finding your pictures, meet with your team again. Go over the list item by item. Have the members show the pictures they brought. Each team gets one point for each accurate picture, drawing, or tracing when it shows its findings to the class. As in any scavenger hunt, the team with the most points wins!

Source: S. Vaughan, S. Crawley, & L. Mountain (1979). A multiple modality approach to word study. *The Reading Teacher,* 32, 435. Reprinted with permission of the International Reading Association.

Additional applications of vocabulary scavenger hunts can be made in any content area. Let's take a look at a few examples.

1. Spanish class

   Categories: things to write with, things to write on, things to erase with, classroom furniture, things found on the wall, people in the classroom

   Words: lápiz, libro de trabajo, mapa, pizarra, cuaderno, profesor(a), goma, relój, escritorio, silla, tiza, papél, estudiante, calendario, pluma, crayon, mesa, borrador

2. Art class

   Categories: ceramics, sculpture, weaving

   Words: fiber, relief, firing, shuttle, clay, modeling, stone, loom, metal, wax resist, flaze, weft, mallet, slab, warp, slip, chisel, yarn, coil.

3. Math class

   Categories: integers, rational numbers, irrational numbers, complex numbers

   Symbols: $-14, 1 + 1, .76, \sqrt{3}, \sqrt{-169}, 89.2\%, -1000, 1^{4/5}, 2\frac{1}{2}, \pi, 2, 23, \frac{1}{4}, 2i + 7, \sqrt[3]{10}, e, 0, 51, 4 + \sqrt{-5}, i$

   (In this situation, the teacher would place these different symbols and numbers around the room for students to locate and put into the correct category.)

4. Computer class

   Categories: types of computers, input/output devices (peripherals), memory devices

   Words: chip, CPU, display screen, desktop, expansion board, floppy disk drive, hard disk drive, joystick, keyboard, laptop, mainframe, mouse, numeric key pad, portable, dot matrix printer, laser printer

   (In this situation, old computers could be disassembled and parts placed around the room for students to locate; pictures could also be used.)

5. Music class

   Categories: percussion, string, woodwind, brass

   Words: flute, clarinet, tuba, bass drum, piccolo, piano, cymbals, English horn, bassoon, baritone horn, snare drum, violin, trumpet, saxophone, bass, tympani, xylophone, bass clarinet, triangle, viola, chimes, French horn, cello, guitar, oboe, marimba

List-Group-Label

This strategy was developed by Taba (1967) and recommended by Readence and Searfoss (1980). It involves having students think about words that may be related and discussing these possible relationships. Students work with concepts and categories when working through this strategy. Let's look at the steps in this strategy.

1. Present your students with a word, topic, or experience (film, filmstrip, experiment, videotape, etc.).
2. Ask your students what they see or what words are related to the topic or word. Record student responses on the board. Try to limit this to about twenty-five to thirty words.
3. Read through the list of words with students.
4. Ask students if any of the words or items belong together. Have students find some basis for grouping these various items. In groups, have the students categorize the words.
5. Encourage students to identify and verbalize their reasons for selecting these categories.
6. Let students discuss their groupings and reasoning with the rest of the class.

For example, you might be studying the unit Living Things in science. You would ask your students to think of as many living things as possible, and they might give you these responses:

squirrel	skunk	deer	fish
fern	sunfish	horse	honeybee
salamander	snake	lizard	chicken
butterfly	apple tree	crayfish	ostrich
human	frog	bat	bear
worm	pine tree	turtle	fox

Working in small groups, students then decide on categories into which these words could be placed. They put each word into the appropriate category and then defend their choices. For the words listed above, students might come up with the following categories: Plants, Animals, Reptiles, Birds, Amphibians, Mammals, Insects, and Fish.

Semantic Feature Analysis

Students' background, or prior knowledge, is of paramount importance when viewing reading comprehension. Words must be introduced and used many times in various situations before they can become part of a student's speaking, listening, reading, and writing vocabularies. Beck, McKeown, and Omanson (1987) recommend that new words be reinforced at least ten times.

In semantic feature analysis (SAF), students search their cognitive structures (schemata) and make associations. They identify likenesses and differences among words in a category. These associations are made through categorization, and this categorization is done through the use of a matrix or grid.

For initial instructional purposes the teacher and students work through the SAF steps together. It is helpful to have a large sheet of chart paper, transparency, or clean chalkboard when engaging in this strategy. The following steps are recommended in utilizing semantic feature analysis.

1. Determine your category. When first learning the strategy, select categories that promote high visual imagery (like Pets, Toys, Clothing, Buildings).
2. List words in the category in chart form down the left side of the paper (for Pets—dogs, cats, birds).
3. List features across the top row of the chart (for Pets—movement, communication, eating, body cover).
4. List subcategories of the features, if appropriate (for Pets—communication: bark, chirp, meow).
5. Go through each word in the category and determine whether it has the features and/or subfeatures in the top row. Put a + or – in feature column next to each word. A + indicates a common feature of the word in the left vertical column. A – indicates that the word does not have this common feature.
6. Talk about the matrix with students. Encourage students to talk about their observations.

The subject area vocabulary reinforcement strategy (SAVOR) was developed by Stieglitz and Stieglitz (1981) and is similar to semantic feature analysis. It, however, is used as a reinforcement strategy after students have studied a topic. Stieglitz and Stieglitz also recommend having students work in small groups (three students per group provides opportunity for all to contribute) and generate their own category, words, and features.

In Example 4.8 the major category is insects. The features of insects are listed horizontally across the top of the matrix, and the specimens students were trying to identify as insects are listed vertically along the left hand side. The only specimen which had all the characteristics of insects was the ant.

Example 4.9 presents a matrix for Mountains. In this example, you will notice that there are four categories of mountains: Volcanic, Domal, Faulted, and Folded. The major features are categorized as Formation, Appearance, Type of rock, and Minerals. Subfeatures are listed under each of these features.

Example 4.8   Semantic Feature Analysis Matrix

Insects

Specimens	Six Legs	Spiracles for Breathing	No Backbone	3 Body Segments	Cold Blooded	Complete Metamorphosis
Cat	–	–	–	–	–	–
Spider	–	+	+	–	+	–
Ant	+	+	+	+	+	+

Example 4.9   Incomplete Semantic Feature Analysis

Mountains	Formation				Appearance			Type of Rock			Minerals		
	pushing	cracks	folds	volcano	rounded	steep slope	folds	igneous	sedimentary	metamorphic	metals	coal	petroleum
Volcanic	−	−	−	+				+					
Domal	+	−	−	−	+			+			+		
Faulted	−	+	−	−		+			+			+	+
Folded	−	−	+	−			+		+			+	

Semantic Mapping

A supervisor walked into a classroom and saw this message on the board:

INSERT YOUR FAVORITE, SHORT, SIMPLE SEMANTIC MAP HERE, LEE.

"Excellent!" said the supervisor, smiling at the teacher. "I see you're using semantic mapping to help your students with vocabulary."

Semantic mapping (Pearson & Johnson, 1978; Johnson, Pittleman, & Heimlich, 1986) helps students categorize and see relationships among the new words they encounter in their reading. Developing a semantic map involves categorizing words in graphic form according to the following steps:

1. Select a word that is essential, or central, to the topic being studied.
2. Write this word on the board.
3. Have students brainstorm words that are related to this essential word. As students contribute words, list and group them in categories on the board.
4. Next, have students brainstorm individually and think of as many additional words as they can that relate to the essential word on the board. They should list these words by categories on a piece of paper.
5. Students give their lists orally and add them to the class map.
6. Students then identify labels for these categories.
7. Finally, as a class, discuss the words and their relationships.

Example 4.10 shows a few of the ideas students shared with respect to the essential item Commercial Building.

Example 4.10   Semantic Map

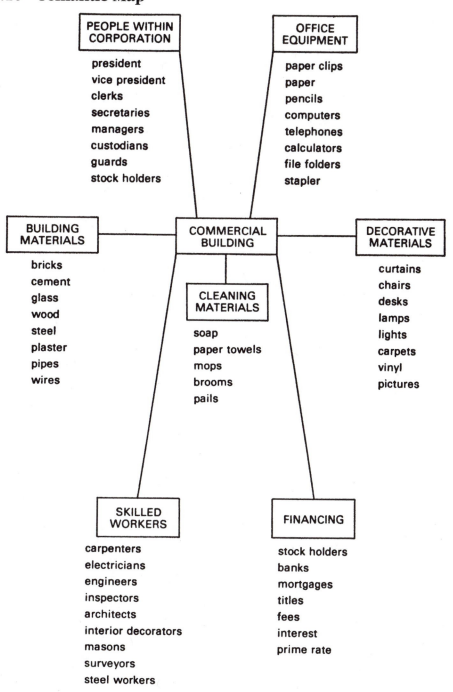

PEOPLE WITHIN CORPORATION

president
vice president
clerks
secretaries
managers
custodians
guards
stock holders

OFFICE EQUIPMENT

paper clips
paper
pencils
computers
telephones
calculators
file folders
stapler

BUILDING MATERIALS

bricks
cement
glass
wood
steel
plaster
pipes
wires

COMMERCIAL BUILDING

DECORATIVE MATERIALS

curtains
chairs
desks
lamps
lights
carpets
vinyl
pictures

CLEANING MATERIALS

soap
paper towels
mops
brooms
pails

SKILLED WORKERS

carpenters
electricians
engineers
inspectors
architects
interior decorators
masons
surveyors
steel workers

FINANCING

stock holders
banks
mortgages
titles
fees
interest
prime rate

Contextual Analysis

To illustrate the use of contextual analysis, take the following multiple-choice test. You must identify the best meaning for each word.

1. dog

    a. to hunt or track like a hound
    b. an animal
    c. a worthless person

2. bird

    a. clay pigeon
    b. to observe or identify wild birds
    c. feathered vertebrate

3. cabinet

    a. a case or cupboard used for storage
    b. a governmental advisory group
    c. exhibition room in a museum

4. model

    a. a miniature representation of something
    b. a person employed to wear a store's or designer's clothes for display
    c. to pattern

5. stage

    a. the height of a river's surface
    b. a part of a theater
    c. to produce for public view

No doubt, you probably had difficulty deciding which was the best answer. If you were to try again tomorrow, your answers probably would change. Now see what happens when you try to identify the best meaning for the same five words as used in the following sentences:

1. Frances Smith is a *dog.*
2. Do you plan to *bird* tomorrow morning?
3. The president's *cabinet* will meet at 9:00 A.M. tomorrow.
4. Making *model* airplanes is a hobby for some people.
5. The river is at flood *stage.*

The meanings you selected for the words in the first exercise probably differed from those in the second exercise because, in the second, you were able to use context. That is, the other words in the sentences helped you identify the word meanings. In the first exercise you had your previous experience with each word to use as a guide to its meaning. In the second exercise the context in which the word was used served as your guide to its meaning.

Textbooks contain many types of context clues that help students understand content materials. There are picture clues and typographical clues such as parentheses, quotation marks, and italicized print. Students can get help in determining word meanings from the syntax of a sentence (where the word is placed in the sentence). And, finally, many types of semantic context clues help students decipher the meaning of unfamiliar material.

Explanations and examples are given here for eight semantic context clues.

- **Direct definitions** or **explanations**. These are the most easily recognized. The words *is* and *means* often are indicators that a definition or example will follow. Example: Sauerkraut is a food made from fermented cabbage.
- **Explanation through example**. Sometimes writers use explanations to help the reader understand the meaning of a new word or term. Example: Mr. Jones has *arthritis;* the joints of his fingers are swollen and painful.
- **Words in a series**. The reader can get an idea about a word's meaning if it is included in a series of related words. Example: The fragrance of the flowers was everywhere. There were *kalanchoes,* temple bells, geraniums, azaleas, and African violets on display.
- **Synonym** or **restatement**. An unknown word is identified through the use of a different word or words that have a similar meaning. These clues are often identified by words such as *that is, in other words,* and *or.* Example: The *velocity,* or speed, of the projectile was 15 kilometers per minute.
- **Comparison** or **contrast**. A new word is compared with a word or idea which is already known. Example: Alva was very *diffident*, whereas Bobby was very outgoing.
- **Familiar expressions** or **figures of speech**. Similes and metaphors are often used to help convey meaning. Example: There is no doubt that our guest was *somnolent*. Francis slept like a log.
- **Inference**. Inferences are statements that provide inferential clues to a word's meaning. Example: The monk looked as though he were going to *macerate* after his long period of excessive fasting.
- **Mood** or **tone**. An author reflects a mood (such as somber, frightening, merry, mysterious) by the words used. An unknown word is likely to have a meaning in harmony with the mood. Example: The carnival noises filled the air with sounds of joy, happiness, and excitement. The evening was *felicitous*.

Cunningham, Cunningham, and Arthur (1981) recommended a three-stage strategy for teaching students to use context clues. Stage 1 is an introductory stage for students who do not know, or may have forgotten, how to use context clues. Stage 2 is for students who are on the road to independence but still need guidance.

Stage 3 is for students who know how to use context clues. Initially, it is a good idea to start students at the beginning, or stage 1. They rapidly can move ahead to stages 2 and 3 as they gain proficiency.

Stage 1

1. After analyzing your textbook, you should select those words you would like to teach using context clues.

2. Write two sentences for each selected word. The sentences should give clues to each word's meaning.

3. List the words, without context clues, on the board, a transparency, or duplicated sheet of paper. Instruct students to write meanings to each of these words. If students don't know a word's meaning, they should write a "guess." Each student should write a "meaning" to every word.

4. Have students volunteer their meanings. Remind students that these are only guesses.

5. Next, show students the sentences containing context clues to the words' meanings. Have students write meanings again, this time based on these clues. Remind students that these are still only guesses.

6. Have students discuss their answers and how they arrived at the definitions. How did the rest of the sentence help them arrive at each meaning?

7. Next, a student should look the word up in a dictionary, read the definitions, and select the appropriate definition based on the context clues.

8. Tell the students where these words can be found in their textbook chapter. Have them read the sections containing each word and discuss their meanings.

Stage 2

9. Move on toward more independence once students have learned how to identify meanings, using the words for which you developed sentences. The second stage may come a week, a month, or many months after beginning stage 1. Provide students with a list of words. Have them guess at their meanings. Tell them where in the textbook the words are located. Have the students identify the meanings using the context of the textbook. Discuss these meanings. Have a student look the word up in the dictionary and locate its correct meaning.

Stage 3

10. The final stage in developing independence involves listing the words on the board and telling students to identify the words' meanings while reading the selection.

While reading a selection in literature, you might find the following words important for your students to learn: *snecked, perambulated, implacable, excised, pandowdy, arduous.* Now, on your own, identify a definition for each of these words. Remember, these are only guesses.

How imaginative were you with your definitions? Now, let's try the second part of Stage 1, seeing the words in context. After reading the following sentences in which these words are used, try to identify their meanings.

1. Unlike Mr. Kelly who never latched a door, Mrs. Wood *snecked* every door in the house.

   The burglar entered easily because the back door was not *snecked*.

2. The old dog *perambulated* lazily to his favorite resting place.

   He *perambulated,* strolled, daily in the park.

3. The school board was *implacable* when the teachers presented their petition for a 20 percent salary increase.

   Unlike the principal, who was easily appeased by the students' explanations, the school superintendent was *implacable*.

4. The surgeon *excised* the diseased tissue.

   The chef *excised,* removed, the excess fat after the meal was cooked.

5. The cook added apples, spice, sugar, and molasses to the pastry to make a delicious *pandowdy*.

   There were pies, cakes, cobblers, *pandowdy,* tarts, and turnovers on display.

6. Although the climb to the summit was *arduous,* the view was spectacular. The first few miles of the marathon were run easily; however, the last three were *arduous*.

Did you do any better at identifying the definitions in the second part of the exercise? You probably did. The context helped you arrive at their meanings and your definitions were probably similar to these: *Snecked* means "latched." You used a comparison-contrast clue and an inference clue to arrive at its meaning. *Perambulated* means "strolled." You used an inference and synonym clue to arrive at this meaning. *Implacable* means "intolerant" or "unyielding." You arrived at these meanings using inference and comparison-contrast clues. *Excised* means "cut out." An inference and a synonym were clues to this meaning. *Pandowdy* is a dessert, more specifically it's "an apple dessert made with sugar, molasses, or maple syrup and covered with a rich crust." You used inference and words-in-a-series clues to arrive at this definition. Finally, did you identify *arduous* as meaning "difficult" or "strenuous"? If so, the inference and comparison-contrast clues led you to this correct definition.

If you were teaching the vocabulary in a geometry lesson, you might use pairs of sentences similar to these:

segment: Mr. Allen told his students to think of a *segment* one unit of measurement long.

He then reminded his students that a *segment* has no area.

area: When the painter painted the inside walls of our house, she was concerned with *area,* not volume.

The decorator who decided to carpet our living room had to calculate the *area* of the floor.

perimeter: We drove around the *perimeter* of the lake.

The square had 4-inch sides, so we knew that its *perimeter* was 16 inches.

volume: The bottle had a *volume*, or holding capacity, of 2 quarts.

Length, width, and height are used to calculate the *volume* of a cube.

If you were teaching a lesson in art, you might use sentences similar to these.

geometric: The triangular shapes in the painting give it a strong *geometric* pattern.

A *geometric* form can be produced easily using the different shapes of geometry.

texture: The *texture* of the rock is very smooth on one side and rough on the other side.

Sanding down the rough spots on the wood carving will give it a more desired *texture*.

value: Adding white to different colors of paint will lighten their *value;* adding black will darken their *value*.

The mood of the picture can be changed to one of sadness by darkening the *value* of colors being used.

Gauthier (1990) recommends several steps you might take to assist your students with the development of vocabulary from context.

1. Select the vocabulary. Start with vocabulary from a short selection (two to four pages). Make a list of words for which students can use the context of the selection to ascertain the meaning.
2. Invite students to take educated guesses about the word meanings.
3. Next, have students read the passage silently. As they read, they locate the words and again speculate about their meanings. Discuss the meanings at which they arrived and how they determined them.
4. After students are familiar with the meanings, they should use the words in sentences.
5. Provide students with opportunities to share their sentences.

In teaching students about semantic context clues, remember that your goal should be to make students aware of the clues that will help them discover word meanings. It is not to have students memorize the names of the specific clues. Whenever possible, help students use the context clues available to them in their textbooks.

Morphemic Analysis

You will recall that a morpheme is the smallest significant unit of meaning. There are two types of morphemes—free and bound. A free morpheme has meaning all by itself. A bound morpheme must be attached to one or more morphemes to have meaning. In the word *wanted, want* is a free morpheme and *ed* is a bound morpheme. In the word *proceed,* both *pro* and *ceed* are bound morphemes.

Direct students' attention to, and model, how knowledge of morphemes can be utilized in determining the meaning of an unknown word. Encourage students to draw on the known to determine the unknown.

The following steps will be helpful in assisting students with morphemic analysis.

1. Identify the unknown word. Let's say it's the word *polytheism*.

2. Divide the unknown word into its morphological components: *poly, theo,* and *ism*.

3a. Identify the meaning of each morpheme:

> *poly* = more than one
> *theo* = god
> *ism* = suffix for a noun

3b. If students have difficulty with step 3a, provide them with several examples of words containing the morphemes (students also can supply some examples):

> *poly*
>
> polygon = many sided
>
> polygamy = more than one wife
>
> *theo*
>
> theologian = a person who studies god(s) and religion(s)
>
> theology = study of god(s) and religion(s)
>
> *ism* = noun form
>
> *polytheism* = more than one God

4. Read the word in the context of the sentence in which it was found.

> The ancient Greeks practiced *polytheism*. There are records of Zeus, Aphrodite, Arthemis, Hermes, Apollo, and Athena.

5. Discuss the meaning.

Burmeister (1976) recommends multiple-choice exercises to provide practice with morphemes. Direct students to identify the best meaning for each word in the exercise. For example, you might present several examples like those which follow when teaching social studies.

1. monarchy
   a. one ruler
   b. two rulers
   c. no rulers

2. bicameral
   a. legislative chamber
   b. two legislative chambers
   c. no legislative chambers
3. union
   a. existing as one
   b. existing as many
   c. not existing

After your students have completed this multiple-choice test, have them locate the words in their texts and identify the correct meaning as it is used in the textbook.

1. The *monarchy* was ruled by a king. (a)
2. Texas has a *bicameral* legislature consisting of a Senate and a House of Representatives. (b)
3. The *union* of states divided into separate factions during the Civil War. (a)

"Folded Morphemes" is a strategy for having students identify the meanings of morphemes in context and providing a study guide for use when studying for a test. Divide a sheet of paper into two vertical columns. In the left column write a sentence that includes a vocabulary word for which the meaning can be determined from context. In the right column write the meaning of the word. Students read the sentences and quiz each other on the words' meanings. Example 4.11 presents a folded morpheme study guide.

Example 4.11   Folded Morpheme Study Guide

Fold this paper along the dotted line so that you cannot see the word meanings. Use your knowledge of the prefix *hyper* ("overly, above, beyond") to arrive at the meaning of the underlined word in each sentence. Unfold the paper to check your answers.

1. Pollution is causing the water in the rivers, lakes, and ponds to become hyperacid.

    1. containing more than the normal acid

2. No matter what anyone did, the hyperactive child could not sit longer than three minutes.

    2. overly active

3. Some physicians believe that hypercholesterolemia may contribute to heart disease.

    3. presence of excessive cholestral in the blood

4. His ability to remember the details of the robbery which took place ten years ago was attributed to hypermnesia.

    4. abnormally vivid or complete memory recall of the past

For "Morpheme Concentration," prepare small index cards showing the prefixes (see Table 4–3), suffixes (see Table 4–4), and roots of words used in your content area. For example, in science you might write: *kilo, meter, hyper, acid, pre,* and *vent* on cards. Now, play the game the way you would play regular Concentration. Shuffle the cards, place them face down on a table or desk, and have students try to turn over pairs of morpheme cards that make a word. When students make a word, they must give its definition correctly in order to keep the pair of cards. The player with the most cards at the end of the game wins. Burmeister (1976) gives another variation of Morpheme Concentration and a list of morpheme families for English, mathematics, science, and social studies.

For "Morpheme Football," place small oaktag cards with prefixes, suffixes, and root words written on them in a box. These prefixes, suffixes, and root words may be related to your specific content area. Draw a football field on the board and divide the class into two teams. Team A draws a card from the box and asks a player on Team B to give its definition.

If the player on Team B gives the correct definition, the player advances the team 5 yards along the field. To move 10 yards along the field, the player must give the meaning of the prefix, suffix, or root word, name a word in the content area that contains the morpheme, and use the word in a sentence. Team B has three plays (may be given three morphemes) to move 10 yards. A first down, 10 yards, gives Team B another play. If Team B makes ten 10-yard advances, it scores a touchdown and the "ball" goes over to the opposite team. If Team B does not move 10 yards in three plays, it goes back to the 1-yard line and picks morphemes for Team A. The team with the most touchdowns at the end of a specified time limit wins.

Before making a reading assignment, prepare students for new words and concepts they will encounter. Select those words students will use most often throughout their lives and those most pertinent to their understanding the content of the reading assignment.

ADDITIONAL REINFORCEMENT ACTIVITIES

Reinforce new words in as many different ways as possible. Use them often in conversation; use filmstrips, demonstrations, actual objects, and past experiences to reinforce vocabulary.

Two types of paper-and-pencil reinforcement activities follow. The first type is called **word play**. These are puzzles students solve to reinforce vocabulary. They can be adapted to your specific content area. The second type of reinforcement activities are related to specific content areas. You will notice that some of these also involve word play.

Word Play Activities

Mountain (1985) presents activities to encourage the development of vocabulary and provide motivation for students. These activities include content-area puzzles, anagrams, graphic puzzles, palindrome puzzles, Tom Swifties, rhyming riddles, and word shapes.

TABLE 4–3 • **Selected Prefixes**

Prefix	Meaning	Sample Usage
a-	in such a manner	aloud
ab-	away from	abnormal
a-, an-	not	asexual
ante-	before	antebellum
anti-	against	antiaircraft
auto-	self	autobiography
be-	treat as	befriend
bi-	two	biweekly
bene-	well	benefactor
co-	together, jointly	coexist
com-	with, together	combination
contra-	against	contradictory
counter-	against	counteract
de-	away, down, reversing	devalue
deci-	a tenth of	decibel
di-	two	dichloride
dis-	apart from, not	disagreeable
en-	to make or become	enslave
equi-	equal	equidistant
ex-	not, out	exclude
extr(a)-	outside, beyond	extrovert
fore-	in front	foreground
hemi-	half	hemisphere
hyper-	overly	hyperactive
il-	not	illegal
in-	not	inactive
inter-	between, among	interdependent
ir-	not	irresponsible
mal-	bad	maladjustment
mid-	middle	midterm
mis-	wrong	misprint
non-	not	nonbonded
out-	beyond	outmaneuver
over-	over	overdose
per-	throughout	pervade
peri-	all around	periscope
post-	after	postdate
pre-	before	prelude
pro-	before, in front, for, forward, forth	proclaim
re-	back, again	regain
retro-	backwards	retrospect
semi-	half	semiannual
sub-	under, below	submarine
super-	above, over	superhuman
trans-	across	transatlantic
un-	not, to do the opposite	unskilled, untie
uni-	one	unicameral

TABLE 4–4 • Selected Suffixes

Suffix	Meaning	Sample Usage
-able, -ble, -ible	tending to, able to	breakable
-age	state of being, place of rest	courage, storage
-al,	pertaining to	directional
-ance, -ence,	state of being, relating to	performance
-ary, -ery	that which relates to, place where	aviary
-ate	act on	activate
-en, -em	having the nature of, to make or become	broken
-er	one who, that which, more in comparisons	writer, larger
-est	most in comparisons	largest
-ful	characterized by, full of	cupful
-fy	make or form into	citify
-hood	state of	statehood
-ic	pertaining to, like	panoramic
-ion	state of, result of a process	hydration, regulation
-ism	quality of	magnetism
-ive	having the nature of, quality of, given to	active
-ity, ty	state of being	deity
-ist	one who	artist
-ish	having the nature of	greenish
-ize	become like	vulcanize
-less	without	helpless
-ly	in the manner of	stately
-ment	resulting state, action of process	excitement
-most	most in comparisons	innermost
-ness	quality or state of being	politeness
-or	one who, state or quality	inventor
-ous	state or condition, having the quality of	prosperous
-ship	office, profession, art, or skill	apprenticeship
-ure	act, process	exposure

Content Area Puzzle

The word puzzle approach can be used to develop content area vocabulary. The rebuses, scrambles, and cryptograms that appear in the *Quiz Book of the American Revolution* (Banks, 1975), for example, can enrich the teaching of history. Your students might enjoy finding the hidden names in the following puzzle (p. 9).

In each sentence a patriot is hidden. We give the first name, but you must find the last name somewhere in the sentence. Underline it when you do.

1. Thomas had radical ideas that sometimes caused pain even to his friends.
2. John knew that sometimes it was the pen, rather than cocked pistols, that could change a man's mind.
3. The cannons roared but Ethan and his boys ran to the fort wall, enjoying the battle.

Did you locate Thomas Paine, John Hancock, and Ethan Allen in these three sentences?

Anagrams

Anagrams help students with spelling as well as vocabulary development. The simplest anagram puzzles involve unscrambling a group of letters and rearranging them to spell a word. The following anagram puzzle is a bit more difficult in that each set of scrambled letters can be rearranged to spell two different words (Edwards, 1977, p. 17).

1. thso   *shot*   *host*
2. aref   _____   _____
3. syla   _____   _____
4. ateh   _____   _____

The full set of answers is (2) *fear, fare;* (3) *slay, lays;* and (4) *hate, heat.*

Another form of anagram, called *Vocabagram* by Nurnberg and Rosenblum (1966, p. 51), involves rearranging the letters of a given word to form the word defined. For example,

wary = twisted (answer = awry)
atom = a ditch surrounding a castle (answer = moat)

Now you try these vocabagrams:

1. rave = declare to be true   _____
2. tore = mechanical memory   _____
3. sure = a trick   _____
4. tome = a speck of dust   _____

The definitions no doubt led you to the words *aver, rote, ruse,* and *mote.*

Graphic Puzzles

Solving a graphic puzzle gives students the same kind of satisfaction a cryptologist gets from breaking a code. Wouldn't you enjoy translating

stand
I

into *I understand?*

Magazines and workbooks are good sources of graphic puzzles. The following examples were chosen from among the contest winners of an airline magazine competition (Kutina, 1981, p. 69).

HEAVEN –PENNIES	YYY MEN	N O T T U B	YOUR COAT	1 3 5 7 9 11 VS. U

If you are a skillful graphics puzzle reader, you came up with *pennies from heaven, three wise men, button up your overcoat,* and *the odds are against you.*

Palindrome Puzzles

Words that are spelled the same way backward and forward are called palindromes (*madam, pop*). Some phrases or complete sentences have this "same backward and forward" characteristic: *Madam, I'm Adam; A man, a plan; a canal, Panama.* For each clue write a word that is exactly the same spelled forward and backward.

    1. midday   *noon*

    2. young dog   _____

    3. observes   _____

    4. mother   _____

Orleans (1977) supplies twenty other palindromes like *pup, sees,* and *mom.*

Palindrome puzzles can even include riddles, according to Espy (1982, p. 72). He suggests that each of the couplets below defines two words, the first the reverse of the second in spelling but otherwise unrelated to it. Guess the words.

> *If I bore you by boasting and putting on airs,*
> *Turn me around, and I'm something one wears.*
>   (*brag, garb*)

> *A river will do this, though shallow, though deep;*
> *Turn it around, and it likes eating sheep.*
>   (*flow, wolf*)

Tom Swifties

A "Tom Swiftie" is a sentence in which the final adverb has a catchy relationship with some of the other words in the sentence. For example,

> "Our *hot dogs* are good," the cook said *frankly.*
> "*Stop* marching,*"* the captain said *haltingly.*

Choose the adverb that fits best in each blank below.

> halfheartedly, stiffly, testily, genially

> "There's too much starch in my shirt," the man said _____.
> "I failed my exam," the student said _____.
> "I think I'll rub my lamp," Aladdin said _____.
> "I tore her valentine in two," the lover said _____.

Tom Swifties can focus students' attention on adverbs, but verbs can be exercised in much the same way. In an issue of *Reader's Digest* (Kinney, 1984, p. 93), these sentences offered possibilities for classroom discussion on choice of final verbs.

> "I wish I were back in the *forest,*" she *pined.*
> "So you think you're a *big wheel,*" he *spoke.*
> "The *cattle* must *move* faster," he *prodded.*

Rhyming Riddles

Rhyming riddles, often called "Hink-Pinks," provide word-puzzle activities for teaching synonyms and definitions as well as rhymes (Tyson & Mountain, 1981).

Here's an example of a lesson to get middle-graders started on composing rhyming riddles. Ask your students for three synonyms of an adjective—for example, the adjective *wonderful.* Perhaps they will reply *great, super, terrific.* Then ask for three nouns that rhyme with the adjectives. Perhaps they will say *great bait, super trooper, terrific Pacific.*

Tell them they have composed the answers to some rhyming riddles. Now all they have to do is come up with the questions, such as,

> What do you call wonderful fishing tackle? (great bait)
> What do you call a wonderful police officer? (super trooper)
> What do you call a wonderful ocean? (terrific Pacific)

Word Shapes

Shape puzzles can help students learn to use context clues. To fill in the triangle below, a reader has to figure out what word belongs in each blank in the following paragraph. Each successive word must contain all the letters of the previous words plus one new letter. For example, a succession of words might be *I, it, sit, tips, strip.*

Try to use determine the words that fit into the equilateral triangle below. The following clues will help.

Betty saw _ man. He was _ _ the corner with his Siamese _ _ _. He stepped on a sharp _ _ _ _ and dropped his _ _ _ _ _ of books.

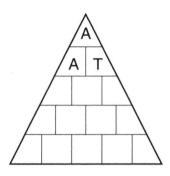

If you used context well, you came up with *a, at, cat, tack,* and *stack.*

Specific Content Area Activities

A variety of activities for reinforcing vocabulary in science are presented below. These activities include association match, fill-in puzzles, and crossword puzzles.

Association Match: Science

Cross out the word in each line that does not belong. Give a reason for your choice.

1. muscles   biceps   ~~lung~~
   (The lung is an organ, not a muscle.)
2. capillary   ~~bone~~   blood vessel
   (Bone has nothing to do with the flow of blood.)
3. divide   multiply   ~~calibrate~~
   (To calibrate is not a mathematical operation.)
4. cartilage   skeleton   ~~stomach~~
   (Cartilage holds the skeleton together.)
5. corpuscle   blood   ~~bone~~
   (Bone has nothing to do with the blood.)
6. lung   ~~neck~~   diaphragm
   (The lung is found in the diaphragm.)
7. ~~blood~~   membrane   skin
   (Skin contains membranes.)

Crossword Puzzle: Science

Using the following clues, complete the crossword puzzle. The words in the box will help you. (Note: This word list may be omitted for more able students.)

cone	algae	amphibian	mammal	extinct
backbone	gill	fungi	spore	lung

Across

1. Simple, green, living things that do not have true stems, leaves, or roots
2. Reproductive part of fungi and ferns
3. Main bone supporting the skeleton
4. Plants that can't make their own food
5. An air-breathing, warm-blooded animal with a backbone and hair somewhere on its body
6. A scaly pod with seeds of an evergreen
7. The breathing organ of an animal that takes oxygen from the water

Down

1. An animal that lives both on land and in water
2. An organ containing air from which the blood takes up oxygen and gives off carbon dioxide
3. No longer found anywhere on earth

Column Match: Math

Combine a prefix or root from column 1 with a suffix or root from column 2 to name a term used in measurement. Write the newly formed word at the beginning of its definition.

Column 1		**Column 2**	
dia-	across, through	*-valent*	well, good
poly-	many	*-(m)al*	belonging to
kilo-	thousand	*-sphere*	round
deci-	a tenth of	*-meter*	measure
hemi-	a half	*-gram*	unit of weight
equi-	equal	*-gon*	angle

1. <u>   Diameter   </u> is the distance through the center of a circle from one side to the other.

2. <u>Polygon</u> is a figure with many sides and angles.

3. <u>Kilometer</u> is a measure of length in metric measure.

4. <u>Decimal</u> is a unit of measure with an unwritten denomination of ten.

5. <u>Hemisphere</u> is a half of a globe or ball.

6. <u>Equivalent</u> means the same or equal to.

Fill-in Puzzles: Math

Use the number of syllables, the number of letters, and the first letter of each word as clues. Fill in the missing letters to complete the puzzling math word.

1. Give a five-syllable word for a four-sided figure whose opposite sides are parallel.

q u a d | r i | l a t | e | r a l

2. Give a four-syllable word for a triangle with one line of symmetry.

i | s o s | c e | l e s

3. Give a four-syllable word for parts of a figure that fit together.

c o r | r e | s p o n d | i n g

4. Give a two-syllable word for an angle greater than 90 degrees.

o b | t u s e

5. Give a three-syllable word for a six-sided figure.

h e x | a | g o n

Fill-in Puzzle: English

The word *valedictory* comes from two Latin roots: *val* ("farewell") and *dic* ("to say"). The suffix *-ory* means "a place" or "a thing for." A valedictory then is the place where an honored student says farewell to a school on behalf of a graduating class.

Using your knowledge of the suffix *-ory* and the clues provided, complete the puzzle with the correct *-ory* words from the list in the box. (You will not use all the words listed.)

salutatory	dilatory	conservatory
history	advisory	observatory
inflammatory	laboratory	dormitory
factory	auditory	mandatory
lavatory	directory	transitory

1. a place for washing or lathering oneself
2. a place for looking at the stars and planets
3. something that greets or salutes a graduation assembly
4. a place for finding directions
5. a position of someone who counsels or recommends
6. something that makes one fiery and angry
7. a place for saving plants from damage or waste
8. something one is commanded to do
9. a place where something is made or fashioned
10. something temporary, changeable, or transferrable
11. a place for working at a craft or science

1. l a **v** a t o r y
2. o b s e r v **a** t o r y
3. s a **l** u t a t o r y
4. d i r **e** c t o r y
5. a **d** v i s o r y
6. **i** n f l a m m a t o r y
7. **c** o n s e r v a t o r y
8. m a n d a t o r y
9. f a c t **o** r y
10. t **r** a n s i t o r y
11. l a b o r a t o r **y**

Morpheme Combining: English

Combine the prefixes below with the Latin root *ven* or *vent* meaning "to come," and fill in the blank spaces. Be aware of any context clues in the examples. (Number 2 has two different answers.)

con-	with, together
inter-	between
ad-	to, toward
circum-	around
pre-	before

1. To (intervene)in a love affair is to come in between the lovers.
2. The (convening , advent) of a new school year causes a mixture of excitement and apprehension in most students.
3. Members of my father's club (convene) once a week for breakfast.
4. Inoculations help (prevent) diseases that might cause severe damage later.
5. Because of his alertness, the sheriff was about to (circumvent) the escape of the thieves.

Homonym Match: English

The sentences below are missing words that are pronounced alike but spelled differently. Fill the blanks in with pairs of these words.

1. Questions were _raised_ about the _razing_ of the historical building.
2. It would take many months before Curley could _earn_ enough money to buy the _urn_.
3. The _fourth_ person in line would have to put _forth_ the greatest effort.
4. Each _choir_ member had a _quire_-sized book of music.
5. _Assent_ was given to begin the _ascent_ in *Lunar 11*.

Association Match: Music

Cross out the word in each line that does not belong. Give a reason for your choice.

1. lines   spaces   ~~notes~~
   (Lines and spaces are part of the staff. Notes are written symbols, "language.")
2. treble   ~~key~~   bass
   (Treble and bass are both clefs.)
3. ~~tempo~~   meter   time signature
   (Meter and time signature are the same thing.)
4. ~~dolce~~   piano   forte
   (Piano and forte are both dynamic markings.)
5. adagio   grave   ~~rondo~~
   (Adagio and grave are both slow tempos.)

Scrambled Letters: Art

Using the clues on the right, unscramble the words and write them in the space provided.

space	**1.** apsce	distance or area between, around, above, below, or within things
line	**2.** nlie	a continuous mark made on some surface by a moving point
form	**3.** omrf	it is three-dimensional and encloses volume
shape	**4.** haspe	an enclosed space determined by other elements such as color
value	**5.** aevul	describes the lightness or darkness of a color

CONCLUSION

Students can develop background in a number of areas to facilitate vocabulary growth. These include knowing word histories and understanding figurative language and word relationships. Being able to use mental imagery, categorize words, understand contextual analysis, and utilize morphemic analysis also contribute to vocabulary growth.

There are a number of guidelines for teaching vocabulary, including the following: teach directly; categorize words; use strategies that promote mental imagery; introduce vocabulary in related schema; involve the learner in the learning process; teach vocabulary that is most valuable; provide many opportunities for students to use the vocabulary; introduce students to books on word study; and teach students how to learn word meanings on their own.

Words change meanings and come into our language through generalization, specialization, amelioration, and pejoration. We also develop euphemisms, coin words, and borrow words from other languages. Acronyms are new words formed from the first letters or first few letters of several words.

Figurative language and idioms contain meanings different from their literal meanings. Some of the specific types of figures of speech are hyperbole, irony, metaphor, onomatopoeia, oxymorons, personification, and simile.

Word relations include synonyms, antonyms, associations, homonyms or homophones, homographs, analogies, classifications, multiple meanings, and denotative-connotative meanings. Facility with these word relations helps students refine meanings and provides a background from which they can draw when they write.

Developing mental images can be facilitated through use of inductive and deductive concept learning, developing word maps, utilizing a vocabulary overview guide, and encouraging motor imaging. As Dale's cone of experiences illustrates, the more concrete and direct experiences are, the more easily learning will occur.

Categorizing can be aided through the use of vocabulary scavenger hunts, list-group-label, semantic feature analysis and SAVOR, and semantic mapping. By helping students see relationships among words, categorizing facilitates learning and retention and provides an organizational framework to which students can refer.

When students use context to determine an unknown word's meaning, they use the surrounding words as aids in understanding the unknown word. Eight types of semantic context clues are direct definitions or explanations, explanation through example, words in a series, synonym or restatement, comparison or contrast, familiar expressions or figures or speech, inference clues, and mood or tone clues.

The use of morphemic analysis provides students with core experiences from which they can build important meanings in your content area. Students use their knowledge of prefixes, suffixes, and roots to unlock the meanings of many new words.

Word play activities are paper-and-pencil games and puzzles that add interest and further motivation to the learning process. They require thinking as opposed to mere memorization.

POSTREADING

INTEGRATING WRITING

In your journal describe students' reactions as they engage in one of the vocabulary strategies described in this chapter. Describe your reactions as you taught the lesson. Now that you have completed Chapter 4, describe the difference between telling students what a word means and teaching them the meaning.

REVIEW

The following is a list of words and concepts related to Chapter 4. Organize them into categories and be able to explain why you organized them as you did. You will have to create your own headings.

amelioration	specialization	acronym
simile	homonym (homophone)	borrowing
irony	contextual analysis	generalization
synonym	attributes	multiple meaning
hyperbole	homograph	pejoration
coining	metaphor	association
concept	antonym	onomatopoeia
denotative	classification	essential
analogy	oxymoron	connotative
euphemism	personification	nonessential

PRACTICE

Do Enabling Activities 7 through 12 in Appendix A.

5

QUESTIONING

"Have you read about the new test kids have to take before entering colleges and technical schools? I understand that the reading section contains a lot of interpretive level questions."

"I know, Phil. Since I read about it, I've been trying to develop a lot of higher cognitive level questions for my students to answer. I have enough questions to last more than a class period. Yet my students don't seem to think when it comes to answering them. You'd think that out of fifty-five questions they would think about some of their answers," replied Ralph.

DISCUSS

What factors might you consider when asking questions? Do you treat boys and girls alike when you ask questions?

PREORGANIZE

Go through the chapter and make a skeletal outline of the major headings and subheadings. This will provide you with a chapter organizer. Predict the contents of the text under one of these subheadings.

OBJECTIVES

After reading this chapter, you should be able to

1. define literal, interpretative, and critical/creative reading.
2. explain how the six levels of Bloom's taxonomy correspond to literal, interpretive, and critical/creative reading.
3. describe Herber's three levels of questions and develop statements at each level.
4. describe and give examples of the various levels of question-answer-relationships (QARs).

5. demonstrate how to improve students' answers to questions through (a) decreasing the number of questions asked, (b) increasing wait time, (c) using verbal and nonverbal reinforcement, (d) probing to have students expand or refine their answers, (e) refining gender interaction, and (f) modeling questioning.

TAXONOMIES

The types of questions we ask affect the levels of our students' thinking. These questions influence whether students will simply read to find out *who, what, when,* and *where,* or whether they will identify fallacies in reasoning, distinguish fact from opinion, and form value judgments about what they have read.

The importance of being able to answer questions at various cognitive levels is evidenced in the testing that takes place in schools. Tests must be taken by people who wish to enter colleges, universities, or technical schools. The *Texas Academic Skills Program Test* (TASP) is one example; Florida's *College Level Academic Skills Test* (CLAST) is another.

The *TASP Test* requires students to read selections of 300 to 750 words and answer multiple-choice comprehension questions keyed to these six skills:

- knowing the meanings of words and phrases;
- understanding main ideas and supporting details;
- identifying the writer's purpose, point of view, and implied meaning;
- analyzing relationships among ideas;
- evaluating materials using critical reasoning; and
- applying study skills to reading.

Clearly, helping students develop their intellect at various levels of cognition is important. Several cognitive taxonomies—hierarchical, organizational structures, or classifications—have been developed to help teachers plan instruction at various levels of cognition. This chapter covers three of these taxonomies.

Bloom's Cognitive Taxonomy

Benjamin Bloom (1956 & 1984) edited a book titled *Taxonomy of Educational Objectives Book 1: Cognitive Domain.* From this book comes Bloom's taxonomy; six levels of cognition. For our discussion we have organized Bloom's taxonomy into our traditional literal, interpretive, and critical/creative levels. The following outline presents the merging of Bloom's cognitive levels with our reading levels.

Literal Reading
  1. knowledge
  2. comprehension

Interpretive (Inferential) Reading
3. applied

Critical/Creative Reading
4. analysis
5. synthesis
6. evaluation

Now, let's consider what is involved at each of these levels.

Literal Reading

Literal comprehension means knowing what the author said, knowing what was written. Your mind acts like a warehouse, taking in and storing exactly what the author wrote.

Using Bloom's taxonomy there are two different levels of literal comprehension: knowledge and comprehension. At the *knowledge* level students recognize the facts and details using the author's own words. Students know the facts (who? what? when? where?). They also recognize details, main ideas, sequence, and cause-effect when these are stated. Students respond to questions using the words of the author.

The second level of literal comprehension is *comprehension*. Students recall what was written, but they respond by using words different from those used by the author. They translate what was written by putting it into another form. Students may rephrase or summarize, compare, graph, classify, outline, or put the information into tabular form.

Let's look at some literal level questions and directions. Can you identify which are knowledge level and which are comprehension level?

1. Compare soccer and football.
2. When was the Magna Carta signed?
3. Explain, in your own words, what the author identifies as the causes of subluxations.
4. How does the author define complex numbers?
5. Who discovered a vaccine for polio?
6. Explain the main idea of this song.
7. Make a graph of the information in this paragraph.

Questions 2, 4, and 5 are knowledge level questions. They require giving back exactly what was written; rewording or translation is not required. Questions 1, 3, 6, and 7 are comprehension level questions. You are required to put the information into a new form—your own words and graph.

Interpretive Reading

At the interpretive (inferential) level your mind becomes a production plant. It helps you identify relationships between your own experiences (actual and vicarious). Bloom calls this level the *applied* level. You apply a rule or a process to a problem, or ideas to new situations, and thus you determine a correct answer.

At the applied level you infer main ideas, cause-effect, time, place, or mood when they are not directly stated. You infer character traits, form analogies, make contrasts, and solve problems that contain a correct answer.

Let's look at some more questions and directions and identify them as knowledge, comprehension, or application.

1. Classify the words at the end of the chapter into more than one organizational pattern. Next, compare the results of these different classifications.
2. Using the definition of folded mountain, identify which of the following mountains are folded.
3. Listen to the following recordings and compare the music of Pachelbel and Chopin.
4. Divide the following artists into the two groups described in the chapter: Romantic and Renaissance.
5. From what country did Cezanne come?
6. Solve the equation $2x + 6 = 14$.
7. In your own words, state the steps for performing with this equipment.
8. Using the definition of an insect, which of these five animals are insects.

Question 5 is knowledge; you are asked to recall a fact. Questions 4 and 7 are comprehension. In 4, the information is given to you, but you are asked to put it into a different form. Question 7 is also comprehension because you are asked to rephrase (use your own words to describe) a process that has already been learned.

The rest of the questions (1, 2, 3, 6, and 8) are applied. In question 1, you go beyond classifying; you have to compare the results, but you are not given any information about the comparison. In question 2, you have to apply the rules of the definition. In question 3, you have to apply what you know about musical theory to answer the question. In 6 you are solving, or applying, what you already know. And in 8, you are applying what you know to a new situation.

Critical/Creative Reading

During critical/creative reading your mind continues to be a production plant. It helps you analyze, produce, and judge. Bloom identifies three levels within this category: analysis, synthesis, and evaluation.

At the *analysis* level you detect fact from opinion, propaganda techniques, and fallacies in reasoning. You identify motives or reasons for something happening. You assess the qualifications of a source of information. You determine evidence to support a conclusion, inference, or generalization. And you draw conclusions and identify motives and causes (why?).

At the *synthesis* level you bring together information. You produce original communications, make predictions, and anticipate outcomes. You write, create, develop, design, and synthesize. Your problems have more than one possible answer. This level is more open ended than the applied level. You consider possibilities, rather than discover one correct way.

Finally, at the *evaluation* level you make judgments. You form and offer opinions; you value and appreciate. You judge the merit of an idea, a solution to a problem, or an aesthetic work. You offer an opinion based on a set of standards.

Next, look at these questions and directions and identify them as critical/creative, interpretive, or literal.

1. Identify what the author listed as the causes of inflation.
2. After reading the editorial, tell why you think the author wrote it.
3. Solve the equation $3y + 7x = 74$, when $y = 6$.
4. Which artist do you prefer?
5. Construct a collage that represents your many emotional sides.
6. What inferences can you draw about the personality traits of the major characters in the play *Hamlet*?
7. How would life be different if people did not pollute the earth?
8. What evidence can you find to support the position that Picasso was a better painter than Bracque?
9. Do you agree with the statement "Learning geometry is necessary"?
10. Classify the mountains mentioned in this chapter as belonging to either the Rocky or Appalachian chains.
11. How can we balance our country's budget?
12. Why is our state's economy in an economic downturn?

Questions 1 and 10 are literal. Question 1 requires you to give back exactly what the author presented—causes of inflation. Question 10 asks you to present what the author presented in a different form—that is, to classify.

Questions 3 and 6 are interpretive. In question 3 you are asked to solve a problem that has a correct answer. Question 6 asks you to draw inferences based on character traits presented in the play *Hamlet*.

Questions 2, 4, 5, 7, 8, 9, 11, and 12 are critical/creative. Questions 2, 8, and 12 are analytical: question 2 asks you to identify motive; question 8 asks you to analyze a conclusion; and question 12 asks you to identify reasons.

Questions 5, 7, and 11 involve synthesis: question 5 asks for the production of an original communication; question 7 asks for a prediction; and question 11 asks you to solve a problem. Notice that these are open-ended questions and allow for a variety of answers.

Finally, on the evaluation level, questions 4 and 9 ask for judgments and opinions: Question 4 asks for a judgment or opinion; and question 9 asks you to evaluate.

We have just reviewed Bloom's six levels of comprehension. These levels are knowledge, comprehension, application, analysis, synthesis, and evaluation. Although we do not recommend an overload of knowledge and comprehension questions, it is often valuable to begin a discussion with knowledge level questions because they can serve as a foundation for higher levels of thinking.

Bloom's taxonomy is useful when you are developing discussion questions or activities for a chapter or unit you are teaching. Bloom's six levels correspond to the three major classifications of reading comprehension—literal, interpretive, and critical/creative. By keeping these classifications in mind, you can provide opportunities for your students to go beyond literal thinking and into the higher classifications of interpretive and critical/creative thinking.

Herber's Three Levels

Herber (1978) identified three levels of comprehension: literal, interpretive and applied. (At this point, you might want to go back to chapter 1 and review Reading as a Thinking Process.) You will recall that we compared *literal comprehension* to a warehouse. You put raw materials into a warehouse and take the same raw materials out of the warehouse at the literal level of comprehension. You're identifying facts the author has written. You read for facts and details and identify the author's main idea if one is stated.

You will recall that at the *interpretive level* of comprehension our factory turns the raw materials at the literal level into a new product. At the interpretive level (sometimes called the inferential level) the reader draws conclusions, makes generalizations, predicts outcomes, and understands the use of figurative language. The reader "reads between the lines."

Herber's third level, the *applied level* of comprehension, is different from Bloom's. At the applied level of comprehension (sometimes called the evaluation or critical/creative reading level), the reader develops new uses for the product that was manufactured. The reader turns what the author said or meant into original ideas. The reader judges the accuracy of the material, distinguishes between fact and opinion, identifies propaganda techniques, and asks, "What can I do with the information I have? Have I had any ideas and experiences...which are similar in principal?" (Herber, 1978, p. 40).

To check your understanding of Herber's taxonomy, read the following selection and identify the statements that follow it as literal (L), interpretive (I), or applied (A).

"Father has been working hard to build that flatboat," Jennie said to her cousin William. "He is anxious to get to the Ohio country before all of the good land has been sold."

The two cousins were sitting on a log beside the Ohio River near a town called Pittsburgh. All along the river whole families worked on flatboats and keelboats. Some of these boats were made with keels. They were called keelboats. The workers were sawing logs and fitting them together.

All of these families planned to float down the Ohio River to find new farms in the Ohio Valley. They had heard that the soil there was rich and that the land was good for farming and the price was low.

The cousins had been gathering wood and were resting now. William said, "I'm glad we finally got here. That trip over the Appalachian Mountains was really hard. It was so steep and rocky, at times I thought the wagon might tip over. I felt sorry for the horses on the steep hills."

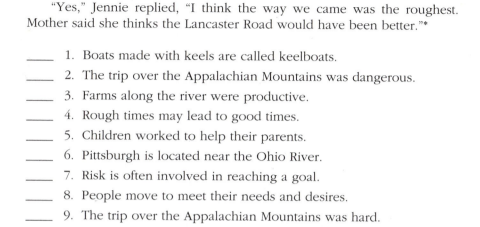

"Yes," Jennie replied, "I think the way we came was the roughest. Mother said she thinks the Lancaster Road would have been better."*

_____ 1. Boats made with keels are called keelboats.

_____ 2. The trip over the Appalachian Mountains was dangerous.

_____ 3. Farms along the river were productive.

_____ 4. Rough times may lead to good times.

_____ 5. Children worked to help their parents.

_____ 6. Pittsburgh is located near the Ohio River.

_____ 7. Risk is often involved in reaching a goal.

_____ 8. People move to meet their needs and desires.

_____ 9. The trip over the Appalachian Mountains was hard.

_____ 10. Families floated down the Ohio River to find rich land at a low price.

You probably identified statements 1, 6, 9, and 10 as literal. Evidence to support your choice of statements 1 and 6 is given directly in the second paragraph. Evidence to support statement 9 is found in paragraph 4. And statement 10 is a summary of paragraph 3.

Statements 2, 3, and 5 are interpretive. Evidence to support statement 2 is given in paragraph 4. Because we are told that the journey was made over steep and rocky mountains and that William thought the wagon was going to tip over at times, we can interpret the trip as dangerous. Statement 3 is supported by the third paragraph. You can interpret that if the soil were rich and the land were good for farming, the farms would be productive. Statement 5 can be supported by evidence in paragraphs 2 and 4. Paragraph 2 states that whole families worked, and paragraph 4 states that the cousins were resting after gathering wood. We may infer that children also worked.

Statements 4, 7, and 8 are applied. Students would have to draw on their own experiences and knowledge of other events in history to support these statements.

Next, read the following selection and identify the follow-up questions as literal, interpretive, or applied.

A little boy went to Curly and told Curly he needed "dough." Curly proceeded to hand him the flour, water, and shortening and suggested that he mix the three ingredients.

"No!" shouted the boy. "I don't want flour, water, and shortening. I don't want to cook. You don't understand. I want green dough."

Curly replied, "You can add green food coloring, and I'll do the cooking."

"You can't get into the movies with that green dough," replied the boy.

*N. Dederick and E. Lindop (1979). Adapted from *Our People of TIEGS-ADAMS: OUR LAND AND HERITAGE,* © copyright, 1979, by Ginn and Company. Used by permission of Silver Burdett Ginn Inc.

"Why sure you can," replied Curly. "Fried green dough would be a delicious snack."

_____ 1. In this story, who wanted "dough"?

_____ 2. What does the boy mean by *dough* in this story?

_____ 3. What would you have said if you were the boy?

_____ 4. Did Curly understand the boy?

_____ 5. Where were Curly and the boy?

_____ 6. Where did the boy want to go?

_____ 7. How do you think the boy felt in this story?

_____ 8. Why did Curly hand the boy flour and water?

_____ 9. Why did the boy say he wanted green dough?

_____ 10. How would you describe Curly?

Did you have difficulty answering the questions? Undoubtedly, no. After drawing on information in the paragraph and your experiences, you probably were able to answer all of the questions.

Now, did you have difficulty identifying the levels of comprehension? You probably did. Let's look at some of the classification decisions you may have made.

Question 1 probably didn't give you any trouble—it was straightforward. The first sentence told you that the little boy wanted dough. It's literal.

Questions 2, 5, 6, 7, and 9 probably didn't give you much difficulty either. These were interpretive. You could answer these questions by reading between the lines in the story. You didn't have to rely on your experience to come up with an answer.

Likewise, you undoubtedly identified question 3 easily. Because you have to go beyond the contents of the story to discuss what you would have done, this is an applied question.

Now, look at question 4. "Did Curly understand the boy?" If you look only at what the boy said in paragraph 2—"You don't understand"—it's literal. If you assume that Curly didn't understand because he gave the boy "flour, water, and shortening," it's interpretive. But suppose Curly wanted to teach the boy a lesson? Suppose Curly knew what the boy wanted all the time but didn't like his use of the word *dough?* Have you ever had such an experience? If so, you may have labeled 4 as an applied question.

Likewise, questions 8 and 10 also could be interpretive or applied, depending on your frame of reference. Did your answers to the questions come entirely from the material in the story, or did you go beyond the story and draw from past experiences or events? Was Curly naive? Or was Curly cleverly trying to teach the boy a lesson?

From the last two comprehension level experiences, you can see that presenting statements to which students respond gives you more control over whether students work at the levels of comprehension you desire. You can more easily direct students' thought processes.

Herber's three levels are useful when you want to direct students' thinking in a particular cognitive way. Using statements at the various levels is a way of modeling the thought process at each level. Statements for response are especially helpful when initiating small group work, and providing a structured situation in which students read and justify (through text and experiences) their answers. You will read more about these three levels in a later chapter.

Question-Answer-Relationships

The question-answer-relationship (QAR) is a procedure for teaching students how to locate and answer comprehension questions. Studies by Raphael (1984) and Raphael and Pearson (1985) show that instruction in QAR improves the quality of students' answers to comprehension questions.

The question-answer-relationship procedure was described by Raphael (1982) and later updated (Raphael, 1986). In QAR, students are taught to identify four types of question-answer-relationships.

Begin by teaching students the two primary sources of information: (1) In the Book and (2) In My Head. Let's look at a text excerpt and examples of the two primary types of questions used to help students understand QAR.

Over 500 ships participated. The minesweepers were the first to come. Then the destroyers came. These were followed by hospital ships, tankers, and cruisers. These ships carried the Allied forces to the beaches of Normandy.

1. What kinds of ships are listed?
2. What event is being described?

Present your students with the text paragraph by putting it on a transparency so that the whole class can see it simultaneously. Next read the text aloud and ask students the first question. The presentation and discussion might proceed as follows:

Ms. Dukes: What kind of ships participated?

Student 1: Hospital ships.

Student 2: Minesweepers.

Student 3: Cruisers.

Ms. Dukes: How do you know these ships participated? Prove it to me.

Student 4: It says so.

Ms. Dukes: Where does it say so?

Student 3:   It says minesweepers, destroyers, hospital ships, tankers, and cruisers.

Ms. Dukes: Come up to the projector and point to where you see these in the story. (*Student comes to the overhead projector and points to the words. Ms. Dukes circles each word as the student points.*)

Ms. Dukes: Yes! The information is in the story. You just read it.

To answer the second question (What event is being described?), students must go inside their heads. The answer isn't found on the page. Ms. Dukes might continue her discussion as follows:

Ms. Dukes: What event is being described?

Students: War.

Ms. Dukes: How do you know? Does the paragraph tell you it was war?

Students: No.

Ms. Dukes: If the paragraph doesn't tell you it's about war, how do you know?

Student 1:   The paragraph mentions specific types of war ships.

Student 2:   Yes, a minesweeper goes ahead of the other ships to clear the path so they won't get blown up. Destroyers are war ships.

Student 3:   I've seen these ships in movies and on TV.

Student 2:   I've seen pictures of these ships in my library book on ships.

Student 1:   I remember reading about the Allied forces. They fought on the U.S. side during World War II.

Ms. Dukes: You used your own experiences to answer this question. That was a good thing to do. Your answers came from inside your head."

Once students can identify the differences between In the Book and In My Head, they are ready for further refining of QARs. In the Book can be further refined to include "Right There" and "Think and Search." In My Head QARs can be further refined to include "Author and You" and "On My Own."
These sublevels of QARs can be explained as follows (Raphael, 1986):

1. **Right There** means the answer can easily be found. Both the word in the question and the words needed to answer the question are in the same sentence.

2. **Think and Search** questions require information from different parts of the story. Words from the question and answer are not found in the same sentence.
3. **Author and You** answers are not in the story. You think about what you already know and what the author tells you.
4. **On My Own** answers are not in the story. You can answer the question without reading the story. You use your own experiences.

In helping students identify Think and Search QARs, the class discussion with Ms. Dukes might continue like this:

Ms. Dukes: When you found the kinds of ships, did you find them in the same sentence?

Students: No.

Student 1: We found one kind of ship in the second sentence.

Student 2: We found another type in the third sentence.

Student 3: We found three types of ships in the fourth sentence.

Ms. Dukes: Right! You found the information in many places. You had to put all of the pieces of information together to form your answer.

Raphael (1982) provides the teacher with several guidelines for developing QAR skills in students. She recommends beginning with two- or three-sentence passages. Next, expand to 75 to 150 words and five questions per passage. Then, increase to the length of a basal reader story (or subsection from a chapter) and develop two questions from each QAR category. Finally, use a passage of about 600 to 800 words and two questions from each category. Raphael further recommends that the teacher have students identify the type of QAR before answering the question.

Question-answer-relationships are especially useful in working with students who look for, and try to give, knowledge and comprehension level answers to all questions that are asked. These are the students who don't know how to search the text and look for relationships among ideas to answer questions. Thinking processes are modeled for them as students explain how they arrived at interpretive and higher level answers. Students receive more structure and guidance when using this taxonomy than with those of Bloom or Herber.

In a meta-analysis of teachers' questioning practices, Redfield and Rousseau (1981) reported that students who had been in classrooms where higher level cognitive questions were asked scored significantly higher on norm-referenced achievement tests than students who were exposed mainly to lower level cognitive questions. Of course, merely asking students higher level questions is not sufficient. The thought processes behind the answers must be discussed and modeled.

IMPROVING STUDENT RESPONSES
TO QUESTIONS

Not only the questions themselves, but also certain questioning strategies, can improve the quantity and quality of student responses. Factors such as reduced numbers of questions, wait time, reinforcement, probing/response elaboration, gender equity in interaction, and modeling can all have positive effects on students' responses. These additional strategies are discussed in this section.

Number of Questions

Studies reveal that teachers ask a lot of questions. Listen to the interaction of students and teachers for a day. How many questions are asked during the typical hour?

As early as 1912, Stevens found that teachers asked a lot of questions. Most of the time teachers talked, they were asking low level questions. Stevens, Dale, and Raths (1945) found that teachers asked as many as ninety questions in several twenty-minute science lessons. Weber and Shake (1988) also found that teachers asked many low level questions during a class.

Needless to say, many teachers need to slow down and cut back on the number of questions they ask during the typical hour.

Wait Time

Pausing, or waiting, after asking a question has been shown to influence the length and quality of students' responses. Teachers often ask questions at a rapid-fire pace and expect students to answer without giving them time to think. The amount of time teachers typically give students to answer a question is less than one second. If we ask questions at such a rate, students don't have sufficient time to think about their responses.

Rowe (1974) conducted a longitudinal, six-year study of the influence of teacher wait time and student responses. She increased the length of wait time from one second to three, and then to five seconds. Rowe found that the quality of cognitive interaction improved as the wait time increased.

Several changes occurred in classrooms where wait time was increased. Students gave longer responses (they increased from an average of seven to an average of twenty-eight words). Students listened more to each other. Fewer students failed to give appropriate answers to questions. Students engaged in higher level thinking. A greater number of students volunteered to give answers. Student-initiated questioning increased. Slower students, who normally did not answer questions, asked and answered more questions.

If an immediate answer is not given, the normal reaction of teachers is to quickly move on to another student or to ask a different question. The silence of no response is uncomfortable for teachers. During this quiet period, resist the temptation to occupy the time with fillers such as *uh-huh, um, okay,* and avoid saying *"Think."* By teaching yourself to wait five seconds, you can dramatically improve the cognitive interaction in your classroom.

Reinforcements

Rewarding the student behavior you desire by verbal and nonverbal means can be an effective tool if it is used honestly and is specific. In an investigation of grade 7 students, Hughes (1973) found that positive teacher reactions improved student achievement significantly more than neutral reactions.

Verbal reinforcement, sometimes called praise, involves statements such as "Right," "Good," or "Excellent!" Another example of verbal reinforcement involves using student ideas for instruction and learning.

Brophy (1981) identifies characteristics of effective and ineffective reinforcement. Reinforcement is ineffective when it

- is delivered without purpose, randomly and unsystematically.
- is limited to global positives such as "Good" and "I like that."
- is the same for all students and all responses.
- rewards participation without consideration of outcome, giving little or no consideration for quality.

Effective reinforcement, on the other hand,

- is delivered when appropriate.
- specifies the accomplishment ("Good, you remembered the primary colors we discussed last week").
- shows variety.
- is individualized toward individual student performance.

A second type of reinforcement is nonverbal. Your body language sends strong messages to students. Do you smile or frown? Where do you stand—close to students or far away? Were do you look—at students or away from them? How do you hold your hands and arms—tightly closed and crossed or relaxed and more open? Do you look interested or bored? These nonverbal cues send strong messages to students.

A word of caution about reinforcement: Mims and Gholson (1977) found that if a teacher did not respond to an incorrect answer, students interpreted the non-reaction as positive feedback and repeated their mistakes. Advise students to erase inappropriate responses from their memory.

If used appropriately, reinforcement can be a strong factor in encouraging and improving student responses. Remember, you must be honest in your praise of students.

Probing

Through probing, or response elaboration, teachers examine the reasons for students' responses and carefully direct students to elaborate, or expand, on their answers. Probing is used to encourage students to be clearer and more accurate in their responses. Duffy and Roehler (1987) refer to this process as *response elaboration.*

The following is a segment of a class discussion in which the teacher uses response elaboration.

TEACHER: Describe the judicial branch of government.

STUDENT: It enforces laws.

TEACHER: How does it enforce laws? Be more specific.

STUDENT: Courts are set up to try people who break the laws.

TEACHER: Explain how the courts function or operate.

STUDENT: I know there is a judge, usually two lawyers, and a jury.

Here is another segment of a probing discussion.

TEACHER: How can we stop littering?

STUDENT: Arrest people. Make people pay fines.

TEACHER: Can we just arrest people and make them pay fines because we don't like what they are doing?

STUDENT: No.

TEACHER: What must happen before we can arrest people and have them pay fines?

STUDENT: People must break laws.

TEACHER: What laws would you make?

STUDENT: I would make it illegal for anyone to litter along the roadside, on the beach, in parks, in parking lots, in forests—anywhere. I would make individual people pay $5,000 fines; and industries would have to pay in the millions—even if it's only a small piece of paper.

TEACHER: Do you think the law would work? How would you enforce it?

Gender Equity and Interaction

Do you treat male and female students the same? You probably believe that you do. Yet studies have shown that this is not so; male and female students *are* treated differently.

Brophy and Good (1974) reported that males received many more reprimands than females. Further, the verbal communication between the teacher and male and female students also differed.

Dweck et al. (1978) studied differences in the praise given to male and female students. Teachers praised boys for performance, how well they accomplished the task or answered the question. And teachers used more probing questions with boys—for example, "That's right. You described all the details. How did the person feel?" As you can see, the teacher told this male student why his answer was correct and encouraged him to elaborate on his response. When making negative evaluations, teachers were more likely to criticize males for sloppy handwriting or for calling out answers without raising their hands.

The results of this pattern of praise and criticism led to males seeing praise as meaningful and criticism as inconsequential. The praise reinforced the positive behavior that they interpreted as coming from their own abilities, but the criticism was something they could shrug off because it was seen as the teacher's attitude toward them, not something within themselves.

Females, on the other hand, were praised for matters that were not as cognitively oriented (like neatness or speaking clearly) rather than for the quality of their answers. Teachers tended to use praise statements such as "Yes," "Good," or "You're right"; but they did not encourage females to elaborate on their answers. As a result, females viewed the praise as meaningless and without substance.

Teachers tended to limit their criticism of females to poor performance, not raising hands, and so on. Because teachers had only criticized them when they did not perform well, females were very discouraged by criticism, and they viewed failure as a result of their lack of ability.

Gender equity is important to consider when teaching. The direction and level of teacher praise *does* affect students' perceptions of their abilities.

Reciprocal Questioning for Modeling

A strategy that encourages students to ask questions independently and to set their own purposes for reading is called *ReQuest,* or *reciprocal questioning.* Manzo (1979a, b) describes the role of the teacher as being a role model for questioning skills and providing feedback to students about their questions. The *Becoming a Nation of Readers* report (1985) specifically recommends this strategy because the teacher engages in direct instruction by modeling questioning skills and because students demonstrate these skills by taking active roles as teachers. The strategy employs the following steps:

1. Tell students that the purpose of the lesson is to help them improve their comprehension, or understanding, of what they read. You and your students will read one sentence at a time. Then you will take turns asking each other questions. They will be able to ask you questions first; and then you will be able to ask them questions about the same sentence. The person or persons answering the questions will have to keep their books closed.

2. You should answer all questions fully, but do not elaborate on low-level (factual) questions your students may ask. If students cannot answer a question when it is their turn to answer questions, ask them to explain why they cannot. Perhaps the question was poorly worded or unclear. Assist the student in rewording the question.

3. As you and your students answer questions, be sure to justify, and have students justify, their answers by referring to specific information in the text.

4. Initially, students' questions will be factual. These factual questions usually will lead to one-word answers and no discussion. When it is your turn to ask questions, you should model questions at higher levels of comprehension.

5. If students ask higher order questions, you should respond with, "That's a good question. I have to think before I answer it." If students' questions are low level, you should merely answer the questions.

6. You and your students should continue through the paragraph until they have developed a purpose for reading the selection. You may have to continue through two or three paragraphs until a purpose is established.

Let's take a look at the following sentence: "Keeping close to the buildings, we cautiously made our way step by step along the street on that cold, windy night." Your students would probably ask: "What time of day was it?" And you might respond, "It was night. The sentence said it was night."

"Where were they walking?" And you would respond, "They were walking along a street. "

When your students have finished asking you questions, you might ask, "How do you think they felt?" Students would have to infer and give clues from the sentence to back up their feelings.

You might ask, "Why do you think they were walking along the street?" Students would have to predict in order to answer this question.

These last two questions could lead to setting a purpose for reading the selection.

Nolte and Singer (1985) found that students' comprehension was increased when teachers used reciprocal questioning. First, teachers modeled appropriate questions (asking about main characters, setting, what the characters wanted to do, what hardships were involved) as students silently read paragraphs, one at a time, to answer them. Then students were placed into small groups where they developed questions about the story and answered these questions. As a next step in the sequence, students worked on reciprocal questioning in pairs.

Palincsar and Brown (1986) also used the reciprocal questioning strategy with students and presented a summary of the results of various studies conducted on the classroom use of this strategy. They found that the comprehension of poor readers increased and that students in large classes performed better on comprehension tests when reciprocal questioning was used. They also found that reciprocal teaching could be used in the content classroom, as well as in conjunction with listening activities.

CONCLUSION

The three taxonomies we studied were Bloom's cognitive levels, Herber's three levels, and question-answer-relationships. Bloom's taxonomy consists of six levels: knowledge, comprehension, application, analysis, synthesis, and evaluation. Each level can be classified as requiring either literal, interpretive, or critical/creative reading skills.

Herber's three levels are literal, interpretive, and applied. The third taxonomy is question-answer-relationships (QARs). Students focus their attention on where information is found—in their heads or in the book.

There are at least six ways to improve students' responses to questions. Decrease the number of questions asked, increase wait time, use verbal and nonverbal reinforcement, ask probing questions, be aware of the verbal reinforcement used with males and females, and model questioning.

POSTREADING

INTEGRATING WRITING

Select a chapter from your content area textbook. In your journal develop three questions on the chapter at each cognitive level—literal, interpretive, and critical/ creative. Observe a classroom and describe the questioning strategies used by the teacher. Describe students' responses to higher level questions.

REVIEW

The following is a list of words and concepts related to Chapter 5. Organize them into categories and be able to explain why you organized them as you did. You may have to develop some of your own category names.

critical/creative	probing	reinforcement
evaluation	synthesis	analysis
in my head	wait time	reciprocal questioning
gender equity	taxonomy	knowledge
three levels	right there	on my own
author and you	applied	comprehension
in the book	interpretive	applied
QARs	literal	think and search

PRACTICE

Do Enabling Activities 13 and 14 in Appendix A.

6

BUILDING BACKGROUND
AND PREDICTING

"Students in my class won't read their texts. They constantly complain that it's boring and means nothing to them," moaned Beth.

"I know the feeling," agreed Al. "My students keep telling me that it's old stuff or they can't get into the chapters."

"It's really discouraging when I spend so much time organizing lectures and then no one in the class seems to care," interjected Laura.

"They either don't have the backgrounds they need," added Al, "or they don't relate their own backgrounds to what they are reading."

"Bob tells me that he doesn't have these problems with his students," said Beth. "I wonder if he'll share his 'magic' with us. Let's ask him what he does."

DISCUSS

What ideas do you have about helping students draw on their background of experiences before reading an assignment? Of what value is it to spend time activating students' experiences prior to reading an assignment?

PREORGANIZE

Go through the chapter and make a skeletal outline of the major headings and subheadings. This will provide you with a chapter organizer. Predict the contents of the text under one of these subheadings.

OBJECTIVES

After reading this chapter, you should be able to

1. describe and construct examples of vocabulary and concept introduction, teacher-prepared assistance, and student involvement strategies for building background.
2. describe and give examples of the following prediction-oriented strategies: think sheet, expectation outline, directed inquiry, and prereading question.
3. identify guidelines for asking and using prereading questions.

Flood and Lapp (1990) write that metareaders—or strategic readers—preview, build background, and set purposes before reading. Previewing involves looking at the topics, subtopics, and pictures, and perhaps reading the introduction and summary. You preview each chapter in this text as you complete the preorganize activity at the beginning of the chapter.

In this chapter we will be studying how to assist students in two strategic prereading activities—building background and predicting.

BUILDING BACKGROUND

The ultimate goal of content area teachers is to have students comprehend the materials in their specific courses. Students, however, don't always have the background to begin reading content area materials on their own. Students may not be aware of how their experiences relate to the topic being studied. For these reasons, it is important to activate students' prior knowledge before they begin reading. It's important to help them predict the contents of the selection.

Read the following paragraph to understand the problems students may face when reading content area materials. Then answer the comprehension questions that follow the paragraph.

From all avib edence no vock fram had ever set fim in this zinny Twiz mage before Eet kump. Eet was pote before sumping that Eet would zobly be a "nart" for the mage; Eet pode this to veam that norgles of my tooption zenderly were reen in Twizland.

1. What kind of mage was in Twizland?
2. What was Eet for the mage?
3. No "what" had ever set fim in the Twiz mage?
4. How often were norgles like Eet reen in Twizland?

Comprehension depends on language awareness. Because of your language background, you probably were able to answer all of the comprehension questions about the selection.

You were able to identify *Twizland* as a proper noun because it began with a capital letter. Using this information, you could refer back to sentence 1 and identify

Twiz as an adjective describing the *mage*. *Zinny* is a word that describes the type of mage in Twizland. Also, you can add *-er* and *-est* to *zinny* and still have it "sound right." The ability to add *-er* and *-est* to a word is a clue that the word is an adjective. The designator noun marker *this* precedes the adjectives *zinny* and *Twiz* and gives a clue that *mage* is a noun.

In question 2, your knowledge of the verb *to be* and the noun marker a led you to identify that Eet was a *nart* for the mage. Question 3 could have been answered easily. The first sentence in the paragraph states that *no vock fram had ever set fim in this zinny Twiz mage.* In answering question 4 you probably recognized *zenderly* as an adverb because it ends in *-ly* and describes time or manner.

In your everyday reading you do not have to resort to such analyses because language, language patterns, and language organization are natural to you. But to many students, reading content area materials is not a natural process. Students have to be led through the process.

You were able to use the passage's syntactic clues to answer the questions. This selection, however, would have made more sense to you if we had taken time to establish background in terms of where Twizland was located, what its people were like, and what it was like to live in Twizland.

Your comprehension would have improved even further if we developed your understandings of *mage, Eet, norgles,* and so on. If these were real, rather than nonsense, words we could have had you draw on your own experiences to establish background. Ausubel (1968) wrote that "the single most important factor influencing new learning is what the learner already knows." Anderson and Pearson (1984) established the importance of background on reading comprehension.

Frager (1993) describes the affective advantages of prereading activities. Prereading activities help students gain confidence. Prereading increases students' interest; interest enhances motivation; and motivation improves learning (comprehension). Thus, preparing students to read is a prerequisite for students' comprehension of the material in their textbooks. Clary (1986) wrote that building background through graphic designs, setting purposes, and making predictions can aid in improving comprehension. The *Becoming a Nation of Readers* report highlighted the importance of building on the knowledge students already possess so that they can see relationships between what they already know and what they are reading.

As you study this chapter, refer to the questioning taxonomies we described in Chapter 5. Use these to help you write questions or statements at various comprehension levels; and remember the guidelines for asking questions. Following these guidelines will improve the quantity and quality of students' responses.

Throughout this section of the chapter we will describe specific kinds of strategies for building background. These strategies will be classified as vocabulary and concepts introduction, teacher-prepared assistance, and student involved strategies.

Vocabulary and Concept Introduction

You can introduce vocabulary and concepts in numerous ways that activate students' prior knowledge. These can range from hands-on experiences to semiconcrete experiences. In this section we view concrete and semiconcrete experiences and drawing as ways to help students build background.

Concrete and Semiconcrete Experiences

Take a minute to review Dale's cone of experiences in Chapter 4. We can build background through direct (purposeful) experiences, contrived experiences, dramatized experiences, demonstrations, field trips, exhibits, television, motion pictures and videos, and we can now add computers to the cone. Direct, purposeful experiences are the easiest to learn and retain.

Drawings

McConnell (1992/93) describes putting mental images into drawings to build background. Students are asked to draw a picture (it can be a simple line and stick-figure drawing) of how they picture a concept being studied. Students are then asked to share their drawings with the class and talk about what they pictured. As the sharing and discussion ensue, similarities and differences are noted in the drawings.

For example, before studying a science chapter on volcanoes, a student's drawing of a volcano might be a simple cone shape with a hole in the middle.

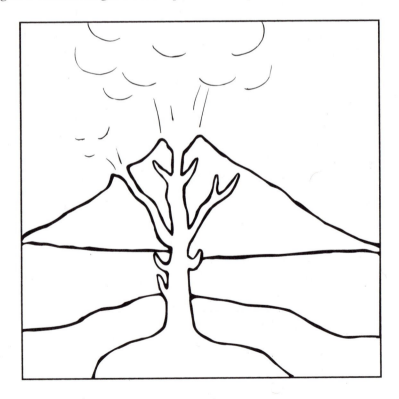

As students are describing their pictures, the teacher makes a list or labels the pictures with words the students contribute. The teacher then organizes these words into a map for student reference. Students can then refer to this map as they read or write.

Later in the discussion students are asked to talk about how they knew the information. They might identify newspapers, books, magazines, movies, TV, radio, videos, other people, or computers as sources of information.

You might like to have students draw a second picture after reading the selection. You and your students can then compare the first and second pictures. For example, the "after" picture of a volcano might include its layers.

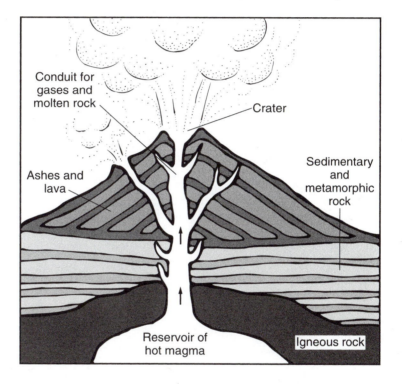

This strategy is appropriate for students at all levels. The visual images enhance retention and provide a reference for students to use in reading and writing.

Teacher-Prepared Assistance

Sometimes the content being studied requires that the teacher do more extensive preparation to help students build background. These strategies involve teachers preparing written materials for students. Teacher-prepared assistance strategies include structured overviews, advance organizers, prereading/reasoning guides, and structured question guide and process sheets.

Structured Overview

The structured overview is a type of cognitive organizer. A structured overview is a graphic or diagrammatic representation showing the relationships among vocabulary or major concepts in a unit or lesson. This strategy was developed by Richard Barron.

Earle and Barron (1973) list the following steps in developing a structured overview:

1. Identify vocabulary and concepts needed to understand the lesson or unit.
2. Arrange the words until you have a graphic or diagrammatic representation showing the interrelationships among vocabulary and concepts necessary for learning the lesson or unit.
3. Add vocabulary terms students already know to the scheme so that students can relate the known to the unknown and the relationships within the discipline as a whole.
4. Check to see if the overview is presented clearly and major relationships are shown.
5. Show the scheme to the students. Explain your reasons for arranging the terms the way you did.
6. As you teach your lesson or unit, relate new information to the organizer.

The structured overview differs from the semantic map (Chapter 4) in terms of development. The semantic map is developed through the brainstorming of students and teacher, whereas the structured overview is prepared by the teacher prior to showing it to students. We have included the structured overview in this chapter on comprehension, but we could just as easily have placed it with semantic mapping. Both are means of developing meaning and seeing relationships before reading. Examples 6.1 through 6.4 are sample structured overviews.

Example 6.1   Structured Overview for Health

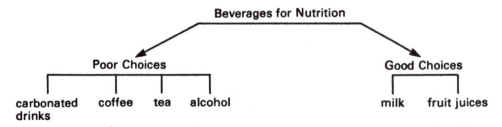

Example 6.2   Structured Overview for Math

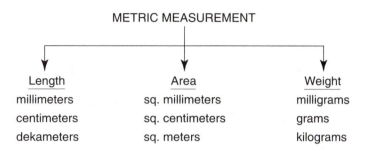

METRIC MEASUREMENT

<u>Length</u>	<u>Area</u>	<u>Weight</u>
millimeters	sq. millimeters	milligrams
centimeters	sq. centimeters	grams
dekameters	sq. meters	kilograms

Example 6.3   Structured Overview for Geography

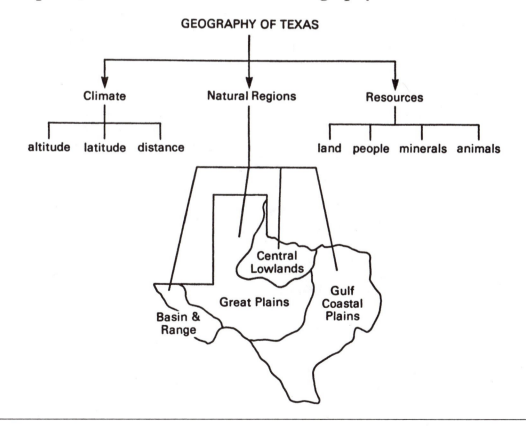

GEOGRAPHY OF TEXAS

Climate   Natural Regions   Resources

altitude   latitude   distance   land   people   minerals   animals

Central Lowlands

Great Plains

Gulf Coastal Plains

Basin & Range

Example 6.4   Structured Overview for Art

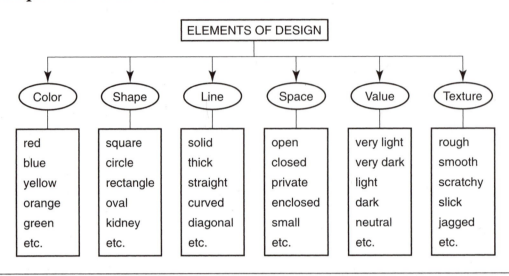

Advance Organizers

Advance organizers are specific types of cognitive organizers. They are a means of helping students relate the new reading material to something they already know.

David Ausubel (1968) is credited with describing and developing the advance organizer. According to Ausubel, meaning does not depend on the method of teaching. Rather, it depends on the learner's background and experiences. If material can be related to the learner's background and experiences (the learner's previously acquired knowledge or experiences), it can be meaningful.

An advance organizer (Ausubel, 1960, 1968) is introductory material presented ahead of the material to be read. Advance organizers are developed by using concept definitions, generalizations, analogies, or illustrations. They should be broad or general enough to incorporate or subsume more specific details in the selection. These advance organizers help the learner relate the material they will read to previously learned material and show relationships between content.

Weil and Joyce (1978) identified two types of advance organizers: comparative and expository. *Comparative organizers* point out major similarities and differences between similar concepts and often are presented as analogies. *Expository organizers* present key facts when learning unfamiliar concepts. Concept definitions or generalizations are utilized in creating expository organizers.

Merely asking students to recall a personal experience or what they did last week, listing for them the objectives of the lesson, or telling them what will be done the following day (Weil & Joyce, 1978) are not advance organizers according to Ausubel's model. Nevertheless, even these cognitive organizers do aid students in comprehending material.

Let's take a look at some examples of advance organizers. Examples 6.5 and 6.6 show an expository and a comparative model.

Example 6.5   An Expository Advance Organizer on Culture

Culture refers to the way people live. The way people eat, the houses they live in, the way they make a living, the language they speak, and the way they worship are all part of their way of life, or culture. Children learn the culture from their parents and other people around them. People learn to talk, eat, work, and worship from their culture.

People throughout the world have the same basic needs. All people must eat. But all people do not eat the same foods. All people must have a place to live. But all people do not build their houses alike. All people speak. But there are many different languages. People in different areas of the world meet their needs in different ways. The different ways people meet their needs make up culture.*

---

*From J. E. Steinbrink (1970), *Comparative Rural Landscapes: A Conceptual Geographic Model* (Geography Curriculum Project, University of Georgia), p. M9. Reprinted with permission of the author.

Example 6.6   A Comparative Advance Organizer on the River System and Circulatory System

A river system is as important to the other elements of the physical environment as the circulatory system is to the human body. It also has some of the same features. A main river, such as the Mississippi River, provides the "life-blood"—water—for plants and animals as well as the agricultural industry and the hydroelectric industry, just as the aorta as a major artery carries blood to the parts of the body. Besides water, it also carries many sources of food for plants and animals. In this respect, rivers resemble the arteries of our body which carry nutrients to the different parts of the body. They are like veins in that they carry many waste products back to the sea. However, a river system differs from the circulatory system in that the food supply and wastes are all carried in one channel. Another similarity is that, like capillaries, streams feed into the river. Therefore, like the circulatory system, the river system functions both as the carrier of sources of energy and as a carrier of waste products.

Just as man can misuse the circulatory system, man can also misuse a river system. When too much waste is carried by the river, it starts to clog up, just as a vein or artery can get clogged. Factories along rivers and soil erosion caused by poor farming methods or poor forestry practices are major causes of clogging. Also, chemicals, fertilizers, and insecticides used by farmers have caused the vegetation along rivers to change. As with the circulatory system, this damage sometimes cannot be repaired, and the repairs, if possible at all, are very time consuming.*

---

*From Eggen/Kauchak/Harder, *Strategies for Teachers: Information Processing Models in the Classroom,* © 1979, p. 263. Reprinted by permission of Prentice-Hall, Englewood Cliffs, New Jersey.

The writing of advance organizers can be time consuming. As you are reading magazines, books, and journals, be alert to advance organizers that are appropriate for your subject area. Once you are aware of the concept of advance organizers, you will begin noticing them when and where you least expect it.

Prereading Reasoning Guide

Prereading reasoning guides are recommended by Macklin (1978) and Bean and Peterson (1981) as a means to help students identify their feelings and beliefs related to ideas or issues raised in a selection. Prereading guides provide a good method of motivating the reading of a selection and following up silent reading with discussion. They are an especially productive strategy for use with newspaper editorials and opinion pieces. To construct and utilize a prereading guide, follow these steps:

1. After you read the selection, identify students' feelings, beliefs, and experiences related to the selection.
2. Develop statements that reflect these feelings, experiences, or beliefs.
3. Prior to reading have students react positively or negatively to each statement. (You can present these statements to students on duplicated handouts or transparencies.)
4. Encourage students to discuss their reactions.
5. Guide students through reading the selection.
6. Have students complete the guide a second time after reading the selection and this time identify the author's perspective as well. Students should identify changes, if any, that have occurred between their responses and the author's viewpoint.
7. Through discussions, students identify differences between their viewpoints and those of the author. Their reasoning must be based on specific information in the selection.

Example 6.7   Prereading Reasoning Guide

Directions: Indicate your agreement with a statement by placing a + and your disagreement by placing a − in the space provided. Complete the anticipation column before reading the selection. Complete the reaction column after reading the selection, and mark what you think the author believes. Do your views change? Do you agree with the author?

Anticipation	*Reaction*	*Author*	
_____	_____	_____	1. It's easier to identify instinctive behaviors in lower animals.
_____	_____	_____	2. The use of drugs is always improper.
_____	_____	_____	3. Positive reinforcement is used in the home and at school.
_____	_____	_____	4. Habits can be broken.

Structured Question Guide and Process Sheet

The structured question guide and process sheet is utilized in the direct discovery approach recommended by Lewis (1979). Lewis draws from the work of Bruner (1961), who recommended discovery learning, and Ausubel (1963), who suggested using written material to present generalizations before reading.

The teacher uses student-generated questions as a motivational device for having students develop concepts and form generalizations. In other words, students work with ideas before reading about them in their textbooks. Reading then serves as a basis for either confirming or rejecting their hypotheses.

Students use a structured question guide and process sheet to aid in their problem solving. They might address such problems as "Should we build nuclear power plants in every state?" "Can solar energy replace oil?" "Will a twelve-month school year ever become popular?" They try to find the answer to such questions as how? why? what? how much? and what will happen if...? They accomplish this by using guide and process sheets that require them to use such process skills as predicting, observing, comparing, classifying, describing, inferring, communicating, experimenting, analyzing, and making deductions.

In science, experiments may be used as a catalyst. After completing the process sheet, students read the textbook and other sources to clarify, confirm, or expand on their conclusions. A question a student brings up during a class discussion might be the catalyst for a lesson in social studies.

Follow these guidelines for using the process sheet:

1. The teacher develops a structured question guide and process sheet around a question of interest or a main idea related to a lesson that is being studied.

2. Students complete the activities in the guide individually and then form groups to compare their answers. The activities may center around experiments or common experiences. (Be sure you leave information which students must gain from reading and not only from discussion.)

3. The students and teacher discuss the group responses and exchange ideas.

4. Finally, the students are introduced to reading material that further develops the concepts covered in the structured question guide and process sheet.

Example 6.8   Structured Question Guide and Process Sheet

Problem: Is pollution having an adverse effect on our environment?

To find out, do the following activities:

1. Possible sources of pollution are listed in column A. In column B, list their harmful effects. In column C, list the benefits these sources of pollution may have to society. In column D, rank these from 1 to 6 according to which you think has the most harmful effects on society. Give a 1 to the one you think has the most harmful effect and a 6 to the one you think has the least harmful effect on society.

A Sources of Pollution	B Harmful Effects	C Benefits to Society	D Ratings
cars			
industries (factories)			
dumping industrial waste			
chemical use (on farms)			
nuclear waste			
other: _____			

2. Compare your answers with group members.
   a. Did members of your group have similar harmful effects listed? Which were the same for most members?
   b. Were the same benefits listed by several members of your group? What were these benefits?
   c. Did any in your group list harmful effects or benefits that no one else listed? Why do you think this happened?
   d. Compare your ratings in column D with others in your group. How were they alike or different?
   e. Why do you think your ratings were different?

3. What can be done to solve the problem of pollution?

As a variation in using a structured question guide and process sheet, let students develop their own question sheets. In this way they will be integrating writing into your content area.

Student-Involved Strategies

Student-involved strategies can be done quickly with students and do not require a large amount of time in teacher preparation. These strategies include question only (QOS), PReP, and opinion poll.

Question-Only Strategy

The question-only strategy, or QOS, is recommended by Manzo (1980). Students try to find out information about a topic by asking the teacher questions.

1. Students are told that they may ask questions to find out everything they can about a topic. After they finish asking questions, they will be given a test covering all the information the teacher thinks is important. If you, the teacher, think information is important, you should cover it on the test even if students haven't asked you questions about it.
2. Students ask you questions and you answer them without a lot of elaboration.
3. Give the students the test and follow up with a discussion of questions the students asked and those they should have asked.
4. Direct the students to listen to your lecture and read the text to learn what they didn't learn in the questioning session.
5. You may give a follow-up test (optional).

QOS is a sound strategy to use when you want students to think, probe, and listen. Students learn what information is important, and QOS equips them with an effective study technique—trying to predict questions the teacher will ask on a test.

Prereading Plan

The prereading plan (PReP) recommended by Langer (1981) assists the teacher in determining what students know about the topic to be studied and the students' ability to express their ideas. The strategy involves these steps:

1. Students are instructed to tell the teacher everything they know about a topic (for example, What does the word *law* bring to mind?). The teacher records students' responses on the board.
2. Next, students are asked why they responded the way they did. What caused you to think of that? For example, Why did you think of criminals, Julio? "I saw them on TV programs." Why did you say *judiciary*, Larry? "People are tried in a court and a judge presides over the court."
3. After students finish discussing their responses, they are asked if they have any new ideas about the topic. Have their views changed? Have they

learned anything new about the topic? Julio said, "I learned that people are tried in courts in the United States, and a judge is in charge of the courtroom."

According to Langer (1981), a teacher can identify three levels of background knowledge students may have by using this strategy. Students who don't have much background usually will mention words that might be similar in sound but not in meaning (e.g., *El Salvador* and *Eldorado*) or irrelevant material. Students with some background usually discuss characteristics or give examples. And, students who have a great deal of background go into detail, use analogies, and present definitions.

Opinion Polls

Opinion polls were described by Crawley and Mountain (1981) as a values clarification strategy. Experience in a decision-making process involves discussing issues and proposing possible solutions to them. It involves judging, on a personal basis, the appropriateness of decisions.

Values play a role in the way we approach a reading topic. We may have incorrect or preconceived ideas based on one experience we have had. Opinion polls provide an opportunity for students to discuss their views and build background prior to reading a selection. The lively debate that may result is good motivation for reading with interest.

Use of the opinion polls strategy requires students to take a stand on an issue and to defend or give reasons for taking that position. Before beginning, write the following labels across the chalkboard (or put them on signs on different walls of the classroom):

WRONG   **MORE WRONG THAN RIGHT**   **MORE RIGHT THAN WRONG**   **RIGHT**

You could substitute a rating scale of 1 to 4 if you want students to begin to think about numeric scales.

Next, read an issue statement aloud to your students. Give your students one minute to decide and take a stand. At the end of one minute each student physically takes a stand, moving to the label that reflects his or her position. The next step is to have students give reasons for their decisions.

The topics you select would depend on topics being studied in your class. Possible topics include the following:

1. Censorship of the arts is good and appropriate.
2. A country's position in war should always be supported by the citizens of that country.
3. Medical experimentation on animals is appropriate for the purpose of finding cures for disease.

4. Non-traditional forms of medical care (like acupuncture and chiropractic) should be covered by medical insurance.
5. All students should be required to take (<u>name subject</u>) (math, art, music, P.E., English, computers, science, law, economics, social studies).
6. Dress codes should be established and enforced.
7. A specific and acceptable hair length should be specified by schools.
8. Students should be required to spend their lunch hour on school grounds and eat specifically planned meals in the lunchroom.

We have reviewed three kinds of strategies for building background. Vocabulary and concepts introduction included concrete and semi-concrete experiences (based on Dale's cone of experiences) and drawings. Teacher-prepared assistance included the structured overview, the advance organizer, the prereading/reasoning guide, and the structured question guide and process sheet. Student-initiated strategies included question only, PReP, and opinion polls.

PREDICTING

You piqued students' curiosity as you built background in the previous section. You can now guide students in making predictions, or setting their own purposes for reading. During silent reading students try to confirm or find they must reject their predictions. This leads to a more active and involved role for the reader. Students interact more with the reading material. Predicting, as you will see, is extremely easy to use.

In this section we will describe the following prediction strategies: think sheets, expectation outlines, directed inquiries, and prereading questions.

Think Sheet

A strategy recommended by Clewell and Haldemos (1983) to help students identify the author's organizational pattern is the think sheet. Students use the think sheets to predict the content of a selection and help set purposes for reading. The strategy includes these steps:

1. Begin with a chapter or section of a textbook.
2. List the headings and subheadings in boldface print. Provide space between each heading or subheading for student writing. If subheadings are not given, use phrases from the first sentences of each paragraph.
3. Working in pairs or small groups, have students discuss (predict) what information will be included under each subheading. Students write this information in the space provided.
4. Students read the chapter and determine if their predictions are accurate.
5. Students meet with their original partners and revise their predictions as needed.

This strategy is especially useful in the social studies and sciences, or in other areas with specifically delineated topics and subtopics. This, you will notice, provides students with an outline of the selection's organization and content. You can vary the procedure by having students, rather than you, list the topics and subtopics. You have been engaged in a variation of the think sheet method at the beginning of each chapter in this textbook. Example 6.9 shows a completed think sheet.

Example 6.9   Think Sheet

A Variety of Drugs
It probably lists different types of drugs.

Drug Use and Abuse
*It probably identifies some of the following misuses: overdoses, withdrawal, and
    shooting drugs.*
Prescription drugs can be misused.

Stimulants and Depressants
What are the differences between the two?

Expectation Outline

The expectation outline (Spiegel, 1981) is recommended for use with science and social studies texts and with factual stories. Several steps are employed in developing this outline:

1.   The teacher asks students what they think (expect) they'll learn as they read the selection—what questions will the selection answer? As students respond, the teacher writes their questions on the board and groups related questions together. What foods do they grow? What do they eat? How do they cook their food if they don't have electricity? What kinds of homes do they live in? What are their homes made of? How do they build homes if they don't have electricity?

2.   When the students have finished asking their questions, the teacher directs their attention to what she has written on the board. "Do you notice anything these questions have in common? Can you think of a heading for this list of questions?" (*Nutrition* or *Food, Shelter* or *Housing*)

3.   Next, students read the selection to find answers to their questions and prove their answers by reading the appropriate material aloud.

4.   Not all the questions students suggest will be answered as they read the selection. There will probably be questions that the students cannot answer based on the information in the selection. You can post these questions in the room and encourage students to use other sources to locate the answers.

You will notice that this activity differs from the think sheet in that student questions, rather than the text outline, form the basis for the content, or study, or outline. Student prediction here also sets the stage for further or extended investigation of the topic.

Directed Inquiry Activity

The directed inquiry activity (Thomas, 1978) is a modification of Russell Stauffer's directed-reading-thinking activity. Students predict answers to the questions who? what? when? where? why? and how? After reading the selection, students' confirm or revise their predictions. The strategy involves these steps:

1. Students survey part of the material they are going to read. This may be only the title in a short selection, more in a longer selection.
2. After surveying, students predict answers to these six questions: *Who? What? When? Where? Why? How?*
3. You record students' responses on the board under the appropriate category.
4. As you record student responses, elaborate on some of their predictions by asking additional questions that might direct students' thinking.
5. As you record responses under each category, you can also help students identify interrelationships among ideas in the various categories.
6. When students have finished predicting, they read to verify their predictions.
7. Follow up the reading by analyzing students' predictions. Material in answer to each question category is added, deleted, or modified.

This strategy works especially well with narrative and social studies materials, but it also can be used in other content areas. You should remember, however, that you must be thoroughly prepared in order to elaborate during the predicting stage.

Prereading Question

The prereading question, by itself, is not a prediction-centered strategy; however, it can be varied to become one. We take time to discuss prereading questions because many textbooks now include them in the teacher's guide.

The prereading question is developed by the teacher or the textbook author, not the students. The student is provided with a brief statement about the selection, followed by a purpose for reading the selection (often stated in the form of a question). Example 6.10 presents several prereading questions.

A word of caution is in order if you are using, or considering using, prereading questions. Faw and Walker (1976) found that factual prereading questions tended to direct students toward looking for specific pieces of information rather than encouraging overall comprehension. You should not disregard the prereading questioning strategy because some students need more direct guidance in developing purposes for reading. Perhaps a more promising strategy would be to have students develop their own prereading questions (Singer, 1978).

Example 6.10   Prereading Questions

1. People encounter many dangers when climbing Mt. Everest, yet some people still try. This selection describes the dangers encountered and the forces that compel people to make the climb. When reading the selection, try to answer the following questions: Why do people undertake the dangerous climb up Mt. Everest? What dangers do these people encounter?

2. This selection describes the three states of matter. Read the selection to identify examples of these states of matter in your life.

3. A boy named Teddy rescues a mongoose named Rikki-tikki-tavi. How do you think Rikki-tikki-tavi shows his loyalty to Teddy and his family? (Make a list of students' predictions.) Let's read the story silently to find out if your predictions are correct.*

4. This selection is part of a letter that King wrote to a group of black clergymen while he was in jail in Birmingham. As you read the letter silently, try to identify King's mood as he was writing.*

5. Life in Canada was very different during the 1820s. How do you think life was different from the way it is today? Read the selection silently to learn more about Canada during the pioneer days.*

Pearson (1985) provides the following suggestions for teachers who wish to use prereading questions for stories:

1. Have students relate the story to previous experiences.
2. Have students make predictions about the story.
3. Use inferential types of questions that will require students to think outside of the story.
4. Have students answer your prereading question immediately after reading.
5. Use synthesis types of activities (dramatization, summarizing) as follow-up activities.

By having students predict answers to the prereading question, we have changed the strategy into a prediction strategy, with three strong advantages: it is (1) simple to use, (2) an efficient use of time, and (3) can be used with all subject areas.

We reviewed four prediction strategies—the think sheet, the expectation outline, the directed inquiry activity, and the prereading question. The strategy you elect to use will depend on the topic being studied and your students. Students enjoy variety!

*From *Jamestown Heritage Readers, Book F (Teacher's Edition)*, pp. 157, 145, 127, by L. Mountain, S. J. Crawley, and E. Fry. Copyright 1991 by Jamestown Publishers, Providence, Rhode Island. Reprinted by permission.

CONCLUSION

The two major topics discussed in this chapter were building background and predicting. Building background has students searching their existing schemata. This search includes cognitive as well as affective knowledge. Background can be built through vocabulary and concept introductions (concrete and semiconcrete experiences and drawings), teacher-prepared assistance (structured overview, advance organizer, structured question guide and process sheet, and prereading reasoning guide), and student-involved strategies (question only, PRep, and opinion poll).

Predicting requires students to make predictions or guesses about the contents of the selection. These guesses provide students with self-knowledge about their backgrounds for the topic and task knowledge as they try to verify their predictions. The prediction strategies included the think sheet, expectation outline, directed inquiry activity, and a modification of the prereading question.

Both of these processes are important metacognitive tasks. Further, the *Becoming a Nation of Readers* report specified that it is important for students to see relationships between what they already know and what they are going to read. Always keep in mind that building background and predicting are *prereading* activities. "Students' prior knowledge of content area topics is supposed to be incomplete, naive, and in some cases completely misconceived; if they knew everything...there would be no need [for textbook authors] to write about it" (Frager, 1993, p. 617).

Many of the strategies described provide opportunities for cooperative learning. Students actively exchange ideas and background. Through this interchange they broaden their background knowledge; and they form a foundation for predicting the contents of the lesson. Building background knowledge, and predicting content improve the comprehension of students as they engage in the reading process.

POSTREADING

INTEGRATING WRITING

In your journal describe how you can use one of the strategies described in this chapter to build students' background. Discuss why predicting is such an easy lesson component to initiate.

REVIEW

The following is a list of words and concepts related to Chapter 6. Organize these into a structured overview and be able to explain why you organized them as you did. You may have to list one or more of your own categories.

question only
student-involved
concrete experiences
structured question guide
    and process sheet
structured overview
expectation outline
prereading/reasoning
    guide

comparative
expectation outline
background
PReP
vocabulary and concept
    introduction
think sheet
drawing

advance organizer
directed inquiry activity
opinion polls
prereading question
predicting
expository
teacher-prepared
    assistance

PRACTICE

Do Enabling Activities 15, 16, and 17 in Appendix A.

7

SILENT AND POSTREADING

"Every night I try to read all the pages you assign for homework, Mr. Valdez, " claimed Mike. "I even read some of them aloud."

"I do too," Judy chimed in, "for all the good it does! I still can't pass your quizzes and tests."

"I just want to give up," Mike complained. "I can't put it all together."

"What am I supposed to do with the stuff I read? I read it and then forget about it," admitted Judy.

Mr. Valdez listened and thought about what his students were telling him. How could he help them use what they read?

DISCUSS

The way into students' heads is through use of what they have read. What strategies have you used, or observed, in classrooms that are effective in having students make use of what they have read?

PREORGANIZE

Go through the chapter and make a skeletal outline of the major headings and subheadings. This will provide you with a chapter organizer. Predict the contents of the text under one of these subheadings.

OBJECTIVES

After reading this chapter, you should be able to

1. describe aids, within the textbook, that can assist students during the silent reading process.

2. describe and construct examples of strategies for discussing and responding to reading assignments.
3. describe and identify examples of organizational patterns around which
   texts are organized.
4. describe and demonstrate the use of team review strategies.

Prior to reading this chapter review the cognitive taxonomies for questioning that
were presented in Chapter 5. Knowledge of these will serve as a basis for developing
statements, activities, and questions in this chapter.

You will also recall that in Chapter 6 you learned some strategies to prepare
students for the reading process. This preparation serves as the foundation for the
silent and postreading strategies we will describe in this chapter.

SILENT READING

Silent reading should always precede any oral reading; and oral reading should be
purposeful—not "round robin," in which every student in the class takes a turn
reading a paragraph of the chapter orally. Silent reading provides students an
opportunity to get a sense of the selection. And it gives the teacher the opportunity
to observe students' reactions and reading habits.

"Round robin" reading, on the other hand, detracts from listening, which is a
vital skill we teach our students. Students attend instead to looking at the words to
be sure they are in the right place when their turn comes. Students also try to
anticipate which paragraph they will be asked to read, and they practice reading it
silently while other students are reading orally. In each situation, students are
focusing on word recognition—decoding—rather than listening to the content and
comprehending what other students are reading. Students should always be given
purposes for reading orally.

Aids within the text and two specific strategies—the gloss and the reading
"guide-o-rama"—can be utilized to assist students during the silent reading phase.

Aids Within the Text

The easiest to use and most convenient aids for silent reading are the aids within
the textbook. Every teacher can make use of these aids by reminding students to
register on headings, subheadings, boldface type, and italics.

Concurrent organization is one type of aid within the text. In concurrent
organization the key words and/or sentences that contain main ideas are underlined
or otherwise highlighted. Sometimes, questions or organizers are presented
at key points throughout the selection. These are called adjunct or concurrent
questions.

A *summary* or *postorganizing statement* is often found at the end of a chapter.
These summary or postorganizing statements may be indicated by *signal words*
such as *at last, consequently, in brief, in conclusion, in summation, therefore,* and *to
sum it up.*

Most textbooks contain other cognitive organizer techniques as well. These include introductions for chapters or sections, visual aids to accompany discussion, outlines, and multiple-choice, fill-in, and true-false pretests.

Gloss

"Gloss notations are marginal notes written to direct readers' attention while they read" (Richgels & Hansen, 1984). Gloss notations are written on sheets of paper keyed to book paragraphs by numbered brackets. The brackets are placed at the edge of the gloss sheet. As students read, they place the gloss sheet next to the page they are reading.

In developing a gloss sheet (see Example 7.1) follow these guidelines:

1. Examine the text to determine what reading skills and strategies are most needed to comprehend the selection.
2. Develop gloss notations according to the skills of your students.
3. Develop gloss notations that have students identify word meanings from context clues, draw conclusions, identify main ideas, and paraphrase.

Example 7.1   Gloss Sheet

Gloss		**Text**
1. The first sentence states the main idea of the selection.	1	One place where water pollution is a great problem in Lake Erie. Find this lake on the map. What states touch Lake Erie? What large cities are near lake Erie?
2. In what three ways has Lake Erie changed? What does the author list?	2	People used to swim in Lake Erie. Fishermen earned money by selling the fish they caught in the lake. People liked to live near Lake Erie.
3. Examples of "pollution" are given. What do you think "pollution" means?	3	But for many years people have dumped sewage into Lake Erie. Little by little, sewage from thousands of homes polluted the lake. Factories helped to pollute it, too. Many of the streams that flow into the lake also became polluted.*

---

*From P. V. Weaver and W. N. Gantt, *People use the earth,* pp. 160–165, © 1972 Silver Burdett Company. Used by permission.

Reading Guide-o-rama

Cunningham and Shablak (1975) suggest preparing a *reading guide-o-rama* as a means of aiding students in developing appropriate reading behavior. The guide-o-rama provides students with guidance in how to read a selection. The following instructions might be included in a reading guide-o-rama.

1. The introduction on pages 332–333 gives you an idea of what Chapter 12 is about. Read this carefully.
2. Two ways in which clouds are formed are described on page 334. Be sure you can describe each of these processes.
3. The way in which clouds are described is discussed on page 335. Be sure to tell what kinds of information are used to describe clouds.
4. The information at the top of page 336 is interesting but not important to understanding the chapter. Read this quickly.

As you can see, this strategy helps students adjust their reading rates for different purposes. If your students seem to read everything at the same rate, you might try this procedure.

POSTREADING

We retain information more easily if we do something with it—if we use it. Postreading activities provide opportunities for students to use and expand on what they have read. Postreading experiences also can incorporate cooperative learning and serve as a motivational device.

In this section we will describe four types of postreading activities: those that provide opportunities for students to discuss and respond to the assignment, those that guide students in using text structure, those that involve team review, and extension activities that offer ways for students to extend their learning.

Discuss and Respond

The use of *discuss and respond* strategies will clarify ideas and concepts. We model our thinking processes *for* others as we explain how we reached our conclusion. We hear thinking taking place at a variety of cognitive levels, not only at the level on which *we* are thinking. We have a chance to broaden our own conceptualizations.

Several strategies are described here that facilitate discussing and responding to assignments. These include graphic organizers, three levels guide, reaction guide, focus, and guided reading and discussion experience (GRADE).

Graphic Organizers

Graphic organizers have been called by various names—webs, pyramids, maps, semantic maps, and networks. Basically they all involve developing a graphic arrangement of ideas. Major ideas are connected to supporting ideas and details by a systematic arrangement of lines, geometric shapes, and arrows.

Four types of graphic organizers (semantic maps) that were identified by Sinatra and Stahl-Gemake (1983) and Sinatra, Stahl-Gemake, and Morgan (1986) are appropriate for content area subjects. These semantic maps include a thematic map that shows the elements and details of text material, the classification map that shows relationships among concepts and details, the comparative-contrastive map that compares and contrasts two or more groups or events, and the sequential-episodic map that shows time order.

The use of graphic organizers has been found to produce significant results in improving comprehension. Notable increases in comprehension were produced with learning disabled students (Sinatra, Berg & Dunn, 1985), students referred to reading clinics (Sinatra, Stahl-Gemake, & Berg, 1984), and freshman college students who had difficulty understanding and organizing written material (Sinatra, Stahl-Gemake & Morgan, 1986). Berkowitz (1986) also found graphic organizers useful in improving the recall of sixth grade students.

Other interesting investigations have been conducted on the effectiveness of using graphic organizers. In one study the investigators found that tenth grade students who were taught to summarize and then to develop graphic organizers had better recall than students who received instruction in outlining or graphic organizers without summarizing practice (Bean, et al., 1986). Moore and Readence (1984) discovered that graphic organizers were more effective when used after reading than before reading. A study by several researchers (Darch, Carnine, & Kameenui, 1986) identified that having students work in small groups to develop graphic organizers produced better comprehension than having students develop graphic organizers on an individual basis.

As you read the Building Background section of Chapter 6, you viewed semantic mapping as a means of activating students' backgrounds of experiences and relating this knowledge to a topic or subject about to be studied. You were having students relate something already known to the central idea of the subject being taught.

In this chapter you will view graphic organizers (webs, pyramids, maps, semantic maps) as a means of having students recall and organize information that they have already read in their content area textbooks. These graphic organizers can serve as a self-testing or evaluation instrument after students have completed their reading assignment. They also serve as a stepping stone to outlining.

Generally, graphic organizers are constructed by identifying main ideas and supporting details. These main ideas, subideas, and supporting details are placed into a visual or graphic form using geometric shapes, lines, and arrows. Clewell and Haldemos (1983) suggested using circles. Hanf (1971) preferred use of lines.

In Example 7.2 you can see that the main idea is Landforms. Subideas are mountains, plains, plateaus, and hills. Descriptive details extend from each subidea. Example 7.3 shows Nutrients as the main idea with lines extending showing the subcategories of fats, vitamins, minerals, water, proteins, and carbohydrates. The details of functions and sources extend as lines from each specific nutrient.

Example 7.2   Web on Landforms

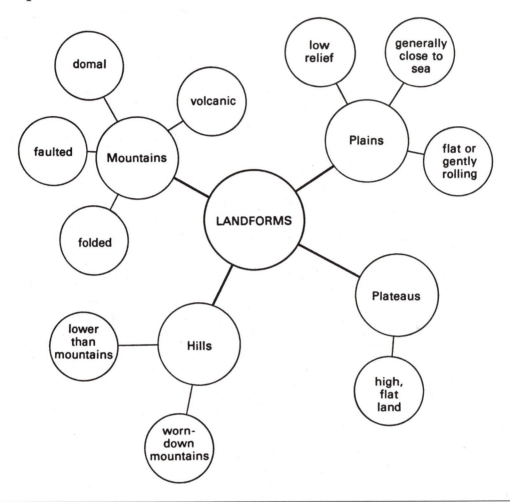

Example 7.3   Mapping of Nutrients

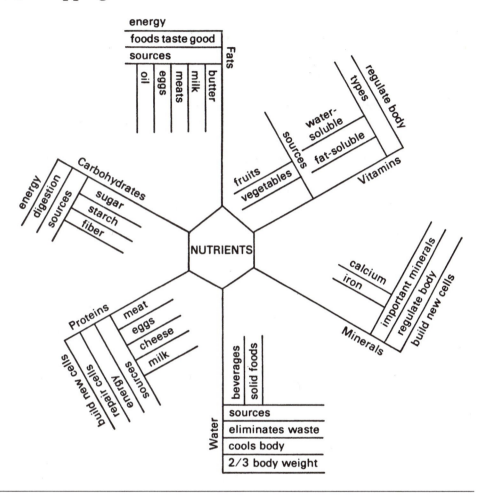

In another form of graphic organizer, Solon (1980) and Clewell and Haldemos (1983) suggest having students create a pyramid of main categories, subcategories, and supporting details. Students label index cards with the information and then build a pyramid. Example 7.4 shows a pyramid of the Inca civilization. The main topic—Incas—is at the top of the pyramid. A one sentence summary statement of the topic appears next. The subcategories that were discussed in the chapter—farmers, arts and crafts, and organization—appear under the main idea. Supporting details fall under these subtopics.

Example 7.4   Pyramid of a Chapter on the Inca Civilization

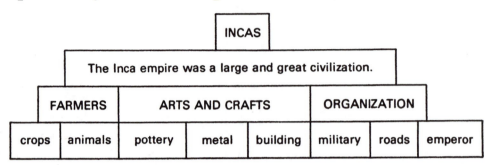

Tierney, Readence, and Dishner (1990) suggest using a herringbone shape to identify *who, what, when, where, how,* and *why,* and *the main idea.* The herringbone can be adapted for the following: *characters* (who), *acts* (what), *scene* (how), *setting* (where), *motive* (why), *time* (when), and *conflict* (main idea). *Resolution* could be added to resolve the conflict. Example 7.5 presents a herringbone for the defeat of the Spanish Armada.

Example 7.5   Herringbone

Who?   England
What?   Defeated Spanish Armada
When?   1588
Where?   English Channel
How?   Battle in Channel
Why?   Philip II thought he could have Armada invade England and seize throne.

Hansell (1978) recommends using arrays. An array organizes major ideas, phrases, or words through the use of lines and arrows. Arrays can take any suitable form. To construct arrays, teachers should select passages of 400 to 800 words that will be read by students. From these passages, the teacher selects ten to twenty phrases or words that are important to the selection and writes these words on separate strips of paper. The teacher then asks one or two questions that get students to think about how the ideas on the strips are related.

Students are placed into groups of three or four (one above average reader, one average reader, one below average reader). The students read the selection and discuss how the words on the strips of paper are related to it. They then arrange the strips showing how the words or phrases are related to one another. Then, they make a copy of their arrangement on a large sheet of paper and draw lines and arrows to show relationships. Hansell found that students' scores on outlining tasks increased by 30 percent after using this approach; scores of other students increased only 4 percent.

In Example 7.6 arrays are used to show relationships among the apple, Adam and Eve, the serpent, and sin.

Example 7.6   Array of Story of Adam and Eve*

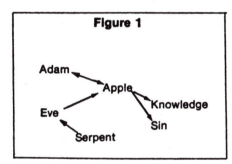 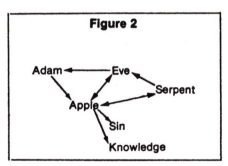

As you can see, graphic organizers come in many shapes and sizes; some even use pictures. Graphic organizers show main ideas, subtopics, and supporting details. This makes their use excellent as a foundation for outlining. Graphic organizers also help students form visual images of the material they are studying. Forming visual images improves retention.

Once you have guided students through developing graphic organizers, they can develop their own for study purposes.

---

*T. S. Hansell (1978), Stepping up to outlining, *Journal of Reading*, 22, p. 249. Reprinted with permission of T. Stevenson Hansell and the International Reading Association.

Three Levels Guide

Herber (1978) recommends using literal, interpretive, and applied statements in three levels comprehension guides. These statements model the types of thinking students would go through if the teacher were to ask them to identify literal, interpretive, and applied information in a selection. (Take a few minutes to review these levels in Chapter 5.)

The effectiveness of these guides has been verified by Hash (1974), Williams (1973), Baker (1971) and Estes (1970). To construct and implement a three levels guide, follow these steps:

1. Read and become thoroughly familiar with the material. Identify statements that support the main idea in the selection.
2. Develop statements at each of the comprehension levels (literal, interpretive, and applied).
3. Develop at least one distractor statement at each of the comprehension levels.
4. Develop clear directions for the students.
5. After reading the selection, students should check off those statements on the guide that they can support based on evidence in the selection.
6. Hash and Bailey (1978) recommend that students respond to the three levels guide individually and then meet with a small group and reach a group consensus.

Herber and Herber (1993) write that "the levels guides provide a link between readers and text in a way that promotes understanding of text and facilitates communication among readers" (p. 219). As students use these guides, they gain greater understanding of thinking at the literal and interpretive levels. When we construct statements at these levels, we are showing students what it means to think literally or interpretively. They must then go to the text to find supporting evidence for each of the statements. (When we ask questions without follow-up, we are testing—not teaching.)

At the applied level students are presented with statements that are broader and more global in nature. Students must be able to relate what the author communicated to their own experiences. They must make the connection between their own experiences and what the author wrote. Group discussions provide a means of expanding this background and seeing relationships.

Example 7.7 presents a three levels guide for literature; Example 7.8 presents a three levels guide for math. (Please note that the page numbers listed in the three levels guide examples refer to page numbers in the students' textbook, not the textbook you are reading. Also, three levels guides usually contain more statements than those listed in the examples.)

Example 7.7   Three Levels Guide for Literature

Read page 299 in your textbook. Place a check on the line if the statement tells what the author said.

_____ 1.   The child in the story was walking with his grandfather.

_____ 2.   Grandfather lived far away.

_____ 3.   The six-year-old had a leaf notebook.

Read the following statements. Place a check before them if they tell what the author meant by what was written.

_____ 1.   Grandfather knew a lot about leaves.

_____ 2.   Even though he was old, Grandfather was still alert and wanted to learn more about life.

_____ 3.   Grandfather had been a teacher.

Read the following statements. Place a check before them if the ideas they contain can be supported by information on page 299. Can these generalizations be drawn? Be ready to give evidence from everyday life and the selection to support your answer.

_____ 1.   Do not squander time, for that's the stuff life is made of.

_____ 2.   One today is worth two tomorrows.

_____ 3.   When the well's dry, they know the worth of water.

Example 7.8   Three Levels Guide for Math

Problem: Max flew on Hooter Air Lines for four hours. The plane flew at an average speed of 365 miles per hour. How many miles had Max traveled when he reached his destination? Place a check beside the correct answers.

Part I: What information is given in the problem?

_____ 1.   Max likes to fly.

_____ 2.   The plane traveled 365 miles per hour.

_____ 3.   The plane flew at an average speed of 365 miles per hour.

_____ 4.   Max was in the air for four hours.

What information is to be found?

_____ 5.   the number of passengers on the plane

_____ 6.   the average speed of the flight

_____ 7.   how far Max traveled

_____ 8. how many miles Max traveled

_____ 9. how much it cost Max to fly

Part II: What mathematical operations could we use to solve the problem?

_____ 1. one plane multiplied by 365 miles per hour

_____ 2. four hours multiplied by 365 miles per hour

_____ 3. one person multiplied by four hours

_____ 4. 365 miles per hour multiplied by four hours

_____ 5. 4 x 365

_____ 6. 1 x 365

_____ 7. 1 x 4

_____ 8. 365 x 4

Part III: What ideas about mathematics can be found in this problem?

_____ 1. Multiplication by two factors gives a product.

_____ 2. Multiplication is like repeated addition.

_____ 3. Multiplication requires two factors.

_____ 4. The commutative law operates in multiplication.

_____ 5. Rate of travel times time of travel equals distance.

_____ 6. Rate of travel times distance of travel equals time of travel.

Focus

One postreading (review) strategy recommended by Herber (1978) is called focus. Broad topics and technical vocabulary of the chapter studied are listed for students. Part I contains broad topics, Part II, technical vocabulary. Students put the technical terms into one or more of the broad topics and explain their reasons for doing so on the basis of what they understand from the material they studied.

In Example 7.9 students were studying the major topic of microorganisms and miniplants. The subtopics they studied were amoeba, paramecium, algae, and euglena. The twenty vocabulary words listed related to these subtopics. After students identified the subtopic(s) to which each vocabulary word belonged, they organized into small groups and discussed their labeling choices. (It is always important to have students justify their answers.)

Guided Reading and Discussion Experience

The guided reading and discussion experience (GRADE) recommended by Mangieri (1977) is a discussion-centered review strategy. The following steps are included in GRADE:

1. Assign a routine reading assignment to your class.
2. When the students have finished reading, divide them into groups of four (three if necessary).

Example 7.9   Focus for Microorganisms and Miniplants

Directions: Use the four labels or topics in Part I. Look at each word in Part II. Fill in the blanks in Part II with the appropriate label(s) from Part I. Be ready to discuss the reasons for your choices.

Part I. Labels for microorganisms and miniplants.

(a) amoeba   (b) algae   (c) paramecium   (d) euglena

Part II. Vocabulary for microorganisms and miniplants.

____ 1.	one-celled	____ 11.	chlorophyll
____ 2.	photosynthesis	____ 12.	dividing
____ 3.	gullet	____ 13.	slipper
____ 4.	colorless	____ 14.	colors
____ 5.	pond	____ 15.	hair-like
____ 6.	seaweeds	____ 16.	diatoms
____ 7.	kelp	____ 17.	reproduce
____ 8.	absorb	____ 18.	protozoan
____ 9.	excrete	____ 19.	water
____ 10.	changing	____ 20.	decaying

3. Assign one student to keep a record of what group members say. If one comment is made more than once, it should be recorded only once.
4. Give each of the other members four minutes to state the major ideas or points of the selection.
5. Walk around the room to keep students on task.
6. The recorder in each group orally shares the group's ideas with the class. Write what is said on the board or on a transparency. The recorders from each group should present only the information not already given by another group.
7. Help the students correct inaccurate contributions and organize and sequence the information. Encourage students to fill in missing points and eliminate unimportant details.

Using Text Structure

When using text structure—the way written material is organized—students identify how facts are related to each other. Students identify signal words and internal organizational patterns; they locate main ideas and supporting details; and they utilize aids within the text. (Review "Aids within the Text" which was discussed earlier in this chapter.)

Signal Words and Internal Organization

Imagine yourself faced with the task of trying to change a flat tire. You have never done it before and you don't know what to do first. Do you first take the hubcap off and unscrew the lug nuts? Or do you jack up the car first? What do you have to do first, second, and third to operate the jack? You are faced with a time order or sequencing problem.

Students are faced with similar problems when they read. They must be able to identify the author's organizational pattern or patterns. Authors of content area textbooks use four basic organizational patterns: time order (sequence), comparison/contrast, cause/effect, and enumerative (listing) order. These four organizational patterns have the following characteristics:

- **Time order or sequence** organization places events into the sequential order that is important.
- **Comparison/contrast** organization shows likenesses or differences between two or more ideas or events.
- **Cause/effect** organization shows how one event or happening leads to another event or happening.
- **Listing or enumeration** presents facts distinctly one after another, but their order of presentation is not important.

Several researchers have identified that students' awareness of text structures are positively related to comprehension. Geva (1983) found that instruction in identifying text structure improved the comprehension of less skilled readers. Three researchers (Meyer, Brandt, & Bluth, 1980) found that the use of organizational patterns contained in texts was important in remembering. Better readers used the organizational patterns of text materials to aid in recall. In another study (Taylor & Samuels, 1983) students who were cognizant of the structure of written materials were able to recall more information from normal passages than scrambled passages. Students who were unaware of text structures did not retain more information from normal passages than scrambled passages.

Knowledge of signal words or connectives can aid students in identifying organizational patterns. Sequence of events is easiest to detect when the events are listed in two separate sentences; the first sentence is the first event or happening in the sequence, and a signal word shows the sequence. Vacca (1981) and Herber (1978) identify the following as signal words with which students should be familiar.

Organizational Pattern	*Signal Words*
Time order	after, at the same time, before, finally, following, in the first place, last, later, meanwhile, not long after, now, on (date), previously, when
Comparison/contrast	as well as, but, but also, by contrast, conversely, either/-or, even if, even though, how-

ever, in contrast, in spite of, instead, not only, on the other hand, opposed to, to the contrary, unless, yet

Cause/effect
as a result of, because, consequently, if/then, nevertheless, since, therefore, this led to

Listing/enumeration
and, first, second, finally, I must add, in addition, in addition to, next, not only, others, specifically, then

Following are some sentences that illustrate these organizational patterns:

Time order: The plane taxied along the runway after being cleared by the control tower.

Comparison/contrast: In contrast to the last president of our organization, our new president is dynamite.

Cause/effect: As a result of the rush of water, the land eroded and left a deep gully.

Listing/enumeration: Of the earlier U.S. presidents, the four best known are Washington, Adams, Jefferson, and Lincoln.

Sometimes, you can find more than one organizational pattern in a sentence. Look at these examples:

Time order and cause/effect: Before the hostages could be released, governmental officials were told they must pay a ransom.

Listing and time order: Looking first at the weather and then at the remaining fuel, the pilot decided to try to fly over enemy territory.

Examples 7.10 through 7.17 present exercises developed for teaching or reinforcing organizational patterns. The examples are divided into the four major organizational patterns just discussed: time order, comparison/contrast, cause/effect, and listing/enumeration. The exercises are further categorized by subject area and specified for above average, average, and below average learners.

Main Ideas

The ability to identify main ideas (or the major topic of the passage or selection) is necessary for summarizing, outlining, and note taking. It is a literal or interpretive level comprehension skill depending on whether the main idea is explicitly stated or only implied. In this section we will outline two strategies for teaching main ideas: the three-stage main idea strategy and the four-stage main idea strategy.

Example 7.10   Science—Time Order
(Below average readers)

Directions: Read the selection starting on page 167 and ending on page 168 in your science textbook. Then read the following questions and circle the correct answer for each.

1. What happened first?
    a. The earthquake was indicated by P-waves.
    b. Surface waves were recorded.

2. What happened second?
    a. Secondary waves were indicated.
    b. P-waves started to fade.

3. What happened third?
    a. Secondary waves were indicated.
    b. P-waves were indicated.

Example 7.11   Science—Time Order
(Average readers)

Directions: Read the selection starting on page 167 and ending on page 168 in your science textbook. Then read the following sentences. Fill in each blank with the correct signal word.

1. P-waves are indicated _____ all other waves.

    before   with   after

2. P-waves start to fade _____ secondary waves occur.

    before   as   after

3. Surface waves are recorded _____ other waves.

    before   with   after

4. Secondary waves occur _____ P-waves.

    before   with   after

Example 7.12 Science—Comparison/Contrast (Average readers)

Directions: Below is a list of characteristics and examples of the marsupial and placental groups of animals. Place each characteristic under the correct category.

well-developed little forepaws
oxygen carried to the embryo by
  blood vessels
born in a developed state
not totally developed when it leaves
  mother's body
totally developed when it leaves
  mother's body

a placenta
produces milk in abdomen
spores
kangaroo
humans
found in Australia

Marsupial   *Placental*

Example 7.13 Science—Comparison/Contrast (Above average readers)

Directions: Using pages 104–107 in your book, list at least five characteristics of the marsupial group and five characteristics of the placental group. Write your answers in the proper category below.

Marsupial   *Placental*

Example 7.14   Math—Listing (Average readers)

Directions: Each word in the list fits under one of the four boldface topic areas or categories. Read the words, then write each word under the proper category heading. Be sure to use all the words.

> one-to-one correspondence
> rectangle
> indirect proof
> relation and function
> biconditionals and conditionals
> slope
> square
> inscribed angle
> central angles, arc, and measure sphere
> rhombus
> linear equation

Logic and Proof   *Circles and Spheres*

Coordinates and Graphs   *Congruent Triangles*

Example 7.15   History—Cause/Effect (Below average readers)

Directions: Some information on dairy cooperatives in Denmark during the middle of the last century is given on this worksheet. In each case, the first event caused a second event to take place. Draw a line from the cause in Column 1 to its effect in Column 2. [You would put this entire activity on one page for your class.]

Column 1: Cause

1. With increased competition from other countries, Danish wheat producers suffered
2. Danish farmers united and formed cooperative dairies.
3. Much land has been reclaimed along the North Sea for dairying.

Column 2: Effect

a. Besides lending money to their members, cooperative dairies also did a lot to improve cattle breeding.
b. To get another source of income, they decided to go into dairying.
c. Danish farmers became prosperous when coastal land was available for raising livestock.

Example 7.16   History—Cause/Effect (Average readers)

Directions: An event in Column 2 was caused by another event. List the event next to the effect it created. The causes and events may be found on page 67 in your textbook. The first one has been done for you.

Column 1: Cause

1. Danish farmers joined together to form cooperatives.

Column 2: Effect

a. Besides lending money to their members, they did much to improve cattle breeding and make sure milk was pure.
b. They wanted another source of income and selected dairying.
c. Farmers became more prosperous because land was available to raise livestock.

Example 7.17   History-Cause/Effect (Above average readers)

Directions: Locate at least six events concerning dairy cooperatives on page 67 in your textbook. Write the cause in the first column and the resulting effect in the second column. The first example has been done for you.

Column 1: Cause

1. Danish farmers joined together to form cooperative dairies.

Column 2: Effect

1. Besides lending money to their members, they were able to improve cattle breeding and make sure milk was pure.

Three-Stage Main Idea Strategy.   Donlan (1980) recommends a three-stage process for teaching main ideas. These three stages involve working with word relationships, working with sentence relationships, and working with paragraph relationships.

In *Stage 1: Working with Word Relationships,* Donlan identified four word relationships that students need to know:

*   **Equal**—such as *general/admiral*
*   **Opposite**—such as *good/bad* and *love/hate*
*   **Superior-subordinate**—such as *world/country,* and *lieutenant/private*
*   **No relationship**—such as *representative/sandwich,* and *Incas/swimming*

Students should identify and explain these relationships as they work with them. Examples 7.18 and 7.19 show ways to help students work with Stage 1, word relationships.

Example 7.18   Science Word Relationships: Superior-Subordinate

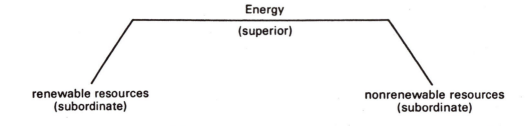

Example 7.19   Social Studies Word Relationships: Superior-Subordinate

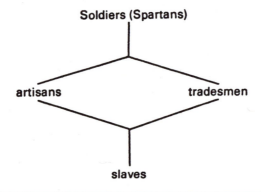

After students are able to identify word relationships, they progress to *Stage 2: Working with Sentence Relationships.* As with word relationships, there are four sentence relationships. These include:

- **Equal**—such as: *Pershing was a general./ Perry was an admiral.*
- **Opposite**—such as: *We experienced love when we married./ We experienced hate when we divorced.*
- **Superior-subordinate**—such as: *The lieutenant gave the orders./ The privates carried them out.*

- **No relationships**—such as: *Our district representative was on TV./ We ate sandwiches for lunch.*

Example 7.20 shows how students might diagram a paragraph according to sentence relationships.

Example 7.20 Social Studies Sentence Relationships: Superior-Subordinate

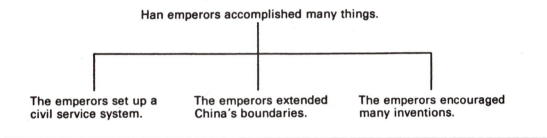

After students understand the relationships among sentences in a paragraph, they are ready to move on to *Stage 3: Working with Complete Paragraph Relationships*. Proceed using activities similar to those in Stage 2, but substitute complete paragraphs for the sentences.

As you view the steps in this three-stage main idea strategy, you will notice that the format resembles a graphic organizer. In this instance, however, students move from words to sentences within paragraphs.

Four-Stage Main Idea Strategy. Dishner and Readence (1977) recommend using a four-stage strategy for teaching main ideas (see Example 7.21). When using this strategy, you should begin by using paragraphs in which the main idea is explicitly stated and later move to implied main ideas. The paragraphs you initially use with students should be close to their independent reading levels to ensure success. You will also notice that the teacher models the identification of main ideas as the students proceed through the steps.

Step 1: Have students identify what each sentence is about. They should identify the key words or topic of each sentence and write a statement that summarizes what each sentence says.
Step 2: Students identify the main topic or one idea that all the sentences have in common.
Step 3: Students write a sentence that states the main idea.
Step 4: Students identify and locate the sentence in the paragraph that states the main idea.

Example 7.21   Four-Stage Main Idea Strategy

Ford's Theater, in Washington, D.C., is the only theater that is a national monument. After Lincoln's assassination in 1865, the theater did not give live performances until 1968. It was used for processing the records of Union soldiers after the Civil War. And it housed the Army Medical Museum. It was used for many things until 1964 when Congress voted to restore it.

Step 1:   Identify what each sentence is about.
1. Ford's Theater is a national monument.
2. The theater did not give live performances after Lincoln's assassination.
3. Union soldier records were processed there.
4. It was used as an Army Medical Museum.
5. It had many uses.

Step 2:   Identify the topic.
Uses of the Ford Theater

Step 3:   Write a sentence stating the main idea.
The Ford Theater was used for many things.

Step 4:   Locate a sentence which states the main idea.
It was used for many things until 1964 when Congress voted to restore it.

Team Review

Team reviews offer students the opportunity to learn together and to cooperate. Through cooperative learning students review material already studied and share knowledge in the review process. In this section we will preview the following team review strategies: triangular review, circle of knowledge, information add, jeopardy, and team bingo.

Triangular Review

A postreading, or review, strategy recommended by Herber (1978) is called triangular review. Students are placed in groups of three. Two students are given a checklist of the words or phrases that represent the major ideas and information in a chapter, or chapter section being studied. The third student in the group reviews the chapter and tells the other two everything he or she remembers about the chapter. This third student does not see the checklist of key words and phrases.

As student 3 recalls information, students 1 and 2 check (✓) it off on their sheets. When the third student can no longer recall additional information, students 1 and 2 ask student 3 questions based on the items not yet checked on their sheets. As student 3 answers these questions correctly, an X is placed next to the appropriate words or phrases. The questioning stops when all the words on the checklist are marked or when student 3 can no longer answer any of the questions students 1 and 2 ask. When the questioning stops, student 3 is given copies of the checklist from students 1 and 2. Any word or phrase not marked represents a key area for the student to study. A key word marked with an X indicates the student needs to review this information.

The two students checking the responses and asking questions also are involved in a review process. They must think about the material, decide if the answers are correct, then decide what questions to ask and how to ask them if the student does not recall information.

The model for movement around the triangle is depicted in Figure 7–1 below. Student 1 starts out checking, then reviews, and finally checks again. Student 2 checks the first two times and reviews the third time. Student 3 begins reviewing and then checks that last two times.

You might prefer to have your students work in pairs. In another variation, a social studies teacher working with a group of slower students assigned one student to ask the question, a second student to locate the answer, and the third student to write the answer. Students then switched roles.

Circle of Knowledge

This small group review strategy is recommended by Dunn and Dunn (1978). The strategy involves the following steps:

1. Small groups of five to six students with chairs (no desks) are placed throughout the room, as far apart as possible. One student serves as a recorder for each group.

2. You present students with a question that has many different answers, such as "Name the capitals of as many states as you can." You also set a time limit for answering the question. The time limit should be short, about five minutes.

3. Each circle of knowledge answers the same question at the same time. Students must go clockwise or counterclockwise in their groups. All students must contribute an answer; no student may skip his or her turn. Students may not give answers to each other, but they are allowed to pantomime hints to the stumped team member. The recorder is the only group member who is allowed to write; he or she records all the group's answers.

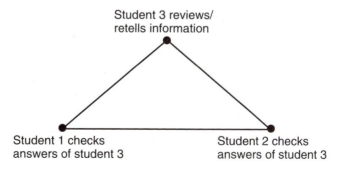

FIGURE 7–1 • Triangular Review

4. When time is up, all recorders must stop writing. Each group makes a note of the number of answers it has.

5. You place numbered columns on the board, one for each team. As you progress from group to group, one team member offers one answer each turn. You write the answer in each group's column. Each recorder checks off all answers (even those given by the other groups) that appear on the group's sheet, so that only answers not yet given will be offered.

6. Award points for each answer written on the board (two, five, ten—whatever you decide the point value will be). The team with the most points at the end is the winner.

7. A team may challenge the answer of another team. If a team's answer is incorrect, the challenging team gets the points. If the challenger is incorrect, the challenger's team loses the number of points assigned to a correct answer.

8. Remember, circles of knowledge are for review purposes only.

9. You may have more than one circle of knowledge competition during a period. Add the number of points the teams earned in each round to identify the winner of the day.

Possible questions for a circle of knowledge include:

How many U.S. presidents can you name?
How many U.S. states can you name?
How many elements on the periodic table can you name?
Name as many battles fought during World War II as you can.
What contributions were made during the Renaissance?
What contributions were made during the Industrial Revolution?
List as many causes of the war as you can.
Find as many solutions as you can to the equation $x + y + 2 = 97$.
List as many of Shakespeare's plays as you can.
Give examples of words that have changed meanings since Shakespeare's time. Be able to give the meaning from Shakespeare's time and the meaning it now has.

Information Add

Information add is a proven and popular strategy for improving listening skills as well as reviewing content. After studying a chapter in science, social studies, or other content area, students recall the information they learned. This is accomplished by having student 1 recall a piece of information. Student 2 must repeat student 1's information and then add another piece of information. Student 3 repeats the information of students 1 and 2 and adds a third piece of information. This procedure continues around the class.

Jeopardy

The Jeopardy review strategy, modeled after the game show *Jeopardy,* fosters cooperative learning, healthy competition, and achievement. First, develop a Jeopardy game board like the one in Figure 7–2, with appropriate categories and slots

FIGURE 7–2 • Sample Jeopardy Board

Category 1	Category 2	Category 3	Category 4	Category 5
$100	$100	$100	$100	$100
$200	$200	$200	$200	$200
$300	$300	$300	$300	$300
$400	$400	$400	$400	$400
$500	$500	$500	$500	$500

for answers. The categories chosen depend on the topic being studied in your class. Questions and answers of increasing difficulty are developed for each category.

The game consists of Jeopardy, Double Jeopardy, and Final Jeopardy. The class is divided into four or five teams. Each group must choose a spokesperson who is responsible for "ringing in" after the team, through discussion, arrives at its answer. Here are the rules:

1. Each spokesperson rolls the die; the team with the highest number goes first.
2. Running tabulations of scores are kept on the board.
3. The degree of difficulty of a question increases with the "dollar" or point value.
4. Correct answers earn applicable points; incorrect answers deduct applicable points.
5. Answers must be in the form of a question.
6. After ringing-in, teams have twenty seconds for the spokesperson to reply with the answer, in question form.
7. If a team answers incorrectly, other teams can ring in.
8. If no team answers within one minute, the statement is thrown out.
9. The team with the lowest score at the end of the first round will begin Double Jeopardy, the second round in which point values are doubled.
10. All, part, or no points can be wagered in Final Jeopardy.
11. The team with the highest score wins.

The Jeopardy board can be placed on a transparency and as items are answered and points earned, the dollar amounts can be covered up.

Team Bingo

This game is played in a manner similar to Bingo. Instead of calling out a number, however, students select a space on the card and must answer the question that corresponds to that space. The following procedures are followed:

1. The class is divided into two equal teams.
2. A Bingo card similar to that in Figure 7–3 is made on a transparency.

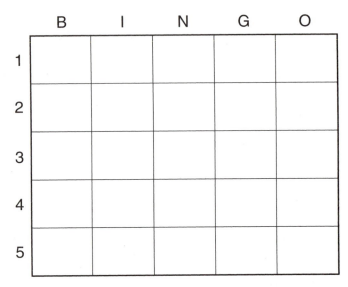

FIGURE 7–3 • Sample Bingo Card

3. Team 1's first player chooses a square, and the teacher reads the corresponding question. Write up the questions and answers ahead of time. For example:

   N-2 Name the three levels of comprehension identified by Herber.

   (Answer: literal, interpretive, applied)

4. If correct, the player's team earns that square and an *X* in the team's color is placed in the square.
5. Team 2's first player chooses another square and tries to win an *X*.
6. If the question is answered incorrectly or the twenty-second time limit for answering the question runs out, the square remains open and the other team may try for it.
7. The team getting a row filled first (as in Bingo) wins.

In a variation of this, students can have individual Bingo cards with terms and/or symbols relevant to the subject on them. The teacher may call out a term and the student covers the appropriate symbol. Or the teacher may show a symbol or read an example, and the student covers the related word.

Extension Activities

Extension involves taking students beyond the content textbook. It involves activities at the analysis, synthesis, and evaluation levels of Bloom's taxonomy, requiring more critical/creative reading and thinking skills.

Extended reading, reading beyond the textbook, is also encouraged. Students might be encouraged to move from nonfiction to fictional reading, or to move from fiction to nonfiction. For example, a student reading an expository textbook in science might be encouraged to read a novel dealing with some scientific phenomena. Or a student reading a narrative that takes place during the Renaissance period might be encouraged to read an expository book about the Renaissance.

Students might determine the qualifications of people for specific activities; compare campaign speeches; compare different biographies of the same person; identify facts and opinions in newspapers, textbooks, and other resources. These are all critical/creative reading skills.

The ability to detect propaganda is another important critical/creative reading skill. Propaganda, or the act of trying to sway or persuade a person to a particular belief, is used by writers, speakers, and advertisers. You will want to familiarize your students with these seven basic propaganda techniques:

1. **Bad names** are used to create or appeal to dislikes, hate, or fear. Words such as *pill, miser, yellow, warmonger* and *communist* are used as bad names. Example: The yellow communist is running for office.

2. Unlike bad names, **glad names** or **glittering generalities** are used to create pleasant feelings. Advertisers often use these labels to describe their products. Words such as *valuable, popular, all-star, nostalgic, American,* and *economical* are used as glad names. Example: A sign reads, "Denwed's economical, super-deluxe hamburgers."

3. The **band wagon** technique appeals to the desire of people to be "part of the group." How often have you or your children said, "Everyone's doing it!" or "Everyone has one." Example: An advertiser picturing many, many people drinking Yammy soda.

4. In **cardstacking** only one side of the "story" or issue is presented. Either the good side or the bad side is presented, not both. What will personnel at a resort area say to entice you to visit? What do advertisers say to get people to buy their products? Example: Rocko cars are bargain-priced, low on fuel use, easily maintained, and stylish.

5. In **transfer** a respected or highly regarded person, institution, or symbol is shown in conjunction with a product or idea. Dentists are shown recommending toothpaste. Example: Tests conducted at leading universities show that people who brush with Zippy Clean have significantly fewer cavities than those brushing with other tooth pastes.

6. Giving the appearance of being one of the ordinary people is the **plain folks** technique. Notice how many advertisements (soaps, fast foods) show plain folks using their products. What about the politician who gets into the crowd and shakes hands with common people and kisses babies? Example: The president of the United States is attending town meetings and shaking hands with townspeople.

7. A **tribute** or **testimonial** is given by popular people to recommend a product, an idea, or a person. We have sports heroes recommending aftershave lotion and paint. Example: Morrow Cloud, the famous football player, says, "Swizzler makes you feel like a man."

The mass media provide excellent avenues for analyzing propaganda techniques. Here are several strategies you'll find easy to use with your students:

1. After reviewing various propaganda techniques, have students collect samples of media propaganda. These may be radio, television, or newspaper advertisements. They may be news articles in which a slanted version of an event is presented. They also may be talk shows in which specific people try to sway the public over to their particular beliefs. Instruct students to identify the propaganda techniques used and how they influence the audience.

2. Have students rewrite news stories and editorials presenting a more balanced approach.

3. Students can search their textbooks and extended reading materials to identify propaganda techniques. Examples of propaganda may be used for a bulletin board display or put into a class book on propaganda.

Other critical/creative level activities might include panel discussions or debates on a controversial issue; deriving principles in science, math, or other content areas; developing media productions (computer, video, audio, art, multimedia); or developing a written piece (poetry, short story, advertisement).

Students might choose to develop and utilize criteria for evaluating or making judgments. They can judge written works, artistic works, beliefs, actions, or emotions.

CONCLUSION

Two major components of a content area lesson were identified in this chapter—silent reading and postreading. Silent reading should always precede any oral reading; and oral reading should always be for a purpose, not "round robin."

Aids within the text help students during silent reading. Teachers can also introduce gloss sheets to help students read for specific purposes and reading guide-o-ramas to helps students adjust their reading rate.

Postreading strategies fall into four categories: discuss and respond, using text structure, team review, and extension. During discuss and respond students react to the material they studied. They use what the author wrote and integrate it with their own experiences. Four helpful discuss and respond strategies are graphic organizers, three levels guide, focus, and the guided reading and discussion experience (GRADE).

As teachers help students become aware of text organization, students learn how authors organize written materials. This knowledge helps students form a mental framework for understanding the author's ideas.

Team reviews provide opportunities for students to review material, to work cooperatively in groups, and to have healthy competition. The triangular review, circle of knowledge, information add, Jeopardy, and team Bingo are recommended team review possibilities.

Extension takes students beyond the textbook. Students work at the critical/creative level. They move beyond reading only the textbook and extend and improve their reading and writing skills.

The ultimate goal of reading is comprehension. By guiding and preparing your students in each content area every year, you will lead your students to independence in reading. Students, however, need guidance. Chapters 6 and 7 of this text have been written in a way to present an organizational sequence for lesson planning and to demonstrate strategies available to you as you prepare your teaching, or lesson, sequence.

Not all strategies will be appropriate for all students or all subject areas every year. You will find that some strategies work better for you and your students than others. We encourage you to select those that work best and use them, keeping in mind that your goal is to provide guidance for your students so that they eventually will become independent learners.

POSTREADING

INTEGRATING WRITING

In what ways can using postreading strategies help meet the needs of students at various levels of achievement in your class? Select one discuss and respond strategy and describe how you might use it to assist students in your content area.

REVIEW

The following is a list of words and concepts related to Chapter 7. Organize these into a graphic organizer of your choice and be able to explain why you organized them as you did.

cause and effect	reading guide-o-rama	circle of knowledge
gloss	focus	critical/creative level
related reading	interpretive level	Jeopardy
main ideas	applied level	expository
team Bingo	grade	graphic organizers
three levels guide	organizational patterns	listing/enumeration
time order	aids within text	arrays
comparison/contrast	literal level	main ideas
triangular review		

PRACTICE

Do Enabling Activities 18 through 22 in Appendix A.

8

STUDY SKILLS

"There's Joe Brooks. I'm glad he's here today," Estelle said with a sigh of relief. "Hey, Joe!"

"Joe, I'm having trouble with my students. They can't seem to study and organize their learning. They just pick up the book, jump in, and don't remember anything when they're finished," said Estelle. "They've given up studying for tests because they say they can't learn what I expect them to learn. They're having trouble memorizing. They take down every word I say when they try to take notes; otherwise, they just sit and gaze at me. They're struggling; and I'm struggling working with them," she continued.

"This isn't anything new," answered Joe. "Your students were taught how to read; now they're expected to use reading to learn. They need a lot of guidance before they can do this successfully. I'll share some ideas with you."

DISCUSS

How and where do you study best? Do you have any strategies that help you remember information more easily?

PREORGANIZE

Go through the chapter and make a skeletal outline of the major headings and subheadings. This will provide you with a chapter organizer. Predict the contents of the text under one of these subheadings.

OBJECTIVES

After reading this chapter, you should be able to

1. identify the various reading rates and explain their uses for reading flexibility.

2. demonstrate activities for developing skimming and scanning.
3. describe the SQ3R, EVOKER, and SQRQCQ study strategies.
4. describe problems students have in studying specific subject areas.
5. prepare a rationale for teaching and using study strategies with your students.
6. describe a system for note taking.
7. discuss guidelines for time management.
8. identify guidelines for taking specific types of tests.

Our goal as teachers is to teach students to comprehend, to understand, our content areas. A goal equally important is to educate students who are prepared, who have the necessary skills, to learn on their own. These "learn-on-your-own" skills are called *study skills*. Gunning (1992, p. 300) writes, "Material can't be effectively learned unless it is first understood. However, just because the material is understood doesn't mean it has been learned or will be remembered: studying is required."

The focus of this chapter is on helping students move from fact orientation to learning. As students are prepared to learn on their own, they will develop reading flexibility, use study strategies, outline, take notes, manage time, memorize in an efficient manner, and utilize test-taking skills. Educating students who can learn on their own is the focus of this chapter.

READING RATE AND FLEXIBILITY

Let's pretend that your car has broken down. A mechanic, who is charging you by the hour, arrives on the scene to rescue you. This mechanic asks you what the problem seems to be, looks the car over, then tows your car to the garage. There, the mechanic takes out the repair manual and begins reading it word by word, page by page, starting at page 1. What is your reaction?

If there were another garage across the street, you would probably leave this garage in a hurry, pushing your car. If there were no other garages in the area, you might pray that the panacea for your car will be covered on the first page of the manual.

This mechanic was reading word by word. Children read word by word or piece by piece. They read everything at the same approximate rate. If they are not taught strategies to develop flexible rates, they will remain as inflexible as our automobile mechanic.

Should people read all material at the same rate? Undoubtedly, no. The rate we select for reading should depend on our purpose. Yet, rate cannot be separated from our decoding ability, motivation, vocabulary, comprehension, and background of experiences. Rate also will depend on the organization of the material being read, the author's style, the style and size of type, the quality of paper used (high gloss, low gloss; heavy weight, light weight), and the way the pages are set up (continuous writing across the page, two columns per page).

How fast can a person read without skimming or scanning? Spache (1962) found that people could recognize and comprehend a maximum of three words per fixation. A person who made no regressions could read ten words in .66 second. This would be equal to fifteen words per second or nine hundred words per minute.

There are three levels of reading behavior: scanning, skimming, and actual reading. *Scanning* is used to locate specific information or a fact. You have used scanning when looking up a number in the telephone directory or looking up a word in the dictionary. In all likelihood, you just ran your eyes down the page until you found the particular bit of information you were seeking.

In scanning, you know what question you are trying to answer. You should work at a speed of about 1,500 words per minute in locating this information; and you should have 100 percent accuracy in answering the question. You use scanning in locating facts in many reference materials—dictionaries, encyclopedias, indexes, almanacs, and statistical tables. You also use scanning in everyday activities—using indexes to locate recipes or an item in a mail-order catalog, using the telephone directory, or locating a program in the TV listings. Remember, your goal in scanning is to locate rapidly a specific bit of information.

Skimming is used to gain an overview or general idea of what the material you're reading is about. It's used to read material in a hurry. When you skim, you do not read every word; you may leave out parts of paragraphs or whole paragraphs. You are just looking for main ideas. Your comprehension should be only 50 to 60 percent (Fry, 1978). Skimming usually is done at rates of about 800 to 1,000 words per minute.

When skimming chapters in a text, you should look at headings and subheadings and read introductory paragraphs, topic sentences, and summary paragraphs. If you are skimming a story, you read the first few paragraphs to get an idea of the mood, setting, and so on. Then you read only key sentences to get the main idea; you skip over the remainder of the paragraph. Just look for important ideas (words, phrases). Then read in full the last two or three paragraphs because they usually summarize.

Actual reading is used to analyze the author's ideas and words. Material that calls for problem solving or critical analysis requires slow, careful reading (50 to 150 words per minute). A moderate rate (250 to 350 words per minute) might be used for reading continuous running material such as magazines, social studies textbooks, or newspapers. A rapid rate (350 to 600 words per minute) might be used for easy, fast-moving novels. Obviously, you need flexibility to adjust to different reading behaviors.

Reading rate is characterized somewhat differently by Carver (1992). Carver describes reading in terms of gears. Gear 1, or *slow reading,* is done at less than 140 words per minute. Gear 2, *learning,* is done at about 200 words per minute. In gear 2 students often are rereading material because of its difficulty. Gear 3, *rauding,* is "the accurate comprehension of the complete thoughts in sentences, whether reading or auding" (Carver, 1992, p. 88). Rauding is usually done at about 300 words per minute and does not exceed 600 words per minute. Gear 4, is *skimming,* overviewing the material. And gear 5, *scanning,* is used to locate a specific piece of information. Scanning is done at 600 words per minute or higher. Flexible readers vary their reading rate, or change gears, according to the purpose and the ease or difficulty of the printed material.

Many techniques and programs have been developed to increase reading rates. One of the most widely known commercial programs is that of Evelyn Wood. Wood claims that some people can read as many as 40,000 words per minute and that her graduates can read at least 1,000 words per minute. Wood's method involves having students move their fingers rapidly down a page in a zigzag pattern. The eyes follow the finger.

Machines are commonly used to increase rate. The Controlled Reader, perhaps the most widely used machine, projects a series of filmstrips onto a screen. Each film contains a story followed by comprehension questions. The reader sees only one line of the text at a time and must read at the projection pace to understand the story. Specific rates are recommended for each film, but the Controlled Reader may be adjusted to other rates. A scanner also may be used with the Controlled Reader. The scanner moves across the line of print in a left-to-right pattern.

The pacer is another machine developed to increase rate. A book is placed under a bar or shade that moves down the page as the student reads. The bar or shade can be set to move down the page at various speeds.

Computers can now be programmed to flash words, phrases, and sentences at increasingly faster rates. This method, too, helps to increase students' reading rate.

In addition to commercial approaches like Evelyn Wood's and machine approaches for increasing reading rate, there also are timed techniques that students can use at home. Under timed techniques, students read short selections and answer comprehension questions about them. Students time themselves and try to read the same amount of material in shorter periods of time or to read more material in the same period of time.

Thomas and Robinson (1972) recommend using an alarm clock graph or a page graph for home practice. With the alarm clock graph, students try to increase the number of pages read during a fixed period of time (half an hour to an hour). When using the page graph, students try to read the same amount of material (ten pages) in less time. Students may write a short summary of what they read to check comprehension. Examples 8.1 and 8.2 show time and page graphs.

There are several techniques you can use to improve students' scanning ability—their skill in reading rapidly to locate specific information. Two general guides apply: be sure your students know what specific information they want to locate; and have students use their index finger as a guide when rapidly looking down a page for key words or figures.

Use the following exercises to teach scanning:

1. Scan a telephone directory to locate a person's name or the name and number of a business.
2. Scan the index of a text to find information on a specific topic or person.
3. Scan an encyclopedia article on a specific state. Locate the state's nickname, bird, flower, capital city, and three important products.

Example 8.1   Time Graph

Directions: Decide how many minutes you will read—10, 20, or 30—and write that number in the space provided. Keep this length of time constant. Use a timing device set for this number of minutes. Try to increase the number of pages you read each time you practice.

I read for _____ minutes each time.

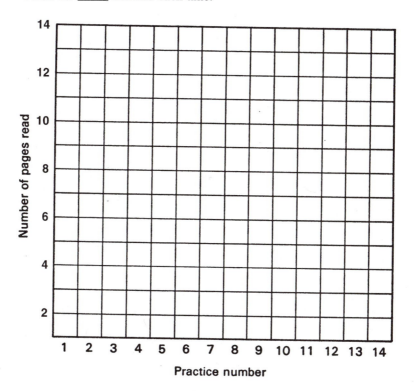

4. Scan the index of a mail-order catalog and locate the page on which specific items may be found.
5. Scan statistical tables to locate specific information.

Skimming, you will recall, is used to gain an overall or general idea of what the material is about. Thomas and Robinson (1972) list eight uses of skimming. Students can skim to preview a chapter, to decide whether they want to read a chapter or article, to determine if a book or article is relevant, or to learn the organization of the material. Students also can skim to learn the writer's opinion, to get a general

Example 8.2   Page Graph

Directions: Decide on a specific number of pages you will read in your book each time—5, 10, or 15—and write the number in the space provided. Keep this number constant. Record the time you start reading. Record the time you finish reading. Figure out how many minutes it took you to read these pages. Try to decrease the amount of time it takes you to read each time.

I read _____ pages each time.

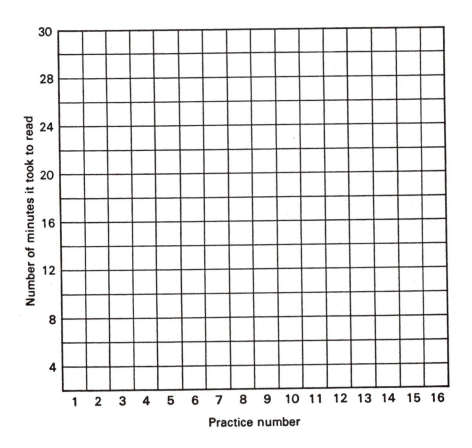

impression of the material, to see if the entire selection fits their purpose, and to review.

Here are three strategies you can use to enhance your students' skimming ability:

1. Give students thirty seconds to skim a news story to find out what happened.
2. Skim an information book. Check the title and subtitles (or subtopics), skim the book jacket (if there is one), skim the preface, look over the table of contents, skim the introduction and the concluding paragraphs.
3. Give students three or five minutes to preview an assigned chapter. At the end of this time, have them write down the main ideas.

Psycholinguists believe that people have limited "processing time." If that time is used up by decoding and other skills, there is less time for comprehension. If students spend too much time and energy decoding words, the purpose for reading can be lost. Therefore, reading rate is a relevant skill as it affects comprehension. Reading rapidly for the sake of speed, however, is rather useless. The ability to be flexible can be the difference between a good reader and a poor reader.

STUDY STRATEGIES

How many times have you seen students pick up a textbook and jump into reading the latest chapter without any preparation—without knowing what to look for, without knowing why? As a result of having no "reason to read," they quickly become bored and lose interest. They don't think about the topic. They don't study.

Studying leads to learning or knowledge, and this in turn will stimulate interest. Interest creates a positive attitude, which is evidenced in a willingness to learn. And skill in the use of facts and principles will create greater interest (Dudycha, 1957).

Textbooks contain a number of aids that can help students learn. Take time to point out these aids to your students. Discuss what these various aids do and what information they provide. Let's take a look at some of the aids commonly found in textbooks.

The *table of contents* shows the major topics that are presented in the textbook and the order in which they occur.

The *index* is much more detailed or inclusive than the table of contents. The index presents an alphabetical listing of every topic covered in the textbook.

New words or vocabulary often occur in *italics* or **boldface** print and are sometimes followed by the written pronunciation and definition in parentheses. If the pronunciation and definition do not follow the word immediately, they may appear as footnotes or in a glossary.

Section headings help students see the organization of topics in the chapter being studied. They help divide the chapter into shorter segments to study.

Paragraph headings appear at the beginning of a series of paragraphs about a subtopic. They let students know when the author is shifting from one subtopic to another subtopic.

Illustrations, such as photographs, diagrams, and drawings, help students visualize an explanation.

Maps provide information about geographical areas and help students see the relationship of one physical area to another.

Exercises at the ends of units or sections test students' understanding and recall of what they read.

General Study Strategies

In addition to these textbook aids, a number of general study strategies have been developed. There are many approaches to studying effectively and efficiently. It is the student's task to find the study approach that best meets his or her needs. It is the teacher's task to acquaint students with these approaches and strategies and help them see their relevance.

Before we read about these study strategies, consider the following example. You receive a registered letter. The letter states that your running team has been selected to run in the Olympic relay race. Imagine the excitement! Imagine the work ahead!

The task of your team is to cross the finish line in the shortest amount of time. So you make a list of the people on your team and their running times, and you establish a training schedule. Getting these people over the finish line first, or in the shortest time, becomes your plan.

Next, you develop a strategy for getting across the finish line first. You know the running times of the people on your team. You identify the running times of the people on the other teams. You identify obstacles on the running course. You set up practice sessions with your team members. You determine who should start the race, run in the middle, and then run last.

The day of the race comes. The television cameras are focused on you. The spectators are watching your team. The race begins. You follow your plan and keep track of, or monitor, how your team is doing.

Finally, when the race is over, you evaluate to see how well you did. Did your team come in first, second, last? What difficulties did your team face? What strengths did your team show?

Students can learn to face study tasks the same way you faced that Olympic race. They plan, form a strategy, monitor, and evaluate. Students survey or look at the plan of the material and develop questions they expect to answer during reading. They form a strategy and read the material section by section. They monitor how well they are reading by answering the questions they formulated. Finally, they evaluate or use self-testing techniques when they are finished. In short, when using study strategies, students are using metacognitive strategies.

Perhaps the most widely used and best known study approach for content area subjects was developed by Francis Robinson (1961). It is widely used with all content area subjects except literature. The approach is commonly known as **SQ3R** (Survey, Question, Read, Recite, Review). Let's take a more detailed look at the steps.

1. Survey. During the survey phase students read the title and view the subtitles in the chapter. The subtitles provide the author's outline and show how subtopics relate to the entire chapter. These visuals assist students with the meaning of new vocabulary and provide a more concrete or visual explanation of something that may be very abstract. Students then read the introductory and concluding paragraphs of the chapter. The survey phase helps students get a general view of the chapter and its main points.

2. Question. Students now work through one section at a time converting subtitles into questions. Students develop questions they would ask if they were the teacher. This questioning step helps students decide what is important and helps them concentrate. It also helps them become independent of the teacher.

3. Read (R1). During this step, students read to answer the questions they formulated. They try to apply what they've read to the world, to give examples, or to make generalizations about their readings.

4. Recite (R2). As students complete reading a section, they should ask themselves what they've read. They should recite the main and important subpoints in their own words. Morgan and Deese (1969) write that the amount of time students spend on recitation will depend on the type of material being read. If students are learning formulas, laws, or rules they might spend 90 to 95 percent of their time on recitation. Well-organized, story-like material might require spending 30 percent of the study time on recitation. Textbooks in political science, psychology, or economics might require spending 50 percent of the study time on recitation. Recitation helps students improve their memories and focus their attention on the task at hand. Finally, it alerts students to material they have misunderstood.

5. Review (R3). The review step involves surveying—skimming over the headings and subheadings again and answering the questions raised in step 2. Students should recite the points they previously read under each heading and subheading, recall the summaries, and check their notes.

Reviews should occur frequently. The first review after the completion of the SQ3R should occur within twelve to twenty-four hours after studying because the greatest amount of forgetting occurs within one day after learning. Encourage students to have a second review a week later, and a third review about three weeks later. Figure 8–1, the so-called curve of forgetting by Thomas Staton, illustrates our point.

The necessity for frequent reviews is substantiated through the psychological factor called *retroactive inhibition*. Have you ever read and understood a chapter in a textbook in the morning, and forgotten what it was about at the end of the day? Psychologists attribute this type of forgetting to what they call retroactive inhibition. This means that the experiences you had after reading the chapter in your textbook

FIGURE 8–1 • **The Curve of Forgetting**

Source: From T. F. Staton (1982), *How to study,* 7th ed. (Nashville: How to Study, P.O. Box 40273), p. 58. Reprinted with permission.

interfered with your retention of the chapter. Dudycha (1957, p. 75) states this another way: "Later experiences have an inhibitory effect on the retention of earlier experiences."

Many researchers have confirmed the relationship between reviews and retention. As early as the 1930s, studies confirmed the importance of review (Peterson et al., 1935; Spitzer, 1939). Later studies by Ausubel and Youssef (1965) and Reynolds and Glazer (1964) confirmed that spaced reviews were more effective in increasing retention than mere repetition. Petros and Hoving (1980) also found that review had a positive influence on retention.

There are many variations of the SQ3R. Thomas and Robinson (1972) added the step *reflect* and developed PQ4R—preview, question, read, reflect, recite, and review. PANORAMA was developed by Edwards (1973). PARS was recommended by Smith and Elliott (1979).

Pauk (1984) modified SQ3R and PQ4R when he developed SQ4R; C2R (Moore, 1981), PSC (Orlando, 1980), and REAP (Monzo, 1976) are some other study strategies educators have developed. Simpson, Stahl, and Hayes (1989) documented a study strategy called PROBE, which integrated predicting, organizing, rehearsal, practice, and evaluation.

Guidelines and Study Strategies for Specific Content Areas

A number of guidelines and study strategies are available for specific content areas (Caughran & Mountain, 1962; Roe, Stoodt & Burns, 1983). Let's take a look at some of these approaches.

Studying Science

Students do not often think of science courses as courses in how to think. Rather, they usually view them as the class in which they must observe experiments and memorize facts. They do not see science as a systematic organization of knowledge.

"This systematic organization is the result of a thinking process which begins with being curious about a problem. It goes through the stages of narrowing the problem to essential facts..., considering possible causes of the problem..., seeking facts which may have gone unnoticed..., selecting the most reasonable cause from a list of possible causes..., and seeking evidence to prove or disprove the solution" (Caughran & Mountain, 1962, p. 313).

Students will do much of their studying about science through reading. The discoveries of scientists, scientific principles, and facts will be included in their textbooks.

Studying History

When studying history, students are not studying one history. Rather, they are studying many different histories. They are reading about the histories of many different people, places, and times.

The historical writer develops a combined history based on the individual histories of many different people, places, and times. The historical writer, generally, has not had firsthand information about these topics but must depend on the secondhand information of earlier historians and on written records (letters, documents) to develop a unique historical point of view. Historians must omit much more information than they can include in a book. Historians make comparisons between people, places, and times and organize these many different histories into topics. The historian thus writes *a* history, not *the* history.

In addition to the many textbok aids that assist students as they read (maps, graphs, charts, tables of contents, indexes, subheadings, vocabulary helps), there are six other ways to help students read to interpret history.

First, have students *check the organization* of their history textbooks. How do the subsections fit into the larger organization of a section or chapter? What is the outline of the chapter or section?

Second, have students *check the names of people*. Think of the people in relation to the places and times in which they lived. Think of the ideas that influenced these people and of how their ideas influence others.

Third, have students *check the location of places*. Names of places are only words until students can locate them on maps and can associate them with people and times.

Fourth, have students *check the dates* and place them into an historic period of time—prehistoric, ancient, Elizabethan, whatever. This will help students understand the significance of the date in relation to the characteristics of civilization during that period.

Fifth, have students *check for elements of civilization*. The study of history is the study of the intermingled elements of civilization. It is the study of changes, sometimes slow and sometimes rapid, as they relate to the elements of civilization.

Sixth, have students *check previously read material for missed interpretations*. Here, rereading means turning back to earlier sections, chapters, or units with reference to what you have just learned. Students will approach these chapters with a fresh, informed point of view.

Studying Mathematics

Let's take a look at some of the reasons why students find mathematics difficult.

Students may write numerals carelessly. As a result, students confuse X's with Y's, 2's with Z's, 4's with 9's, and so on. When solving problems, these students are confused by their own writing and solve the problems incorrectly.

Students may copy the examples carelessly. The problem in the book is $X + 18 = 43$. Careless students may copy the problem $X + 18 = 34$.

Students may look only at the sample problem in the book and follow the sample when solving all other problems. They don't read the explanations. As a result, they don't learn the vocabulary of mathematics and don't understand the teacher's oral explanation.

You probably are familiar with students who glance at the problem and then turn to the answer key without even trying to work a solution. Through trial-and-error guessing, these students fit numerals into the problem until they obtain the right answer.

When learning a new concept in mathematics, students may forget anything that they previously learned. They think that what was learned in the past no longer is necessary.

Students may read their assignments too fast. They read the assignments and problems as though they were reading the newspaper comics, with little or no attention to comprehension. They read the explanation, but skip the problems.

Students need to learn that mathematics has its own specialized vocabulary and system of expression. Mathematics is learned through use and practice, not just by reading about it. This requires the careful reading and analysis of problems.

Fay (1965) developed a special study strategy to help students read mathematics. The strategy is called **SQRQCQ**. Let's look at the steps in SQRQCQ.

1. **Survey.** Read the problem rapidly to gain a general understanding of it.
2. **Question.** Determine what the problem is asking you to find out.
3. **Reread.** Reread the problem to determine what facts are given and what their relationships are.
4. **Question.** Determine how you should go about solving the problem.
5. **Compute.** Solve the problem.
6. **Question.** Check to determine if your answer is correct.

Studying Literature

The type of reading used for the study of history or science is not appropriate when reading prose, poetry, or drama. There are several obvious differences between reading fiction and nonfiction that account for the need for a different style of reading. Fiction is often written in the past tense, it often contains incomplete sentences, and the characters may be introduced by first names only.

Students not only have to be aware of these obvious differences, but they must be aware of the time period in which the selection was written and the different meanings words take on over a period of time. What was the value of $50 in the 1600s as compared with its value today? Was an *undertaker* during Shakespeare's time the same as an *undertaker* today? What were the life-styles of people during the period of time about which the selection was written?

Unlike seeing novels, short stories, or plays acted out on screen or stage where a director interprets mood, settings, and scenes, students must do this interpretation themselves. They must be able to read between the lines to discover the meaning of the author. Does the author have a meaning other than what is the obviously stated, literal meaning? Students must be able to judge the significance of the actions, events, and characters.

Students will recognize poetry by its physical appearance. The right margin is uneven and does not go to the end of the page. Each line usually begins with a capital letter. Stanzas are equal in length. There is usually a rhythm or beat to poetry. (We refer to this rhythm as stressed and unstressed syllables.) Sometimes poetry contains a rhyming scheme.

Poetry sometimes is more difficult to understand because it is very compact. Authors often suggest, rather than explicitly state, what they mean. Very specific words are used to convey meaning.

Reading drama can be a difficult and frustrating experience because it originally was intended to be seen and listened to rather than read, especially read silently. Students must be given the proper background for understanding the ideas presented in the text of the play. The reading of drama should be done orally with students taking parts to give the words an aura of conversation. If possible, encourage students to act out the drama.

The reading of prose fiction, poetry, and drama demands close attention. It requires students to interpret the precise meaning the author intended to convey to readers, to go from a superficial meaning to depth in meaning, to go from the general to the specific parts that make up the whole. Pauk (1963) outlined a study strategy to help students read imaginative prose, poetry, and drama. The strategy is called EVOKER and consists of these six steps:

1. **Explore.** Read the entire selection silently without stopping. This will give you an overall view of the author's message.
2. **Vocabulary.** Underline or note key words in the selection. Look up words that are unfamiliar. Familiarize yourself with names, events, and places mentioned.
3. **Oral reading.** Read the selection aloud with good intonation or expression.
4. **Key ideas.** Locate key ideas and determine the author's organization.
5. **Evaluate.** Analyze the key words and ideas in detail. Note how the key words help develop mood and shades of meaning.
6. **Recapitulate.** Put the parts back into the whole selection by rereading the entire piece.

OUTLINING

Outlining is a means of organizing ideas and showing how they fit together. In a way, outlining is similar to sending a telegram. For a telegram, a person selects only the most important words or ideas from a letter. For an outline, a person selects the most important ideas from a larger piece of written material, or presents an organization for something the person will expand on at a later time.

Pyramiding, mapping, herringbone, and webbing strategies were discussed in Chapter 7. Each of these graphic organizers is excellent for developing outlining skills. In this chapter we will discuss techniques other than those that have already been covered.

Hofler (1983) believes that we should show students how to outline through classification exercises before introducing them to indexing or using numbers and letters for outlining. You can begin with simple classifications such as types of dogs. Lassie and Laddie are collies. Rin-tin-tin and Mack the bionic dog are German shepherds. This strategy involves several stages, as follows:

1. List concrete items.

Wind River Range
Teton Range
Front Range
Smoky Mountains
Green Mountains
Catskill Mountains

2. First classification.

Rocky Mountains	Appalachian Mountains
Teton Range	Smoky Mountains
Wind River Range	Green Mountains
Front Range	Catskill Mountains

3. Second classification. (Notice that the columns in the second classification are placed one above the each other, thus resembling an outline.)

Mountains

Rocky Mountains	Appalachian Mountains
Teton Range	Smoky Mountains
Wind River Range	Green Mountains
Front Range	Catskill Mountains

4. Add outline format using Roman numerals, capital letters, Arabic numerals, and lowercase letters as follows. (See Example 8.3 for the expanded outline format.)

Mountains

I.	Rocky Mountains	1.0
	A. Teton Range	1.1
	B. Wind River Range	1.2
	C. Front Range	1.3
II.	Appalachian Mountains	2.0
	A. Smoky Mountains	2.1
	B. Green Mountains	2.2
	C. Catskill Mountains	2.3

Before beginning outlining, students should be able to (1) select main ideas and important details, (2) classify, (3) write in telegraphic style, and (4) change the order of words in a sentence to create a clearer meaning. (For example, "The nuclear accident created many unforeseen and potentially dangerous problems" would be rewritten, Problems of nuclear accidents.)

Once students are able to cope with the above skills, they are ready to begin a systematic introduction to outlining. At first, the outlines should be very simple (just main headings) and the teacher should fill in some of the answers. Gradually, the outlines become more difficult. See Example 8.4 for a kind of outlining exercise.

As a teacher, you should take time to show your students how the chapter titles and subheadings fit together and often form the skeleton of an outline. Show students that this skeleton outline helps them see the chapter organization during the survey step in SQ3R.

Example 8.3   Outline Format

Title

I.   Main Heading or Topic
   A.   Subtopic supporting I
      1.   Detail supporting A
         a.   Detail of secondary importance, supporting 1
         b.   Detail of secondary importance, supporting 1
      2.   Detail supporting A
   B.   Subtopic supporting I
      1.   Detail supporting B
      2.   Detail supporting B
         a.   Detail of secondary importance, supporting 2
         b.   Detail of secondary importance, supporting 2
II.   Main Heading or Topic
   A.   Subtopic supporting II
      1.   Detail supporting A
      2.   Detail supporting A
         a.   Detail of secondary importance, supporting 2
         b.   Detail of secondary importance, supporting 2
   B.   Subtopic supporting II
      1.   Detail supporting B
      2.   Detail supporting B

Outlining is an important organizational skill for students to master. It not only assists students in seeing relationships, but it is a valuable skill to know for note taking.

Grant (1993) recommended integrating outlining into a study procedure through the use of SCROL—survey, connect, read, outline, and look back. The procedure contains the following steps:

1. **Survey the headings.** Look at the headings and subheadings and determine what you already know about the topic; then predict what information the author might present.
2. **Connect.** When you have finished reading all the headings and subheadings, look at the overall organization and determine how the topics relate to one another. Construct a skeletal outline of the headings and subheadings by writing down key words.
3. **Read the text.** Read the text section by section. Use the headings and subheadings to identify important ideas related to the section. Highlight important ideas and details.
4. **Outline.** On the skeletal outline you created in step 1, fill in major ideas and supporting details. Try to write the heading and fill in the ideas and details without looking back at the text.

Example 8.4   Outline with Words Listed at Bottom of Page*

Peanuts

Peanuts are not really nuts; they are members of the pea family. Peanuts bear pods that usually contain two seeds. These seeds are called peanuts and are found underground.

There are two types of peanut plants—the bunch and the runner. Bunch peanuts are straight, bushy plants. Runner peanuts are vinelike plants that spread along the ground.

Peanuts are useful in many ways. As a food, they are popular when ground into a paste for peanut butter. Peanuts also are used in making bakery goods. Peanut oil is used in cooking.

Peanuts also have industrial uses. The oil may be an ingredient in lubricants and paints. Peanut shells may be ground up to make plastics.

Peanuts are a major crop in the United States. Over 1.5 million tons are grown annually in this country. Leading peanut-growing states are Georgia, Texas, North Carolina, and Alabama.

Peanuts

I. *The peanut plant*
  A. *Pods*
    1. *Two seeds called peanuts*
    2. *Found underground*
  B. *Types of plants*
    1. *Bunch*
    2. *Runner*
II. *Uses of peanuts*
  A. *Food uses*
    1. *Peanut butter*
    2. *Bakery goods*
    3. *Peanut oil*
  B. *Industrial uses*
    1. *Lubricants*
    2. *Paints*
    3. *Plastics*
III. *Peanut production*
  A. *Tons produced*
  B. *Peanut-growing states*
    1. *Georgia*
    2. *Texas*
    3. *North Carolina*
    4. *Alabama*

Bunch	Uses of peanuts	Plastics
Paints	Runner	Peanut-growing states
Georgia	Peanut butter	Two seeds called peanuts
Peanut oil	Texas	Alabama
Pods	Industrial uses	Bakery goods
North Carolina	Tons produced	Found underground
Lubricants	Types of plants	

   5. Look back. Now use the text to check your accuracy. Correct any errors.

As you can see, SCROL integrates elements of the study procedure we discussed earlier with outlining skills. Note that the important issue is not that students can create a neat outline, but that they can use the outline for study and review purposes.

NOTE TAKING

Note taking is an important skill. Most students consider it essential for college success. However, students often are not given any instruction in it. Take time to practice some of the following strategies with your students.

Listening Guides

Listening guides can be used as an initial step toward note taking. Castallo (1976) describes the strategy as a means of helping students identify the important points of a lecture. The listening guide is an outline that includes main ideas and subtopics and leaves students space to include details. Example 8.5 presents a listening guide. The underlined sections are those that you would leave blank for students to complete while listening to your presentation.

Two-Column Strategies

As students mature in their ability to listen to lectures and succeed at initial note-taking strategies, they are ready to begin more advanced strategies of note taking. Students usually aren't ready for advanced note taking until about grade 9. However, most teachers in high school don't show students how to do it.

Palmatier (1971) studied student use of four different note-taking strategies. Although the results were not conclusive because of the brief training period, Palmatier wrote that the two-column strategy appeared to be most useful in studying.

Several two-column procedures include the NSL two-column note-taking system (Palmatier, 1973; Aaronson, 1975); the VSPP, verbatim split page procedures (Readence, Bean, & Baldwin, 1981); the Cornell note-taking system (Pauk, 1974, 1984); and the DNA, or directed note-taking activity (Spires & Stone, 1989).

Pauk (1974, 1984) also recommends using a two-column note-taking strategy. This is more commonly referred to as the Cornell note-taking system. The student divides an 8 1/2-by-11-inch sheet of paper into two vertical columns. The columns are 2 1/2 and 6 inches wide, or approximately one-third and two-thirds of the page width wide, with the narrower column at the left side of the paper. In the wide column, the student records the lecture as fully as possible. In the narrow column, the student writes key words and brief summaries of the lecture. These are used as cues in studying. Then, looking only at the key words, students recite aloud as

Example 8.5   Listening Guide

Land Formations

I. Plains
- A. Physical description
  1. *broad, level*
  2. *lack steep hills*
  3. *rarely entirely flat*
- B. Benefits to people
  1. *most economical to build highways and railroads on*
  2. *most of world's food grown*
  3. *world's largest cities built*

II. Mountains
- A. Physical description
  1. *rapid changes in elevation*
  2. *highest elevation*
  3. *greatest local relief*
- B. Types
  1. *volcanic*
  2. *faulted*
  3. *domal*
  4. *folded*

III. Hills
- A. Physical description
  1. *lower elevation than mountains*
  2. *many are worn down mountains*
- B. Formation
  1. *wind erosion*
  2. *water erosion*

IV. Plateaus
- A. Physical description
  1. *level land*
  2. *higher than surrounding land, except when between mountains*
- B. Few benefits
  1. *little rainfall*
  2. *small population*

much of the material from the lecture as they can remember. Reciting aloud forces students to think rather than daydream.

By using a two-column procedure, students can use the key ideas on the left side of the page as cues for reciting information for study purposes. They can, in essence, quiz themselves using the left column, and check their responses responses using the right column. As we mentioned with outlining, the critical issue is not the neatness of the notes, but that the notes are useful for study and review purposes. Do not encourage students to rewrite their notes. Rewriting takes away from study time and tends to be merely mechanical.

After reviewing research on underlining (or highlighting) and note-taking strategies, McAndrew (1983) made the following recommendations.

Underlining

1. Give students preunderlined material whenever possible.
2. Provide training for students in effective underlining.
3. Have students underline major general ideas.
4. Remind students to underline sparingly.
5. Remind students to spend the time saved by underlining in studying.
6. Underlining is not always the best study strategy. Other techniques may be better.

Note Taking

1. The value of note taking lies in its use as a way of storing material for later study, not in the act of taking notes.
2. Try using a spaced lecture method with your students.
3. Highlight and emphasize the structure of your lectures. This can be done through verbal cues, like "It is important that..." or gestures.
4. Write material on the board if you want to be sure students include it in their notes.
5. Students are unlikely to put information from slides or overhead transparencies into their notes because the material usually is complex and the instructor usually talks at the time it is being shown. Preview and review the material on the board if you want students to get it into their notes.
6. Tell students the type of test you will give.
7. Whenever possible, use handouts with plenty of space for students to write their own notes.

TIME MANAGEMENT AND STUDY AIDS

With all that we have to do in a day, when do we have time to study? How can we organize our time better? Conley (1992) uses the term "persistent procrastination" to describe how many students study. They keep putting study off until the last minute, sometimes never getting around to the assignment. Other times, they work a little, stop for a long period of time, work a little, stop for another long period of time. More time is spent off the task than on the assignment. You and your students can benefit from following time management guidelines.

We can save a lot of time by *doing while we are waiting*. Think of the hours we spend waiting. During this time we could review notes, survey reading assignments, and the like. Use this time wisely. Don't idle around.

Plan a specific time each day for studying. Some people study early in the morning because it is quiet. Once the habit of studying at a specific time is established, studying becomes easier and more natural.

Think positively. Negative thinking interferes with meeting our goals. Use positive affirmations. Place cards with positive affirmations written on them in the place where you study, on your mirror, and other places around the house where you will see them. Affirmations might include these: *I like to study. I like to study (name of subject). I do well in (name of subject). I am a genius, and I successfully use my genius in everything I do.* Keep the affirmations in the present and positive. Even if you don't think you like the subject or you aren't doing well in it, keep telling yourself that you like it and you are doing well in it. Believe what you are saying. We can change our lives if we change our thinking.

Be sure that you know specifically what the assignment is and what you are expected to do. You can waste a lot of time trying to figure out what you're supposed to do, doing the assignment incorrectly, or even more time doing the wrong assignment.

Review often. Spaced review enhances learning. Spend about fifteen minutes reviewing previous assignments before beginning a new assignment.

Reward yourself for a good study session. When you have finished, have a favorite snack or watch a favorite video.

Make good use of study periods. Use the time between classes to study rather than driving off campus.

Plan a daily schedule for yourself that includes study blocks. Follow this schedule so that you do not ignore study time.

MEMORY ENHANCEMENT

Affective factors and self-esteem play important roles in how well students learn. Listen to what students say about themselves; listen to what they "say," or show, through body language about the subject. How students communicate with each other, verbally or nonverbally, can give you important clues to their self-esteem. Building positive self-esteem is a major part of improving memory and learning.

Organization and use of material is important for retention. Putting material into visual images, mentally or through mapping, can help with organization. By doing this you "chunk," or group, materials into meaningful units for retention.

Be sure that you have a purpose for reading and studying. Having a purpose provides direction.

Recite or practice what you've learned. Say it aloud, and often, after initial learning; then review once a week. This leads to overlearning for easy retrieval. Study the material even though you have already learned it.

Break long pieces of material you must memorize into shorter units. Learn a section, then review this and add another section to it.

Use *mnemonic devices* to aid in learning. We all remember "Thirty days hath September, April, June and November;" or "Every good boy does fine." There are several types of mnemonic aids: acrostics, acronyms, key word associations, and ordering.

An *acrostics* is a verse or sentence used to remember material; the words of the sentence, or their first letters, are clues or reminders. A group of students devised the acrostic shown in Example 8.7 for learning about the planets.

Acronyms are another mnemonic device. We learned about acronyms when we studied the chapter on vocabulary. You will recall that an acronym is a word made up of the first letter, or first few letters, of several words. Some common learning acronyms are: FACE—for the note spaces between the staff lines in music; UNESCO—United Nations Educational, Social, and Cultural Organization, and HOMES—the Great Lakes, Huron, Ontario, Michigan, Erie, and Superior.

Developing *key word associations* is another mnemonic device. The word *rushing* might help you remember the word *Russian*. You might think of the name of a friend and try to associate it with people and places you are learning.

Ordering, or placing items in chronological or alphabetical order, aids in retention and memorizing a list, especially when key words or associations don't work.

Audiotapes also have been developed to improve memory. Three examples of such tapes are:

Super Learning, by Sheila Ostrander and Lynn Schroeder. Sound Editions by Random House.

Example 8.7   Acrostic for Learning About Planets

Key Word	Planet Order	Identity Detail
mild	Mercury	no weather patterns
volatile	Venus	sulfuric acid atmosphere
embryos	Earth	life, liquid water
must	Mars	rust-red appearing
jump	Jupiter	largest planet
seven	Saturn	seven major rings
ugly	Uranus	gas "giant"
naked	Neptune	"green" planet
pipsqueaks	Pluto	smallest planet

Acrostic: Mild, volatile embryos must jump seven ugly naked pipsqueaks.

Improve Memory and Concentration, by Larry Garrett. Garrett Hypnosis Clinic. *Accelerating Learning,* by Steven Halpren. Sound Rx.

TEST TAKING PROCEDURES

Test making is a big business. Prell and Prell (1986) write, "In 1983, school systems purchased an estimated $500 million worth of commercial achievement tests—an estimate that does not even include IQ, diagnostic, or most minimum competency tests" (p. 1). Despite the many objections to testing, it is still growing. Because of education's emphasis on testing, it is important to teach students "test-wiseness." That is, teach students how to use the test format and testing situation to achieve higher test results.

Some students earn lower scores on tests than their knowledge or ability demonstrates they should score. Their test scores are lower because they lack test-wiseness. They do not understand the characteristics of various tests or the test-taking procedures necessary for scoring higher.

The best way to prepare for a test is to master the subject matter by studying and reviewing periodically. Only through study can a person walk into a test with confidence. Just as an athlete needs to train, and train, and train to become skilled in his or her sport, a student must study, and study, and study in order to become knowledgeable in academic subjects.

Take the following test. The sentences in this test contain dangling participles. Rewrite the sentences correctly.

1. We viewed the autumn leaves gliding along in our sailboat.

2. Flipping through the pages, my eyes were caught by a shiny red Moped.

3. Leaping out of the water, the trainer fed the dolphin a fish.

4. We saw a bear riding along in our new Honda.

How did you feel when you first saw this exercise? You may have felt uncomfortable because you weren't prepared. Had you forgotten what a dangling participle was? *Study and preparation* are essential to good test taking.

If students follow a study procedure that involves periodic reviews, studying for a test should be mainly another review. Students should review their notes and the important ideas and details they noted in their textbooks. This test review, however, should be more intense than the periodic reviews.

Students' test scores depend on several factors. These success factors include experiential background, attitude, motivation, interest, and reading comprehension.

Students can get a good idea about what to study from course goals and objectives, class notes, knowing a teacher's likes and dislikes, visual aids a teacher uses to emphasize a point, past quizzes, and reviews. If a teacher uses the word *discuss* during a review, it's a good clue that the test probably will be in essay format. If the teacher uses the word *know* during a review, the test probably will be objective; the student will have to know more details.

Students need to know themselves better in order to make the best study plans. Do they study best in the morning or evening? Do they study better in quiet or do they need some "sound" around them? Do they study better sitting at a desk, sitting in a comfortable chair, or lying on the floor or bed? Students need to find a study place that fits their learning styles.

Encourage students to develop their own study aids. One valuable study aid is a reference file. Advise your students to keep copies of corrected homework, quizzes, tests, and notes in a subject file folder.

The use of flashcards is another study aid. Use index cards. Write review questions on one side and the answers on the reverse side. Have students go though the cards asking the questions, answering them, and then checking their answers by turning the card over.

As we discussed in previous chapters, textbooks provide many study aids for students. Highlighted topic sentences, summaries, chapter tests, or review questions, boldfaced type and italics all point to important information. Direct students' attention to these textbook features.

It is difficult to study for any test without memorizing some information. Be sure students understand what they are memorizing. Show students that categorizing information by putting it into chronological order, alphabetical order, or any other grouping of items with similar characteristics aids in memorization. It is easier to memorize categorized items than those that have no groupings or associations. It is also easier to memorize smaller amounts of information than large pieces.

Using the memory enhancements discussed in the previous section also will help students improve their test taking skills.

Guidelines for True-False Questions

In true-false questions, students are given a choice of two answers (true or false) but only one is correct. Direct your students to remember these guidelines when taking true-false test:

1. Certain qualifiers such as *all, never, always, none,* and *only* tend to make statements false.
2. Broad, general statements that contain the words *sometimes, perhaps, seldom,* and *generally* are likely to be true.
3. Don't try to figure out a pattern. A well-constructed true-false test does not contain a pattern.
4. The longer the statement, the more likely it is to be true.
5. If there are two parts to a true-false statement, both parts must be true for the answer to be true.

Guidelines for Multiple-Choice Questions

Multiple-choice questions contain a stem (an incomplete statement or question), a flower (the best answer), and thorns (distractors or incorrect answers). Here are some guidelines for taking multiple-choice tests:

1. Eliminate answers that do not complete the stem grammatically or logically.
2. Longer answers tend to be correct because more information needs to be included to make them correct.
3. Discard any answers you know are incorrect and concentrate on the possible correct answers.
4. Look for answers that are stated so carefully that they probably are correct.
5. If one answer includes correct material from other possible choices, it is probably the correct answer.
6. Correct answers are often found in the middle of your choices. When in doubt, select **c**.
7. If you have two opposite choice possibilities, one of the answers is usually correct.
8. When taking a multiple-choice test, read the stem and try to complete the answer before looking at the possible choices.

Guidelines for Matching Questions

In a matching test students are asked to make pairs from two lists of facts or ideas. The following guidelines will assist your students:

1. Work from the column with most information to the column with the least.
2. Check to see if any of the answers can be used more than once.
3. Answer the questions you are sure of first. Go through the entire list before starting from the beginning a second time.
4. Cross out items as you use them.

Guidelines for Fill-In Questions

In fill-in types of questions the student must complete a statement with names, dates, symbols, or other correct words. Acquaint your students with the following guidelines for taking fill-in tests:

1. Be sure to use capital letters if the fill-in is at the beginning of a sentence or a proper noun. There may be penalty points for not doing this.
2. If the fill-ins are in paragraph form, read the entire paragraph before completing the blank spaces.
3. If you don't remember the exact word, write a synonym. You may get partial credit.
4. The length of the blank spaces or separations between blank spaces may give you a clue to the length of the word or the number of words required to complete the answer.

Guidelines for Essay Tests

In taking an essay test students must be able to assemble, organize, and present material in a coherent manner. Direct your students' attention to the following guidelines:

1. Be sure you do what the essay questions ask.

    illustrate: Provide the best analogies or examples you can think of.
    compare: Present the similarities and differences.
    outline: Present the information in outline form using main ideas, subtopics, and supporting details.
    explain: Tell about, define, or describe using an illustration.
    summarize: State the main points or principles without going into a lot of discussion.
    trace: Show a detailed history of the topic, event, or subject.

2. Set time limits for answering each question.
3. Outline your answer to organize your ideas.
4. Give your own examples or illustrations. Don't parrot back examples from the text.
5. Do not include a lot of extraneous information or padding in your answer.
6. Do not try to bluff your way through a question.
7. If you don't have time to fully answer a question, provide an outline of your answer. You may get partial credit.
8. Check your answers for correct spelling, grammar, and punctuation.
9. Be sure your handwriting is legible.

Another Test
Answer the following questions in writing.

1. If an electric train were moving along the track at 88 km/hr, would the smoke blow to the back or the front of the train?
2. If a truck backed into a peanut tree at 80 km/hr, would peanuts fall on the truck?
3. Which would weigh more, a kilogram of feathers or a kilogram of lead?
4. If a baby bull got hurt, would it go to the mother bull for comfort?

Were you able to answer all of these questions? Did you read the questions carefully? Let's see. In number 1, electric trains don't have smoke. In number 2, peanuts don't grow on trees. In number 3, a kilogram is a kilogram; it would just take more feathers than lead to make a kilogram. And, in number 4, the baby couldn't go to the mother bull because bulls aren't mothers. Finally, did you write your answers to the questions in cursive, or did you use manuscript?

Remember, studying the material on a test is not the only prerequisite to scoring well. Test-wiseness is also necessary.

CONCLUSION

In this chapter we discussed seven major areas of study skills: reading rate and flexibility, study strategies, outlining, note taking, time management and study aids, memory enhancement, and test taking.

When children begin school, they read word by word or piece by piece. As students progress through school, they need to develop the ability to vary their reading rates according to the material they are reading and their purpose for reading. Scanning is used to locate specific information or a specific fact. This is a very rapid rate of about 1,500 words per minute. Skimming is used to gain an overview of what the material is about. Skimming is done at about 800 to 1,000 words per minute. During actual reading a student is critically analyzing the author's ideas and words. Actual reading is done at 150 to 600 words per minute, depending on the difficulty of the material and the reader's purpose for reading. The controlled reader, pacer, time graph, and page graph are methods for increasing reading speed.

There are many different study strategies. The SQ3R is probably the best-known general study strategy. The SQRQCQ strategy was specifically developed for reading mathematics. EVOKER was developed for reading imaginative prose, poetry, and drama.

Outlining is a means of organizing ideas and showing how they fit together. Classification exercises provide a good introduction to outlining. From basic classification exercises students can work into completing outlines in which teachers supply some of the information and gradually work toward outlines in which students supply all of the material.

Note taking is an essential skill for students to develop but it does not come naturally. Students need to be taught how to take notes. Two strategies include the use of listening guides and taking notes in two columns.

Time management and study aids stress using time efficiently, knowing what you are supposed to do, maintaining a positive attitude, and rewarding yourself for a job well done.

Memory enhancement is being able to learn more, more easily. Affective factors influence memory. Organization and practice also affect memory. Various mnemonic aids—acrostics, acronyms, key word associations, and ordering—help improve retention. Audiotapes also have been developed to improve memory.

Thoughtful test-taking strategies and test-wiseness are needed for success in school. The use of reference files, flash cards, and categorizing strategies for memorization can aid students in test preparation. But students don't only have to study the material in courses, they must also understand test-taking procedures. True-false, multiple-choice, matching, fill-in, and essay tests all have specific features that students should understand to increase their chances for success.

Good study strategies are necessary for success in school. They provide students with organizational frameworks with which to approach learning.

POSTREADING

INTEGRATING WRITING

In your journal describe your first attempts at note taking and compare that with the Cornell system.

REVIEW

At the beginning of this chapter you made a skeletal outline of the chapter's contents. Now, using this skeletal outline, try to fill in as much information as you can recall. Using the Cornell system, develop a more complete outline. Develop a list of words related to Chapter 8. Organize these into a graphic organizer and be able to explain why you organized them as you did.

PRACTICE

Do Enabling Activities 23 and 24 in Appendix A.

9

INTEGRATING WRITING

"The students in my class just finished writing research reports," commented Terry. "They really got carried away and wrote forty-page reports!"

"That's going to be a lot of grading for you to do," said Celeste.

"I'd like to have my students do more writing, but I can't grade too many sets of forty-page reports each year," sighed Terry.

"I know what you mean. I used to get so overwhelmed with papers that needed to be graded that I didn't have a minute to myself. I hate to admit it, but I've given up on having my students write. The reports are just too long to read and grade," said Celeste defensively.

"I overheard you talking about writing," interjected Julie. "When I was teaching at Westside, we realized that we were requiring too many research papers. And we weren't integrating writing into our courses as much as we could. I'll share the handbook of ideas we developed with you if you'd like."

"Great!" said Celeste.

"That would be terrific," Terry added. "We could use some different ideas."

DISCUSS

In what ways do reading and writing interact with each other? How do you go about writing? What process do you use? How might writing be incorporated into your content area?

PREORGANIZE

Go through the chapter and make a skeletal outline of the major headings and subheadings. This will provide you with a chapter organizer. Predict the contents of the text under one of these subheadings.

OBJECTIVES

After reading this chapter, you should be able to

1. develop a rationale for including writing in content area classes.
2. describe and demonstrate the use of instructional frameworks for writing.
3. describe and develop writing lessons in the categories of journal writing, critical/creative thinking, categorizing, and specific skills.
4. list additional writing activities.

Writing is a process that requires time and concentration. Students spend hours writing greeting cards or letters to friends and family. They want to be sure they write the exact ideas they want to communicate. Yet when it comes to classroom writing assignments, students think they should be able to complete the assignment in a short period of time. Some students may even turn in papers with very few well-developed ideas.

Just as football and basketball players do warm-up exercises before playing a game, students need to be given warm-up activities to start their "creative juices" flowing before beginning a writing assignment. In this chapter. we'll look at the role of writing in content area teaching. And we'll discuss journal writing, critical/creative thinking, categorizing, and specific skills writing strategies.

WRITING AND THE CONTENT AREA TEACHER

For many years teaching writing was viewed as the sole responsibility of English teachers, and content area teachers today are still reluctant to incorporate writing into their classes. Content area teachers don't feel that they are experts in the use of language. Content area teachers believe that writing assignments must be long. They fear that students cannot develop their own writing topics. They hear about writing conferences and can't imagine what takes place in one. Perhaps their greatest concern is in the area of evaluating and grading papers.

In spite of these concerns, writing *does* take place in most content area classrooms. Florio and Clark (1982) observed writing during school and identified four functions of writing. These functions include writing to take up free time, writing to become involved in the community, writing to know oneself and others, and writing to demonstrate academic competence.

The most effective content area assignments are ones that encourage students to have an informed opinion. These assignments are also ones that can be written within a reasonable time and length framework (Murray, 1968).

Reasons for Including Writing

Tchudi and Yates (1983) advance five reasons for including writing in content area classes.

1. Writing about a subject helps students learn better. When writing in the content areas, students must utilize concepts and ideas in the subject.
2. Practice in content area writing provides a basis for becoming a more skillful writer as an adult.

3. Content area subjects can be highly motivating for students—computers, space adventure, medical advances, and the future spark high interest.
4. Other language skills are developed as writing skills are utilized. Students read to gather information, interview people, and discuss their topics in class with other students.
5. Finally, thinking is a skill being given emphasis in our schools. And thinking is at the basis of writing. Students must select and organize information, then present it in a logical sequence.

Several research studies can be cited that highlight the effectiveness of writing in content area classes. Research by Taylor and Beach (1984) showed that paragraph writing improved students' reading of expository material. Writing essay responses to questions improved students' quality of reading (Petrosky, 1982). Note taking and summary writing have been shown to help students' comprehension of content material (Anderson, 1980; Taylor, 1982). Newell (1984) found that essay writing was more effective than note taking in learning information.

Building Background

In reading, you take time to build students' background before they engage in the assignment; so too, in writing, you also prepare students by building backgrounds. This preparation for writing can take many forms. If you look back at Dale's cone of learning in Chapter 4, you will see a hierarchy of experiences, with direct concrete experiences as the most powerful. As you have students engage in small group or class discussions you are providing a background of experiences for students.

Building background is the most important phase of the writing experience. Without background students have nothing to write about. Students need to recognize that they *do* have something to write about—they *do* have something to say. This idea is based on the language experience philosophy: I can talk about what I see or experience. I can write about what I say. I can read what I or someone else writes.

Developing Topics

Students should be encouraged to develop their own topics or subjects within frameworks set by the teacher. Graves (1983) identifies several classroom activities that can help students generate writing topics.

1. Students can share their work with each other. As students read paragraphs or early drafts of their work to each other, the topics may stimulate other students' interests.
2. Publishing or binding students' writing and making it available to other students is another way of adding to students' repertoire of writing topics.
3. Reading selections by different authors aloud to students stimulates the flow of creative ideas.

4. Encourage students to keep writing folders and to list future writing topics on the inside cover of the folder. These topics may be the result of listening to other students' sharing of writing, TV programs viewed, or an element of a topic that was originally too broad.

Content area journals can provide additional ideas for writing (Fulwiler, 1980); for example:

defining terms in a personal way
writing summaries or questions about the day's lecture
evaluating a topic
writing opinions about current events topics
describing what is seen
describing feelings after listening to music
identifying attitude changes

Conferences

As students write, they should meet with the teacher for conferences. Set aside conference periods, times during the week when students meet with you to discuss progress being made and problems encountered in a writing assignment. Frequent, short conferences in which you tackle only one problem at a sitting are the most effective (Murray, 1982).

During a conference session encourage the student to sit beside you—on your right side if you're right-handed, on your left side if you're left-handed. As you meet with the student, concentrate on one problem with which the student is having difficulty. Take your student one step at a time. If you cover too much during the conference, you'll only confuse the student (Graves, 1983).

Calkins (1983) recommends beginning the conference with predictable questions: "What are you planning to do next?" "What new problems did you run into?" "How is this draft different from the earlier one?"

Once the conference has begun, you may use follow-up questions to keep the student talking or ask process questions to focus the student's attention on his or her writing. Graves (1983) provides several examples of process questions: "I notice that you changed your lead. It is much more direct. How did you do that?" "If you were to put that new information in here, how would you go about doing it?" "What strategy do you use for figuring out where one sentence ends and the other one begins?"

Calkins (1983) recommends four categories of follow-up questions. Here are her categories and a few of her examples:

1. Questions that help writers focus:
   a. Have students identify the most important things they are saying.
   b. Have students identify a reason for choosing the topic. What makes the topic important to them?

    c.   Have students identify the most important part and why it is important.

    d.   Have students identify where they got the main idea.

    e.   Have students identify anything that doesn't seem to fit.

2. Questions that help writers "show, not tell":

    a.   Have students read their best description. Also have students identify what makes this section better than others.

    b.   Have students identify places where they could be more descriptive.

3. Questions that help writers expand their pieces:

    a.   Have students tell you about an idea in their own words.

    b.   Have students identify questions other people might have after reading their papers.

4. Questions that help a writer reconsider the sequence:

    a.   Have students tell what came first, second, third. (Make a list.)

    b.   Ask if the events could be arranged in any other way.

    c.   Ask students why they decided to put their ideas into the specific order.

Peer Editing

Ultimately, students should be taught to assess their own writing. Peer editing can reduce teacher grading to a reasonable level in several ways that have been highlighted by Tchudi and Yates (1983):

1. The responsibility for revision is placed with the writer.

2. While students are working in editing groups, the teacher has time to meet in conferences with individual students.

3. Papers turned in after peer editing are better than those that are dashed off without revision.

Calkins (1983) suggests the following format for peer conferences:

1. Writers should begin by explaining where they are in the writing process and what help they need. For example, the writer might say, "I'm on my second draft and can't decide which ending is more effective."

2. Next, the writer reads the piece or important section aloud.

3. The writer then calls on listeners to retell what they've heard.

4. Finally, students ask questions or make suggestions that will help the writer.

To avoid the "It's all wrong, again" or "Isn't anything I write ever any good?" reaction that students sometimes have when writing assignments are returned, Lyons (1981) recommends using a PQP (Praise, Question, Polish) strategy. The PQP strategy was developed to promote a positive and constructive atmosphere in which to carry on writing assignments.

Students read and comment on each others papers using these questions as guides:

P(Praise):	What do you like about my paper?
Q(Question):	What questions do you have about my paper?
P(Polish):	What kinds of polishing do you feel my paper needs before it can be published?

Initially, students should work through this process one stage at a time. The teacher might show a couple of examples to students and practice the Praise step as a class. Then students should spend several sessions working with each other on this step.

The same procedure would be followed for the Question and Polish steps. In the question stage students look at the paper's clarity, organization, and elaboration of ideas. In the Polish stage proofreaders suggest what should be done to the paper to make it suitable for publishing. Students correct mechanical problems during this third stage.

Publication and Sharing

In the writing process students should be encouraged to write for an audience, not just for themselves individually and their teacher. Through sharing their writing, students broaden their audience and thus establish a reason for writing in a more interesting and informative manner.

INSTRUCTIONAL FRAMEWORKS

As your students engage in writing, you might want to consider these two organizational structures for integrating writing into your classroom: The guided writing procedure and the directed writing activity.

Guided Writing Procedure

The guided writing procedure (GWP) was developed as a means of integrating writing into the content classroom. The strategy involves a series of steps that first identify students' knowledge about a topic before instruction, then sample and evaluate students' writing in various content areas, and finally improve written expression and provide a means of aiding learning through writing.

Smith and Bean (1980) outline the following steps to the guided writing procedure:

Day 1: Diagnosing Students' Knowledge of Content and Writing

1. Students state everything they know about the topic you are going to teach.
2. You write everything the students say on a transparency or on the board.

3. Students identify major ideas and organize their responses in outline form. Initially, do this as a group. After students have gained skill in this procedure, they may do the outline individually.
4. Using the outline, students independently write two short paragraphs. This serves as each student's first draft.
5. Collect these papers. Use a checklist that includes correct spelling, sentence structure, correct punctuation, and paragraph structure as a guide for evaluating the papers. Check off those areas in which each student is strong, but do not write on the student drafts.
6. Finally, students read about the topic and compare their written papers with the information learned during reading.

Student	Correct Spelling	Sentence Structure	Correct Punctuation	Paragraph Structure
John	X		X	
Mary	X	X		

Day 2: Teach Topic and Writing

1. Return the papers to your students, and display the checklist in a place where every student can see it. Display selected paragraphs on the overhead, and have the class edit these examples together.
2. After editing several paragraphs with students, have them edit their own papers, paying attention to content as well as spelling, structure, and punctuation. Collect students' second drafts and compare them on the checklist to their first drafts. There should be an improvement.
3. Give students a quiz on the material they were to read.

Directed Writing Activity

The directed writing activity (DWA) was developed by Blake and Spennato (1980) as a framework for teaching writing. It serves the same purpose as the directed reading activity, a similar framework for teaching reading. The DWA contains the following steps:

1. **Prewriting.** Prepare pupils for writing. Help them select and narrow a writing topic. Assist students in identifying information sources.

You've decided to have your class write about the broad topic of *Disease*. Your first step is to help students narrow the topic. You might start out by having your students brainstorm about more limited subtopics. Some of their subtopics might include: infectious diseases such as pneumonia, influenza, chicken pox, and mumps; noninfectious diseases such as pellagra, rickets, and cancer; past ideas about causes of disease; antibiotics; famous physicians and scientists such as Alexander Fleming, Joseph Lister, and Edward Jenner.

2. Framing the writing assignment. Encourage students to formulate questions relevant to their topic and to which they will seek answers. Once students have a list of questions, they can decide which questions interest them most and focus on those.

During the framing stage a student who selected to write about influenza might develop the following questions:

    a.   What is influenza?
    b.   How do people get influenza?
    c.   Is influenza an infectious disease?
    d.   How many people get influenza each year?
    e.   How can people avoid getting influenza?
    f.   Is there a treatment for influenza?

During this stage your students might also identify how they can go about obtaining information. Students might visit the health department, interview a doctor, go to the library, or use an encyclopedia.

3. Writing the assignment. Students organize their information into a draft. They delete unwanted or unneeded information or add information needed to answer questions formed during step 2. Next the writer reads his or her paper to another student or teacher. The student or teacher makes suggestions that will help the student clarify his or her thoughts.

4. Revising the draft. Using the suggestions from students or the teacher, the student revises and rewrites the first draft.

5. Editing. Each student should have an editing notebook. This includes editing symbols that you, or other students or adults, will use, along with their descriptions (e.g., m–margin, c–capital letter needed). The person correcting the paper should use these symbols.

6. Final draft. The author (student) rewrites the paper using the editing information.

In using any process or framework, you should realize that steps don't always follow a sequential horizontal or vertical line. For example, people don't always plan, research write, and revise in this strict sequence. Sometimes people begin by planning, do a little writing, go back to planning; they may do more writing, revise, plan, write, and so on. The elements of the writing process are there, but the sequence may not be a perfect step-by-step process.

WRITING STRATEGIES

In this section we will consider strategies for incorporating writing into our content classes. Some of the strategies described may take a couple of days, others will take only ten minutes. All are specifically designed to have students use and review the content of the lessons you are teaching. The strategies are classified into four categories: response journal writing, critical/creative writing, categorizing, and specific skills writing.

Response Journal Writing

Response journals are simply a form of informal written communication between two or more people. They are a discussion or response vehicle for what students have heard, experienced, or read—personal reactions to experiences related to the content area. They are also a form of purposeful social interaction.

Response journals can take any form—formal-looking bound diaries, spiral-bound notebooks, or simply several sheets of paper stapled together.

Students should be encouraged to experiment with different kinds of responses in their journals. They might describe their feelings, write a letter, use poetry or rap, develop a chart, write a song, create cartoons, predict, summarize, or question.

Teachers respond to students' journals. The responses should be personal, "Your description of the play was very vivid. You used good descriptive words." Avoid corrective "red lettering."

Gauthier (1991) describes the journal's use in a social studies classroom. The teacher introduced the concept of *coordinates* and pointed them out on a world map. Students were given time to respond to the lesson in their journals. The teacher reviewed the journals and found that students did not see the value of knowing coordinates and confused longitude and latitude. These journal comments gave the teacher a direction for the next lessons.

Critical/Creative Writing

Critical/creative strategies are those that get students to generate new ideas from which comparisons can be drawn and/or relationships developed. The critical/creative strategies include matrix, visual synetics, and brain writing.

Matrix

In this strategy students brainstorm and develop a matrix from which they can develop various writing topics.

1. Select a topic.
2. Have students generate a matrix of ideas related to the topic.
3. Students then use this matrix, to select possible topics for writing. (Naturally, not all relationships are logical or useful. These should be eliminated.) When using the matrix, students look for intersections between the horizontal and vertical coordinates. Students would not select the intersections A,A or B,B. Example 9.1 shows a matrix on the topic Pollution.

Example 9.1   Matrix for Pollution

A.   Buffalo, Los Angeles, and New York have high pollution rates.
B.   Pollution standards should be tougher.
C.   Polluters should be required to clean up their pollution.
D.   Polluters should pay very heavy fines.
E.   Polluters should be arrested.
F.   Industries pollute.
G.   People pollute.
H.   The government pollutes.
I.   Pollution is harmful.

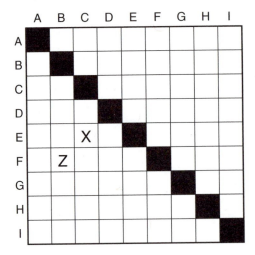

Looking at Example 9.1, a student who believes in punishing polluters might choose to expand on the topics in box C, E on the grid (labeled *X*) and write about how polluters should be required to clean up their pollution and how they should be arrested. Another student might lay claim to box B, F (labeled *Z*) and write about tougher pollution standards for industry.

Visual Synetics
In visual synetics students relate a topic to a picture or object that appears unrelated to the topic. The following steps make up the visual synetics strategy:

1.   Assign a topic to the class.
2.   Show the class a picture that has no obvious relationship to the topic.
3.   Students brainstorm about what they see in the picture.
4.   Another student writes the students' descriptions on the board.

5. Students discuss how the picture might be related to the topic.
6. When students have exhausted their ideas, they begin to write.

For example, you might have been studying corruption in government. You bring in a picture that shows different types of erosion and ask students what they see in the picture and what thoughts they have about the picture. Your students respond that they see areas that have been blown or washed away by running water, ice, wind, and people. The vegetation that was removed once protected and preserved the soil from being blown and washed away. If erosion is not controlled, the land will be destroyed.

You then ask your students how this picture of erosion could possibly be related to corruption in government. Corruption is the wearing away or decaying of moral principles. It's caused by the greed of people for money and power. The function of government is to preserve and protect the rights of people. If corruption is not controlled, government for the people will be destroyed.

Or, you might be studying the five fundamental building blocks of music—melody, harmony, rhythm, form, and expression. Bring a cake into class and ask students what possible relationships exist between the cake and the fundamentals of music. Through brainstorming and discussion students arrive at the generalization that just as specific ingredients are necessary to make a cake, the five fundamentals of music are necessary to make music.

Brainwriting

In brainwriting students work in groups and aid each other in developing ideas about a topic. Here's how brainwriting works:

1. Divide your class into groups of four or five students.
2. Have each student individually list ideas about the writing topic on a sheet of paper.
3. After each student has written three or four ideas, the papers are placed in the middle of the group.
4. Each student takes a different paper and adds ideas to it.
5. The group poses or generates questions about the ideas.
6. The group selects the best ideas.
7. Finally, students write about the topic using ideas they want.

Categorizing

Through categorizing strategies, students put concepts and vocabulary into categories. This categorizing, or organization, then serves as the basis of writing, which may be done individually or in groups. These strategies include: prereading and postreading writing, vocabulary into essay, writing organizers, writing approach to reading, list-group-label-write, and RAFT.

Prereading and Postreading Writing

A writing strategy that requires students to preview headings and subheadings, predict information that will be included under these headings, and then read and verify is the prereading and postreading writing strategy recommended by Karlin and Karlin (1984). The headings and subheadings serve as a basis for categorizing ideas. The following steps are utilized with the strategy:

1. Have students list the headings and subheadings of a chapter.
2. Next, have students write paragraphs based on the headings and subheadings. Drawing from their backgrounds, they write what they know and anticipate what information will be included in the selection.
3. Students discuss what they have written.
4. After reading the selection students verify, revise, add to, and rewrite their original paragraphs. They also compare their organization of the material to the authors'.

Vocabulary into Essay

Nichols (1985) recommends the vocabulary-into-essay strategy (see Example 9.2) that requires students to categorize and write paragraphs from these categories, as follows:

1. Provide students with a list of technical vocabulary terms and categories. Have students place the technical terms into the correct categories.
2. Have students check with you to see if they have categorized the words correctly.
3. Have students write a paragraph on each category of words. Their paragraphs should incorporate as many of the listed terms as possible.
4. Remind your students to start with a good topic sentence and end with a good closing sentence.
5. Review your students' uses of the terms. Then have students rate themselves on a scale customized to the subject.

Example 9.2   Vocabulary into Essay

Directions: Place the following words into the correct categories.

Ice Age	dinosaurs	writing
compass	archaeologist	Stone Age
space flight	Copper Age	glaciers
anthropologist	automobile	Bronze Age
printing press	Iron Age	geologist

Prehistory   **History**   **Scientists**

Check your answers with me when you have categorized all the words.

Now, write a paragraph for each of the categories. Use as many of the words as possible in your paragraphs.

Remember, begin each paragraph with an opening or good topic sentence. End each sentence with a good summarizing or concluding sentence.

Check with me to see how many of the words you used correctly. Then, rate yourself on the scale below.

Number Correct	Rating
15	You are a world famous archaeologist.
13–14	You are an established archaeologist.
11–12	You are an amateur archaeologist.
9–10	You are on your first dig.
7–8	You got lost on the way to the dig.

Here are some examples for other classes:

Social Sudies Class

Categories: legislative branch, documents, executive or judicial branch

Vocabulary: override, filibuster, bill, closure, veto, law, rules committee, pocket veto, constitution, majority report, record(s), unconstitutional, public hearing(s), Supreme Court

Music Class:

Categories: rhythm, melody, dynamics

Vocabulary: leap, piano, sixteenth note, eighth note, forte, step, pianissimo, half note, skip, fortissimo, quarter note

Math Class

Categories: have students create their own

Vocabulary: origin, base, polynomial, coordinate plane, degree, exponent, quadrants, *x*-axis, *y*-axis, algebraic expression, slope of line

Writing Organizers

To grow in their ability to develop and organize paragraphs, students can participate in a strategy (writing organizers—our own strategy title) that leads them through a process that helps structure paragraphs for them (see Example 9.3). Arthur (1981) recommends selecting a story that is about two typewritten pages long. Give the students a copy of the first half of the story. Then give them a second sheet with ideas from the second half of the story, but not the story itself. These ideas are listed in random order. The students then organize the ideas into main ideas and supporting details. This arrangement of ideas serves as an outline for their writing the end of the story. Be sure to tell students that they will have to add supporting sentences to those they developed by using their outlines.

Example 9.3   Writing Organizer

Directions: Read the following passage. Then outline or organize the words below the passage into a story sequence. Using your outline as a guide, develop the next episode of the story.

For weeks Joe had been looking forward to this moment. Now it had come! Here he was, inside the museum's time machine, ready to travel into the past. His friends had told him so much about this time machine. He could hardly wait for the museum man to start him off.

The man pushed a button that lit up four control panels. "These panels control the four adventures you'll have in our time machine," he told Joe. "Your first stop may be back in the age of dinosaurs. Your last stop will take place between 1800 and now."

Joe glanced at the dates on each of the four panels. "Wow! This is going to be fun. Can I start now?"

The museum man nodded. "Wherever you land, you'll know the language. You'll be dressed like the people of that time. They won't know you're from another time and place."

"How do I get from one time to another?" asked Joe. "And how do I get back here?"

"Through certain passages and entrances, on certain roads, over certain bridges..." The museum man's voice trailed away.

Clouds of cold gray fog rose around Joe. For a few moments he felt as light as a leaf, floating through the fog. Then suddenly he knew there was something solid beneath his feet again. A second later everything came into focus, and he saw a plane.*

trip	officer	shorter
December 1940	out and falling	don't know how
like floating	could do it	present
line	looking down	World War II paratroopers
closed eyes`	falling	cold gray fog
leaping	stand at door	museum
pushed	over	cold wind
	wouldn't be scared	

Writing Approach to Reading

The eight steps in the writing approach to reading (Hennings, 1982) lead students from oral through written activities, helping them build schemata (frameworks

---

* From *Attention Span Stories: Time Trip,* by Lee Mountain, Ed.D., p. 9. Copyright 1978 by Jamestown Publishers, Providence, Rhode Island. Reprinted by permission.

based on prior knowledge) for comprehending content materials (see Example 9.4). These steps are as follows:

1. **Factstorming.** Students call out information on a topic and a recorder writes these words or phrases on the board, chart paper, or transparency. A movie, videotape, laser disk, or story may serve as a basis for factstorming.

2. **Categorizing facts.** Students organize the information into categories and label these categories. You may have to guide students through this process if they have not had much classification experience.

3. **Drafting cohesive paragraphs.** After students have categorized the facts, they can write short paragraphs about each of the categories. You may want to begin with teacher-guided group writing if students lack writing experience with categorizing. In small teams, students may write paragraphs using the remaining categories. If each group writes about a different category, these may be put together at a later time.

4. **Sequencing paragraphs into a logical whole.** The paragraphs, written by groups, are shared and then organized into a logical sequence. Students discuss the advantages and disadvantages of the various orders into which they can be arranged.

5. **Drafting introductions and conclusions.** Once the paragraphs have been organized, students think about an appropriate introduction and conclusion. As a group, students write a beginning sentence and several supporting sentences, which become the introduction. The same procedure is used for writing a summary paragraph or concluding generalization.

6. **Organizing parts to a cohesive whole.** After students have written their introductory and concluding paragraphs and developed a sequence for the body, the paper is put into a whole using subheadings.

7. **Interpreting similar pieces of discourse.** Students next apply their schemata in reading. They study content materials and look for the same structures they have been using in their own writing. Questions recommended by Hennings (p. 13) include the following:

> What are the major categories of information with which this writer is dealing? How do we know?
>
> What system of heads and subheads is this writer using?
>
> What does the system of heads and subheads tell us about the way the topic will be developed in this section?
>
> What is the main—or most important—topic of the section? How do we know?
>
> What kind of information has the writer put into the introduction to the section? What clues have been given in the introduction as to the organization of the material to follow?
>
> What kind of information has the writer put into the concluding section? Are any clues given as to the most important points included in the conclusion?

8. Summarizing, synthesizing, and judging writing. Students can complete data charts after reading a particular selection. These data charts can be used as a basis for additional writing.

Example 9.4   Writing Approach Chart for Vitamins and Minerals

Vitamin/ Mineral	Foods (Sources)	How It Helps Your Body	Health Problems from a Deficiency
Vitamins			
A			
Bl			
B2			
niacin			
C			
D			
Minerals			
calcium			
iron			

Choose one of the following writing assignments related to this summary chart:

1. Write one paragraph that describes how minerals help the body.
2. In two paragraphs discuss how the B vitamins help your body and what problems may arise because of a vitamin B deficiency.
3. Write a paragraph telling which vitamin deficiency you would elect to have, if you had to have a deficiency, and why.
4. Write a paragraph describing a well-balanced dinner. What foods would you include?

List-Group-Label-Write

Take a few minutes to review list-group-label in Chapter 4. Wood (1992) recommends adding a "write" step for mathematics classes. At the end of a unit of study, students brainstorm concepts and vocabulary related to the unit. The teacher lists these on the board. Students, in small groups, classify the terms. They then write a paragraph on the category of their choice. The paragraph should reflect students' understanding of the vocabulary as it is used in math. Naturally, this strategy can be adapted for any content area.

Role-Audience-Form-Tense (RAFT)

Dueck (1986) suggests that you provide students with four key elements before they begin writing. These four elements—role, audience, form, and tense—are essential building blocks for clarifying students' writing assignments. Examples 9.5 through 9.8 are useful samples.

Example 9.5   RAFT for Social Studies

You are the emperor of the Han dynasty in 1350. You are telling the future emperor about the accomplishments of the past Han emperors. Write a dialogue in which you and the future emperor talk about the Han accomplishments.

Role:	Han dynasty emperor
Audience:	Future emperor
Form:	Dialogue
Tense:	Present, because you're talking to the next emperor

Example 9.6   RAFT for Science

You are a tornado. You have just blown through the Florida Keys. You're telling the people of the area how you formed. Write a paragraph explaining why you caused the destruction.

Role:	A tornado
Audience:	Residents of the Florida Keys
Form:	Paragraph
Tense:	Past, because you're telling what happened

Example 9.7   RAFT for Music

You are the young composer Haydn living in Europe in 1761. You are talking to a reporter about what it is like working for Prince Esterhazy of Hungary. Write the reporter's interview with Haydn to inform the public about the composer's life.

Role:	Haydn
Audience:	Reporter
Form:	Dialogue
Tense:	Present, because you are taking to a reporter

Example 9.8   RAFT for Art

You are the artist Picasso living in Spain in 1937. You're talking to an art critic about your art work. Write an interview between Picasso and the critic in which you tell the world about your successful style.

Role:	Picasso
Audience:	Critic
Form:	Dialogue
Tense:	Present, because you are talking to a critic

Specific Skills Writing

Specific skills writing capitalizes on students' needs to develop three specific skills: listening, using organizational patterns, and summarizing. The pertinent strategies are: dictation, cloze adaptations, paragraph frames, summarizing, translation writing, sustained student summary writing, and paraphrasing.

Dictation

Dictation is recommended by Stotsky (1982) as a means of improving listening skills, comprehension, and attention spans. Students also become more aware of the syntactic and semantic structures of language as they engage in dictation. There are five basic steps to dictation:

1. Select a passage of four or five sentences from your content area or literature.
2. Read the passage through completely while students listen to you. Students gain insight into the meaning of the selection in this step.
3. Slowly read the passage in phrases and pause at the end of each phrase to allow students to write what you have read. Do not repeat phrases in this step.
4. Read the passage a third time at normal speed. This gives students a chance to check spellings, check punctuation, add omitted words, and correct capitalization.
5. Have students proofread their written passage against the original passage.

Cloze Adaptations

Harris (1985) describes a way to adapt the cloze procedure to writing. By using cloze techniques the writer becomes aware of the role of prediction in both reading and writing. The strategy also reinforces the skill of using context. Follow these steps:

1. Copy passages from content area textbooks and delete a specific part of speech (e.g., all the verbs, nouns, transition words).
2. Type spaces of equal length where the words were deleted.
3. Have students read the passages and supply the missing words.
4. Let students compare their versions with the original text. Is the meaning different? In what way?

If verbs are deleted, students must pay attention to meaning and tense agreement (see Example 9.9). If transition words are deleted, students must pay attention to relationships among different ideas.

Example 9.9   Cloze Adaptation with Verbs Deleted

If you _____ outside on a cold winter day the wind usually _____ from the north. Winds that _____ from the north _____ _____ north winds.

If you __*go*__ outside on a cold winter day the wind usually __*is coming*__ from the north. Winds that __*blow*__ from the north __*are called*__ north winds.

Paragraph Frames

Nichols (1980) discusses using paragraph frames as a structured strategy for assisting students in organizing material read and placing it into written format. Words specific to different organizational patterns are provided for students, with blank spaces before or after them. Students must fill in these spaces with information from the text. In most cases they will have to use more than one sentence to complete the blank. Examples 9.10 through 9.12 are useful samples.

Example 9.10   Comparison-Contrast Frame

The climate and vegetation of _____ and _____ are very different. The climate of the tropics is characterized by _____ while _____ .

The vegetation in both regions also is very different. Because of _____ . In contrast, _____ .

Example 9.11   Simple Listing Frame

The Chinese under the Han dynasty became noted for many practical inventions.
To begin with _____ .

In addition to _____ , they also invented _____ .
This is a method _____ .

I must add that the first _____ .

Example 9.12   Cause-Effect Frame

Precipitation forms in three steps. First _____ .

Next _____ .

As a result of _____ .

Miller and George (1992) expanded on this idea and developed *expository passage organizers,* which provide a framework for an essay. The framework contains an introduction, a two-paragraph body, and a concluding paragraph. Utilizing expository passage organizers made a significant positive difference in both reading and writing (Miller & George, 1992).

Translation Writing

Arthur (1981) discusses the translation writing strategy as being a process of having students rewrite text materials. The following steps are recommended:

1. Use short selections at first.
2. Teach the important vocabulary and concepts of the selection to your students.
3. Give students a copy of the important vocabulary with definitions. List the words in outline form.
4. Use one of several methods to present the text material to students. You may read the selection aloud to your class. Students may listen to a tape recording of it. Good readers may read the material to poorer readers.

Older students may come into your room and read to a group of students. Students, if they can, may be encouraged to read the material silently.

5. Students should take notes on the material during reading or listening. The vocabulary list helps students with spelling. The person who is reading from the text should pause to allow students time to write.

6. Next, the students write their own text using their notes as a guide. You may display several good examples for students to read.

7. Give students a list of questions related to the information about which they wrote. If they cannot answer these questions from their rewritten text material, they should find the information and include it in their passages.

8. Have students put the vocabulary outline, their rewritten or translated text, and the questions into a folder or notebook for future reference and evaluation.

Sustained Student Summary Writing

Sustained student summary writing (SSSW), developed by Cunningham and Cunningham (1976) and recommended by Thelen (1986), requires students to rephrase or put new concepts into their own words. The strategy is best used toward the end of a class. Students spend five minutes writing summaries of the material covered during class. At the end of the five-minute period the teacher randomly selects one of four activities from these options:

1. Three students may be asked to read their summaries to the class.
2. The teacher may collect and read all the papers.
3. Students may work in pairs and read their summaries to each other.
4. Nothing may be done with the papers.

It is important that the teacher *randomly* select what will be done with the summaries to avoid having students feel that the teacher is "out to get them." Imagine having a student who has been very conscientiously writing excellent summaries for an entire week, but you elected not to collect them. Then on Friday, this student was preoccupied and did not get any writing done. You had been walking around the room during this time and walked by this student's desk. At the end of class you decided to have all students hand in their summaries. What would this student, who had worked hard at the summary writing all week, think?

Random selection may be accomplished in a number of different ways. Drawing a red disk from a box may indicate #1. Drawing a blue disk may indicate #2, and so on. You may use numbered slips of paper or any other means you can think of to incorporate random selection into the process.

The way in which you grade these summaries is an individual matter. You may grade for content only. You may grade for punctuation, use of capital letters, or complete sentences. But it is important to add criteria other than class content very gradually.

Paraphrasing

In paraphrase writing, students rewrite content material in their own words, restating the author's message as concisely as they can. Shugarman and Hurst (1986) identify activities for paraphrasing.

1. Ask students to identify good and poor paraphrases of a short passage. This is accomplished by giving your students a passage to read, a poorly written paraphrase, and a well-written paraphrase. Students discuss the strengths and weaknesses of each paraphrase.
2. Have students write one- or two-sentence captions to comics, maps, graphs, or charts.
3. Divide your class into groups or teams and appoint a "panel of experts." Each team must read the same passage and write a paraphrase of it. The panel of experts selects the best paraphrase and gives reasons for the choice.
4. Give students a handout containing words to a popular song. Play the song and have your students paraphrase it.

ADDITIONAL WRITING TOPICS

The following activities do not contain step-by-step procedures; however, they should provide you with additional ideas of topics that might be appropriate for your class. Enrichment activities are limited only by your imagination.

Writing a newsletter requires students to practice using interesting and informative ideas, edit, revise, and write succinctly. Couch (1983) describes how her experiences in an aerobics class led to the possibility of newsletter writing. Here are some of her suggestions for "bodyworks" writing:

1. Interview people who experienced good results from exercise classes. Incorporate these interviews into the newsletter.
2. Summarize major articles or books on fitness.
3. Write recipes of seasonal foods for fitness.
4. Feature interviews with staff members or body-building experts.
5. Write about how to get into shape.
6. Answer questions about what happens to your body when you work out.

Berry (1986) suggests book-making applications across the curriculum. Even in the primary grades, after a unit on plants, each student could write one page for a class book about plants. Typewriters and computers in many classrooms make production of class books and newspapers an easier job.

Hipple, Wright, Yarbrough, and Bartholomew (1983) highlight forty activities that are appropriate topics for student writing assignments. Some that are especially suited to content area writing are listed below.

1. **Test items.** Tell each of your students to prepare test questions (two essay questions, two easy questions, three hard questions, and three average questions).
2. **Point of view.** Have your students pretend that they are objects—a building, a house, a street, a traffic light—and have them write about the problems these objects might experience during the day. These topics might include noise pollution, taxes, people defacing them, and the weather.
3. **Paraphrasing.** Have your students select a paragraph from their textbook and rewrite it so that a much younger student would understand it.
4. **Writing characterizations.** Have your students develop a list of a hundred words that describe people. Select a well-known person and have students check all the words on the list that describe that individual. Then have students write a characterization using those yes words. (Students can write similar characterizations for people in history, music, art, math, science, literature, physical education, or any other area.)
5. **Question writing.** Have your students develop a list of questions they would ask during an interview with a famous person.
6. **Dialogues.** Outline a scenario between two people in history (military leaders, scientists, explorers, psychologists). Then have your students write a dialogue that might occur between the speakers.

CONCLUSION

Writing in the classroom can no longer be considered the sole responsibility of English teachers. Research studies produce evidence that writing in conjunction with content area classes improves the comprehension of students. Writing assignments do not have to be long, and there are many ways of developing writing topics. Conferencing and peer editing can serve as two valuable tools in the writing process.

Two frameworks or general instructional strategies that apply to most content area writing are the guided writing procedure and the directed writing activity.

Writing strategies have been classified as journal writing, critical/creative, categorizing, and specific skills-oriented writing. Journal writing is a form of communication between two or more individuals. Categorizing strategies have students classify prior to writing. Prereading and postreading writing, vocabulary into essay, writing organizer, writing approach to reading, list-group-label-write, and RAFT are categorizing strategies.

Specific skills-oriented writing builds student strengths in listening, organizational patterns, and summarizing. Dictation, cloze adaptations, paragraph frames, translation writing, sustained student summary writing, and paraphrasing are skills-oriented writing strategies.

POSTREADING

INTEGRATING WRITING

Think back to one of your first school experiences in expository writing. In your journal, describe what you learned about teaching from this experience that will have an effect on *your* teaching. Describe how you can use one of the critical/creative or categorizing writing strategies in your content class.

REVIEW

Make a list of concepts and vocabulary presented in this chapter. Then arrange these terms into a graphic organizer.

PRACTICE

Do Enabling Activities 25, 26 and 27 in Appendix A.

10

MEETING STUDENTS' NEEDS

"It's time for my three-month conference with Mrs. Simms," commented Sam. "So I'm working on my self-evaluation sheet. How is she in these principal-teacher conferences?"

"She's great," said Danna. "She keeps lists of everything we do right. I'll bet her evaluation of what you're doing with your class will be better than your self-evaluation."

"You don't know what my class is like," sighed Sam. "Some of my students can't read beyond the primary level. Others can manage our textbook, but learn better by listening. Some won't read the textbook unless I use special motivational strategies. Others profit more from group work than from book work. They're all so different!"

Danna laughed. "Welcome to the world of reality! Have you been making any variations in your teaching style?"

"Some," replied Sam, "but I really don't know what else to try."

"Mrs. Simms will give you some good ideas. And I know of some strategies that might work," said Danna. "See me after your conference. I know you'll be feeling great after you talk with Mrs. Simms."

DISCUSS

Should classroom teachers play a major role in adjusting materials and using motivational strategies to meet students' needs? What special materials adjustments or motivational strategies have you used or observed in classrooms?

PREORGANIZE

Go through the chapter and make a skeletal outline of the major headings and subheadings. This will provide you with a chapter organizer. Predict the contents of the text under one of these subheadings.

OBJECTIVES

After reading this chapter, you should be able to

1. develop a rationale for using cooperative learning in classrooms.
2. describe cooperative learning strategies and create lessons using them.
3. describe computer-assisted instruction and how it is used in classrooms.
4. demonstrate the use of three listening strategies to improve learning.
5. describe four materials adjustments that teachers can make.
6. describe and demonstrate the use of newspaper activities to teach specific content lessons.

As we walk into a school, one of the first things we will notice is the wide diversity of students. This wide diversity is reflected in the achievement levels of students. Some students learn quickly and easily; others learn slowly and need a great deal of assistance.

Many of the strategies discussed in this text have been developed to meet the wide diversity of students' needs. The focus of this chapter is on five more generalized avenues through which we can help meet students' needs. These five avenues are cooperative learning, computer-assisted instruction, listening, adapting materials, and using the newspaper.

COOPERATIVE LEARNING

Sometimes students will not read because they lack motivation. At other times, you cannot give students the individual tutoring they may need. In such situations, small group discussions of material presented in class can be a beneficial strategy (Alvermann et al., 1985). Increased student achievement and improved intergroup relationships were reported (Slavin, 1985) as positive effects of cooperative learning. Information intermix, student teams–achievement divisions, teams-games-tournament, jigsaw, and the group investigation model are grouping organizational patterns, designed to motivate students.

Cooperative learning is not new; we can trace it back to the pioneer days of America when people came together for barn-raising. People worked together, and young people learned by participating in this group activity. John Dewey advocated having students work in groups to solve problems and investigate. More recently, Robert Slavin and David and Roger Johnson have advocated a strong thrust toward cooperative learning.

What is *cooperative learning?* Slavin (1987b) defines it as "instructional methods in which students of all performance levels work together in small groups toward a group goal. The essential feature of cooperative learning is that the success of one student helps other students to be successful" (p. 8). As you can see in this definition, there are two essential ingredients for cooperative learning to be effective. First, there must be a group goal toward which students work. Second,

TABLE 10–1 • Comparison of Cooperative Groups and Small Groups

Cooperative Groups	*Small Groups*
Positive interdependence: we sink or swim together. Face-to-face oral interaction.	No interdependence. Students often work on their own, occasionally checking their answers with other students.
Individual accountability: each person must master the material.	Hitchhiking. Some students let others do most or all of the work.
Teacher systematically teaches social skills needed for successful group work.	Social skills not taught.
Teacher monitors students' behavior.	No direct observation of student behavior. Teacher often works with other students or prepares next lesson.
Feedback and discussion of students' behavior.	No discussion of how well students worked together, other than general comments like "Nice job" or "Next time, try working more quietly."

Source: From *Cooperative learning: Getting started,* by Susan S. Ellis and Susan F. Whalen, p. 15. Copyright © 1990; Scholastic, Inc. Reprinted by permission of publisher.

individual learning of all group members must be required to reach this goal (Slavin, 1978a).

From an interview with David and Roger Johnson, Brandt (1987) identifies five basic elements of cooperative learning. First, students must believe that they are dependent on one another. Second, there must be a lot of verbal interaction; students learn from talking to each other. Third, everyone must contribute; everyone is accountable for learning and assisting others. Fourth, students must develop social skills. If social skills have not been developed, much of the benefit of cooperative learning is lost. Fifth, periodically, students must evaluate how they are working together.

In Table 10–1 Ellis and Whalen (1990) summarize the differences between cooperative learning and our traditional small groups.

Groups generally should be composed of three to four heterogeneously grouped students to provide opportunities for maximum interaction. In a group of three, you would place one accelerated student, one average, and one slow student. In a group of four, there would be one accelerated student, two average students, and one slow student. If a group of five were formed, there would be three average students.

In order to encourage interdependence Ellis and Whalen (1990) recommend several measures. First, provide only one set of materials for students to use. Second, assign different roles to group members: finder (researcher), reader, writer; or encourager, time-keeper, and checker. Third, give each group member a specific task to complete: doing different steps in an experiment; writing different paragraphs; or doing different problems alone and as a group. To keep communication under control, encourage students to speak in "16-inch voices," allowing only members to their group to hear.

Several strategies for encouraging cooperative learning include: information intermix, student teams–achievement divisions, teams-games-tournaments, Jigsaw II, and the group investigation model.

Information Intermix

According to Capuzzi (1973) information intermix is a small group learning strategy that takes advantage of student-to-student interaction to learn information. It is based on several assumptions:

- Students will learn best when they are responsible for teaching others.
- Students can accept responsibility, within limits, for their own learning.
- Students are more likely to grow—socially, emotionally, academically— when they are growing or learning with a group.

Follow these procedures when using intermix:

1. Give students some basic instructions: Everyone in class is expected to learn. Each of you will be responsible for your own learning and the learning of others. When I give a signal (such as turning off the light), everyone is to be quiet, pay attention, and listen to instructions.

2. Assign students to groups of three or four. If there are twenty-five students in your class, you should have 7 groups of three and 1 group of four. If there are thirty students in your class, you should have 6 groups of four and 2 groups of three.

3. Each student is given a task to learn. Capuzzi (1973) refers to giving students "concept slips." (See Example 10.1 for a typical concept slip.)

4. Students spend a specified amount of time learning the material on their concept slips. They may make notes, underline, or use any other study strategy to learn the material.

5. When learning time is up, each group member teaches the other group members the information on his or her concept slip. In this way, all three or four group members will teach one lesson and learn the information taught by the other group members. Each group member should be a teacher once and a learner for others in the group three or four times.

6. When each student has finished teaching, students must share with the others in their group all they have learned.

7. The class comes together for discussion and clarification with the teacher.

As students are working in their groups, the teacher circulates and notes how they are working together. The teacher may also clarify any questions students may have or instigate challenges to their thinking.

Example 10.1   Concept Slip

There are different forms of energy. Some of these forms include electric, nuclear, light, sound, and mechanical. Moving machines produce mechanical energy. A power lawnmower, a rolling wheel, and a turning windmill all produce mechanical energy.

Mechanical energy can be turned into other forms of energy. A turning windmill can produce electric energy to light our homes. Heat energy can be turned into mechanical energy to run our cars.

1. What is energy?
2. Why is a moving car a form of mechanical energy?
3. What kind of energy is a flashlight?
4. Give an example of how light energy can be turned into mechanical energy.
5. Using only a pencil and your hands, create heat energy.

Student Teams–Achievement Divisions

Student teams–achievement divisions (STAD) emphasizes cooperation within groups and competition among groups. STAD is effective with any subject. In student teams–achievement divisions the teacher starts by teaching a lesson to the whole class and then forming study groups. The study groups work on written assignments given by the teacher. Students discuss answers and how they arrived at them; students help one another understand the concepts and processes. At the end of the study time, sometimes a couple of days, students take individual quizzes or tests to check their understanding. The test scores of team members are averaged for a group grade, but students' individual scores are the basis for achievement divisions, in which high-scoring students earn points for their team.

Slavin (1978, 1980) emphasizes the following steps in the strategy:

1. Students are assigned heterogeneously to teams.
2. The job of each team is to prepare its members to score high on a quiz.
3. You give a class presentation on the topic being studied. Students are then given worksheets or reading materials that reinforce and extend the topic.
4. Members of the team study together and quiz each other on the material.
5. Team members display what they have learned on a quiz.
6. Students from each team are assigned to a group based upon previous achievement. The quiz scores of students who scored highest on the last quiz are compared. Quiz scores of the next highest group are compared, as are scores of the lowest group. Only scores of similar achieving students are compared. In all cases achievement groupings are based on scores students obtained on the previous quiz.

7. The student having the highest score in each achievement group earns 8 points for his or her team. Students' scores are compared with past averages, and points are awarded based upon the difference between the present test scores and past test score averages.

8. It is possible for the achievement divisions and groups to change due to bumping. Different students may be the highest to score on quizzes each time the strategy is used.

Teams-Games-Tournament

Like STAD, the teams-games-tournament (TGT) strategy emphasizes cooperation within groups and competition among groups. It is an effective tool with any subject area. Slavin (1978), DeVries and Slavin (1978), and Slavin (1980) describe the strategy this way:

1. Students are assigned heterogeneously to teams of different abilities, sexes, and races.
2. The job of the team is to prepare its members to do well in the tournament.
3. You give a class presentation on the topic being studied. You then give students worksheets or materials to read that reinforce and extend the topic.
4. Members of the team study together and quiz each other on the materials.
5. Team members then display what they have learned in a tournament.
6. Students from each group are assigned to tournament tables on the basis of past achievement. High-achieving students compete against high-achieving students. Low-achievers compete together.
7. At each table students compete at games that test their knowledge of the topic. The scores of each team member are added together to get a team score.
8. The team with the highest score wins.

There are many ways to run a tournament competition. You could play a game such as "College Bowl." Students on each team compete by answering questions and receiving five points for each correct answer. The team with the most points wins.

A checkerboard could have a question in each square. In order to move a checker, the student must correctly answer the question on the empty space. Five points are given for each question correctly answered.

Jigsaw II

Jigsaw is a team learning strategy in which students work together, and teach each other, so that each student will do well on a quiz. There are no group scores, only individual scores, and there is no group competition on the quiz. Sharan (1980) writes that jigsaw focuses on peer cooperation and tutoring in the classroom.

Slavin (1980) and Aaronson (1978) suggest these procedures:

1. Assign students to small heterogeneous teams.
2. All students read all the material.
3. Divide the material to be learned among the various team members.
4. Each student studies his or her section with members of other teams who have the same section.
5. Students come back to their original teams and teach others the material.
6. All team members take a quiz on the material that was learned and taught.

In Jigsaw II students start out reading the entire text, then rereading a specifically assigned subsection. They meet and talk with members of other teams assigned to study the same material. There is then "home-team reporting" and individual test taking. Jigsaw II is most effective in science, social studies, literature, and foreign languages when literature is being studied. It is effective in any subject that involves continuous text reading.

Group Investigation Model

The group investigation model (G-I) is a strategy that emphasizes data gathering by students, "interpretation of information through group discussion, and synthesis of individual contributions into a group product" (Sharan, 1980, p. 250).

Sharan (1980) identifies the following steps in the group investigation model:

1. Students select subtopics within a topic you have specified. Students then organize into task-oriented groups.
2. Students, with teacher guidance, form a plan for learning the information in the subtopic.
3. Students engage in a wide variety of learning experiences. The teacher keeps a close check on the progress of groups.
4. Students analyze and evaluate the information they find. They also plan how to summarize it and present it to the class.
5. Groups give interesting presentations on the subtopics they studied.
6. Students and the teacher evaluate each group's presentation and/or the presentations of individual students.

For a group inventigation project in astronomy, you might identify the planets as a topic for investigation. Possible subtopics students might select would be Copernicus, Kepler, Mercury, Venus, Mars, Jupiter, Saturn, Uranus, Neptune, and Pluto, or even how to observe planets. Your students now organize into task-oriented groups and identify reference sources for research. In this example your students might interview an astronomer, visit a planetarium, read science magazines, journals, and newspapers, find books in the library, or view and read information on laser disks.

After writing and revising their reports, your students might elect to present their information to the class as a group using pictures, posters, models, slide-tape or video presentations, or possibly laser disk presentations. (Students feel more comfortable giving a presentation when they have something to manipulate or show.)

Several questions you might keep in mind when evaluating your students' reports include

Did your students put the material into their own words?
Was the presentation well organized?
Were grammar and usage correct?
Did the group incorporate a variety of resources in developing the report?
Did the presentation keep the attention of other students in the class?

The group investigation model, as the name implies, is effective in any subject in which library research is encouraged.

Many of the strategies we described in previous chapters can be adapted for use in cooperative learning structures. Cooperative learning takes time and patience to incorporate into your classroom. Initially take small steps, concentrating on building social skills, then expand. Cooperative learning is an excellent vehicle to use in the practice and reinforce steps of the teach-practice-reinforce-review cycle of learning.

COMPUTER-ASSISTED INSTRUCTION

The next century will bring new instructional systems into not only the schools but also the homes of students. In Chapter 1, we described reading as a technological process and suggested some of its ramifications for instruction. "Technology should serve educational goals, not direct them" (Dockterman, 1991).

Computer Technology Uses

Blanchard, Mason, and Daniel (1987) identify twelve applications of computer-assisted technology in the classroom: testing, information and instruction management, drill and practice, tutorial/dialogue, simulations, telecommunications/information retrieval, word processing, utilities that support educational activities (software for crossword puzzles, banners, and so on), interactive fiction in which students create their own stories from computer-generated story fragments, video-disks and compact disks, speech synthesizers, and programming and problem solving. As you can see, the list appears to be almost limitless, especially when you combine your imagination with any of these uses.

Mountain (1992–93) and Allen and Mountain (1992) write about telecommunications networks that can be set up in homes. Small, computerlike terminals come complete with monitor and keyboard. They can be plugged into a standard telephone jack at home to deliver electronic educational programs that help students with aspects of math and reading. Most important, these terminals are very inexpensive compared to actual computers.

Each evening, students can log on to programs that give (1) this week's assignments, (2) last week's assignments, and (3) other programs to explore. A week of assignments might address, for example, reading a folktale and establishing a sequence of events on Monday, trying predictions on Tuesday, analyzing and solving math word problems on Wednesday, and playing Math Bingo on Thursday. Among the many "other programs to explore" are an on-line encyclopedia that is frequently updated, biographies of current sports figures, up-to-the-minute news services, and sports information.

The service can be expanded so that teachers, tutors, pen pals, and students can send messages back and forth to one another. This type of correspondence generates valuable reading and writing practice for students.

Additional uses of computers were discussed in Chapter 1 under Reading as a Technological Process. Take a few minutes to review these uses.

Set Your Direction

Decide how the computer can help you go where you want to go or accomplish what you want to accomplish. Don't let the computer direct you. The computer is a tool, not the curriculum. First, list your goals and objectives. Next, list the methodology you want to use in meeting your objectives (role playing, discussion, drill, lecture and demonstration, whatever). Once you have identified what you want to do and how you want to do it, identify how the computer can help you in your desired delivery—methodology. A computer is only a tool to help you deliver the content you choose using the methodology you desire. This tool, however, can be very powerful if used properly.

Information on Hardware and Software

You can obtain information on computer hardware and software from a number of journals. *Curriculum Review, School Library Journal, Educational Technology, Technology and Learning, Electronic Learning, Computers in Schools, Journal of Computer-Assisted Learning,* and *Computers and Education* are just some of the journals that offer specific information. Journals related to specific content areas (such as *Journal of Reading,* and *Modern Language Journal*) also provide reviews of software.

As with any new technology, be cautioned about overuse. There is growing evidence that neck problems, carpal tunnel syndrome, hypertension, and cataracts can occur from the overuse and/or misuse of computers. Avoid giving students a total diet of technology.

LISTENING STRATEGIES

In most situations students' listening comprehension is above their reading comprehension. By providing listening experiences in your classroom, you can communicate information to students who may not be able to read the textbook. You also may aid students in further developing their ability to listen and to identify specific information. Their long-term memory and critical listening skills will also improve as you stress listening in class.

Directed Listening Activity

The directed listening activity was developed by Cunningham and Cunningham (1976) as an aid to content learning. It contains three major steps, as follows:

I. Readiness Stage
  A. Motivating the lesson
  B. Introducing new or difficult concepts
  C. Introducing new or difficult words (five per lesson maximum)
  D. Giving students a purpose for listening
II. The Listening-Reciting Stage
  A. Students listen to answer the purpose-setting question
  B. Teacher asks students several questions (literal and interpretive) related to the purpose
  C. Students discuss their answers
  D. Teacher rereads sections if there are points students do not understand
III. Follow-up
  A. Students engage in activities related to the material they listened to
  B. Activities may be art, discussion, writing, reading, observing, or data collecting

---

Example 10.2   Directed Listening Activity for Science or Social Studies

Readiness: Ms. Krantz's class was studying a unit on sources of energy. She motivated her students by giving them figures on how the cost of various forms of energy has increased and/or decreased over the past twenty-five years. She also told them about the Arab embargo of oil during the 1970s and showed them pictures of the long lines of cars waiting for gas. She then introduced the terms *renewable* and *nonrenewable* energy sources and brought in samples (where possible) of the different energy sources. Ms. Kranz's purpose for students' listening was this: Listen to identify which energy sources are renewable and which are nonrenewable.

Listening-Reciting: Students discussed the supply of energy sources in comparison to their cost. They also classified ten sources of energy as either renewable or nonrenewable.

Follow-up: For one week, students kept a record of the types and amounts of energy sources they used. They later calculated the cost of using these energy sources.

Guided Listening Procedure

Another listening strategy designed to improve students' understanding of content materials is the guided listening procedure (GLP) developed by Cunningham and Cunningham (1976). The purpose of this strategy is to increase students' long-term recall. Cunningham and Cunningham recommend that this time-consuming strategy not be used more than once every two or three weeks. The GLP contains these steps:

1. Tell students to "listen to remember everything they can."
2. You lecture, read, or play a prerecorded selection. If you are lecturing or reading, record the material.
3. When you have finished reading, ask students to tell you everything they can remember. The students' responses, even if inaccurate, are written on the board by you or two students.
4. After students have finished adding information, have them listen to the tape of your lecture or reading. This time they listen to find omissions or errors in the material on the board.
5. You, or the two students, make changes in the information on the board as students indicate.
6. Ask students which ideas on the board seem to be the main ones. Students can categorize the notes.
7. During a discussion, ask literal and interpretive questions important to understanding the material.
8. Erase the board and give a short-term memory test consisting of true-false or multiple-choice items. This test should not be a measure of students' reading and writing abilities.
9. In several weeks, give another test containing similar (but not the very same) items. This will test long-term memory.
10. Let the students grade their own papers and keep a record of their scores. Does their listening ability improve as you continue to use GLPs?

Planned Inferential Listening Lesson

According to Cunningham, Cunningham, and Arthur (1981), planned inferential listening lesson (PILL) was patterned after PIRL (planned inferential reading lesson). Developed to improve students' listening comprehension, PILL contains the following steps:

1. Teachers prepare for the lesson by listening to a selection and writing several true statements. Some of the statements should be literal and some inferential (interpretive). It's best to begin with a short listening selection and gradually increase the length of selections.
2. Give students the list of statements. As they listen to the selection, they are to decide if they actually heard the statements or if they had to figure them out. (Example 10.3 is a PILL selection with response statements about Eskimo life.)
3. If students think a statement is inferential, they must remember and tell other students and you the parts that helped them figure out the inference.
4. Once students can distinguish between literal and inferential statements, they are ready to identify true (supported) and false (unsupported) inferential statements.

5. Students identify which statements are true according to the information they hear in the selection.

6. After students can listen for inferences, you can divide the next lesson into two parts. The first part would have students listening for inferences. The second part would have students reading to find inferences in a continuation of the same material used in the listening portion.

7. When teaching lessons to students, you would mix up the order of the statements as you asked students to identify them.

Example 10.3   Planned Inferential Listening Lesson

During the winter months Eskimos lived in sod houses with several rooms. These were built by digging a hole one to two feet deep. A frame of whalebone, stone, or wood was constructed and packed with sod.

During the winter Eskimos hunted seals by waiting near holes in the ice where seals came for breathing. Dogs pulled sleds on which they carried their dead seals.

If Eskimos could not find enough food during the winter, they traveled to a place where there was better hunting. Their temporary houses were made of blocks of hardened snow. The blocks were placed upon each other in smaller and smaller circles until a dome shape was formed. A snow house could be built by two Eskimos in about an hour.

1. Eskimos lived in sod houses during winter. (*actually stated*)
2. Eskimos lived in igloos. (*correct inferential*)
3. All Eskimos lived in igloos during the winter. (*incorrect inferential*)
4. Life for Eskimos was rugged. (*correct inferential*)
5. Eskimos hunted seals. (*actually stated*)
6. Eskimos' homes were comfortable. (*incorrect inferential*)

MATERIALS STRATEGIES

The way you use the content area materials available to you can make a difference in your classroom. Four ways you can use or alter materials to meet the needs of your students are presented in this section. These adjustments involve varying the length of assignments, using multilevel textbooks, utilizing similar passages, and adding supplementary materials.

Varying Lengths of Assignments

Not all students work at the same rate. Some students are naturally slow workers; others do not have the basic skills to work rapidly. To meet the needs of these students, consider shortening the assignments. If you are giving a reading assignment, have Louise read ten pages instead of twenty. Instead of having Ralph solve twenty word problems, perhaps you could reduce his assignment to ten, the rationale being that it is better to have Ralph solve ten problems correctly than get twenty wrong.

Multilevel Textbooks

In some school systems you are fortunate enough to have several textbook series from which to choose. In such situations select different textbooks for different students in your class or select different textbooks for different classes.

Consider the factors discussed in Chapter 2 of this text when you select textbooks. Five critical areas outlined by Glenn and Lewis (1982) will refresh your memory.

1. Be sure the textbook meets the goals and objectives of your course.
2. Be sure the content of the textbook is accurate.
3. Be sure the ideas in the textbook are presented at the appropriate cognitive level for your students. If your students are not reasoning at abstract levels, do not select a textbook in which 80 percent of the content requires students to work at the formal operational stage of reasoning. Your primary concern is with *how* concepts and generalizations are presented.
4. Identify the readability of your textbook.
5. Be sure the textbook has students practice and apply knowledge they previously learned or now are learning for the first time. You will provide many opportunities for students to practice and apply ideas, but the textbook also should provide such opportunities.

Similar Passages

When reading about a new topic, students can select passages from textbooks and articles of varying levels of difficulty. If students begin by reading the easiest material, they can gain background on the subject and proceed to materials of higher levels of difficulty. Also, some textbooks and articles may present material more clearly or memorably than do other reading materials.

Supplementary Materials

Develop a collection of supplementary materials you can use with your students. These may include old trade books, old textbooks, periodicals, applications and forms, do-it-yourself manuals, audiotapes, compact disks, videotapes, and games.

One teacher had a series of old *Reader's Digest* magazines he had organized at various levels from grade 1 to adult level. He cut the magazines apart and placed the selections into topic files containing information on different reading levels. These topics were ones the class was going to study during the year. Students selected articles on various topics at levels they could read comfortably. The same procedure can be followed if you have old textbooks at a variety of levels.

Multimedia materials are excellent for meeting needs of students with various learning styles. Auditory learners can listen to audiotapes. Visual learners can view videotapes and read. Kinesthetic learners can play games and work on constructions or demonstrations.

USING THE NEWSPAPER

The newspaper can be a highly motivating instructional tool for content area reading. Use the newspaper in class for collecting data, map reading, labeling, problem solving, and critical thinking. Let's look at some newspaper activities for mathematics, social studies, science, and language arts.

Mathematics

1. Have students play the stock market. Students "buy" and "sell" shares of stock and keep track of their profits or losses.
2. Prepare menus and look at advertisements to find out which foods they can purchase most reasonably.
3. Transform data in the newspaper into charts and graphs.
4. Give students a set amount of money (say $75) and tell them to "order" the weekly groceries from ads in the newspaper.
5. Locate ways in which math is used in sports (batting averages, standings).
6. Look for words that express size, measurement, and time.

Social Studies

1. Role play events in the newspaper.
2. Identify occupations in the classified section of the paper.
3. Pretend you are interviewing a famous person in the news. Write a list of questions you would ask and the person's probable replies.
4. Use newspaper articles as the basis for values education discussions. (Should punishment for stealing be the same for all people?)
5. Write a letter to a famous person in the newspaper.
6. During election year trace the campaigns of politicians.
7. Use the obituary section of the paper and make a chart listing the genders and ages of people who died. What conclusions can you draw from this information?
8. Have students construct a scrapbook related to a specific problem (pollution or crime for example).
9. Locate examples of propaganda techniques in ads and editorials.
10. Locate local, state, national, and international events on maps.

Science

1. Use charts to keep track of temperatures in different cities.
2. Locate symbols used in science.
3. Plan a balanced menu (food pyramid) using ads from the paper.
4. Use weather maps to follow and forecast the weather.
5. Conduct a study by tracing information through the newspapers on a particular topic. (For example, trace global ecology issues in the United States, Russia or China.)
6. Locate science words in the paper.
7. Locate articles on how to care for plants.
8. Locate articles on health and medicine.

Language Arts

1. Display photographs to show causes and effects (floods, tornadoes).
2. Have students write letters to the editor.
3. Have students pretend to be reporters and write an account of an event.
4. Have students locate main ideas by matching headlines with articles.
5. Cut the dialogue out of comic strips and have students create their own.
6. Have students prepare and give speeches on current events topics.
7. Locate weekly vocabulary words in the paper.
8. Locate examples of overused phrases or common clichés.

Contact your local newspaper or a newspaper from the nearest large city for ideas and cooperation on using the newspaper in your content area. Many newspapers will provide materials on newspaper in the classroom and have consultants on staff to meet with teachers and demonstrate activities.

CONCLUSION

Throughout this book we have presented various strategies for teaching content to your students. In this chapter we have looked at some solutions to general problems with learning content.

Cooperative learning strategies can serve as motivational strategies for those students who enjoy peer interaction. Information intermix, student teams–achievement divisions, teams-games-tournaments, Jigsaw II, and the group investigation model are strategies that can provide students with peer interaction.

Computer-assisted instruction provides another alternative for meeting the needs of students and meeting your objectives. Computerlike machines in the home, simulations, drill and practice, information retrieval, word processing, and interactive videodisk learning are only a few of the many possibilities for instruction. Remember, you control the use of the computer to meet your instructional objectives. The computer should not control your goals and objectives.

Listening strategies can be used to communicate information students cannot read, to improve long-term memory, and to develop critical listening ability. We discussed three listening strategies: the directed listening activity, the guided listening procedure, and the planned inferential listening lesson.

Materials adjustments can be made in a number of ways. The length of assignments may be varied. Multilevel textbooks, supplementary materials, and smiliar materials at lower readability levels may be used. Computers also provide self-paced, immediate feedback, reinforcement for students.

The newspaper is another aid that often is overlooked by teachers. It contains maps, charts, pictures, cartoons, news articles, feature stories, editorials, obituaries, sports, and classified sections from which you can develop lessons. A number of activities related to mathematics, social studies, science, and language arts were highlighted in this chapter.

Teachers can vary their strategies to meet students' needs and thereby help students learn more. Variety produces more interesting classes for both teachers and students; and interest produces motivation. The more motivated students are to learn, the more they will learn.

POSTREADING

INTEGRATING WRITING

In your journal describe your observances of the effective use of cooperative learning or computer-assisted instruction for teaching.

REVIEW

Make a list of words and concepts related to Chapter 10. Organize these into a graphic organizer. Be able to explain why you organized them as you did.

PRACTICE

Do Enabling Activity 28 in Appendix A.

11

MULTICULTURAL LITERATURE AND TEENS

"Mr. Hull, why do you read books other than our textbook?" asked Peter.

Mr. Hull thought for a minute. "For one thing, I enjoy reading and think that reading is important. The more I read, the more I get to know about other people."

"I love to read," interjected Diana. "Everytime I read, I learn something new. It's relaxing and fun for me."

"Peter," asked Mr. Hull, "do you like to read?"

"I like to read if it's something I'm interested in," replied Peter.

Mr. Hull added, "Let's find out what interests you. I am sure we can find books related to our class that you'd enjoy reading."

DISCUSS

Of what value is using literature in content areas? What literature have you used in your content area? How can you interest your students in reading books other than the textbook?

PREORGANIZE

Go through the chapter and make a skeletal outline of the major headings and subheadings. This will provide you with a chapter organizer. Predict the contents of the text under one of these subheadings.

OBJECTIVES

After reading this chapter, you should be able to

1. name the functions reading for pleasure serves.
2. identify reasons why students don't choose to read.

3. identify possible ways to overcome students' negative attitudes toward reading.
4. identify pre- and postreading activities that motivate teenagers.
5. cite information books students enjoy reading.
6. define multicultural literature and identify its functions.
7. formulate questions for discussion of fiction and nonfiction literature.
8. construct an interest inventory for specific books in your content area.

In order for something to be read, it must first be written. The author Hadley Irwin is actually two people who write together and use the one name. They describe why they write (Nilsen & Donelson, 1993).

- Because life is so terribly funny. It's a way to express all those ridiculous, funny times in life.
- Because life is so terribly difficult. It helps people understand that hardships can be overcome.
- Because life is so precious.
- Because life is so exciting.
- Because, most of all, writing allows us to live hundreds of lives, share what we know and what we guess, laugh at ourselves and the world.

People read for the same reasons that authors like Hadley Irwin write. Reading gives people the experiences of laughing at life, crying about life, overcoming difficulties, experiencing the preciousness and excitement of life, and living hundreds, thousands, of different lives.

In this chapter we will view literature's role in our classrooms.

INTERESTS

How much time do you and your students spend reading? The amount of time we and our students spend reading varies greatly. It might not surprise you, however, that students who spend the most time reading have higher than average standardized test scores.

Reading for pleasure serves several basic functions and is a necessary component of learning. Shefelbine (1991) identifies some functions reading serves.

1. Reading improves reading. The more students practice reading, the better they will be at reading.
2. Reading rate and comprehension increase as students recognize more words at sight more rapidly.
3. Students recognize the meanings to more words as the amount of reading they do increases. Vocabulary is the basis for comprehension.

4. Students become more aware of the syntactic structure used in books. Sentences in books are longer and more complex than the sentences we use in everyday conversation.
5. The vicarious experiences of books expands students' views and understanding of the world.
6. Reading releases students from the isolation and insecurity they often feel as teenagers. They see that others have had the same feelings and faced the same problems they do and have moved forward successfully.
7. Reading provides students with a leisure-time, stress-releasing activity.

Our challenge as teachers is to motivate those teenagers who won't read. Gentile and McMillan (1977) help shed light on some reasons why students won't read.

1. Students may equate reading with failure, ridicule, or exclusively for school use.
2. Some students prefer direct, concrete experiences to the ideas presented in books.
3. Some students have difficulty sitting for long periods of time.
4. Teenagers are involved with themselves; they are egocentric. They don't see books as relating to themselves.
5. Students have become accustomed to extrinsic rewards and want to be entertained. Reading presents intrinsic rewards.
6. The persistent pressure at home and school to read! read! has turned students off on reading.
7. Reading materials are not available to students in the home. They do not see the important adults in their lives reading.
8. Reading is not seen as the "in" thing to do. Peer pressure creates an atmosphere that is not conducive to reading.
9. Many textbooks look and read like encyclopedias. They are dull.
10. Teenagers often reject the adult world, and they see reading as part of the adult world.

Viewing the reluctance of teenagers to read, Mathison (1989) writes that student interest can be captured by using analogies relating new information to what students already know, relating personal experiences that make things more "real," disrupting students' expectations by presenting them with material expressing conflicting views, and presenting students with factual information that clashes with their beliefs and experiences.

Clary (1991) identified additional steps teachers can take to ameliorate the intensity of these negative attitudes toward reading.

1. Allow adolescents to read adolescent fiction and nonfiction. Don't pressure them into adult literature.
2. Try to determine your students' interests.

3. Give students choices in ways to share their books. Not all book reports need to be written.
4. Provide some time during the school day for students to read silently and independently. Uninterrupted sustained silent reading (USSR) is one way of building in this time.
5. Motivate students through talking about books, showing videotapes, and having games and contests.

Perhaps the biggest motivator, however, is to be excited about books yourself. Students will model your behavior.

In an effort to ascertain the kinds of pre- and postreading activities that motivate teenagers, Livaudais (1985) surveyed students in grades 7 through 12. She found that students preferred the following twelve prereading activities:

Selecting their own books
Watching the stories at the movies or on TV or video
Participating in book fairs
Utilizing a class library
Matching books with students on the basis of their interests
Listening to audio recordings of books
Visiting the library regularly
Having the teacher read the first few interesting pages of books
Scheduling time each day when everyone in the building reads
Having teachers teach with books written especially to teenagers
Hearing authors speak about their books
Having a file of student book reviews

Livaudais (1985) also found that students' twelve top choices of activities after reading included:

Sharing and talking about books with friends
Relating the book to a movie or television production of it
Talking with a small group of students in class about books they like
Using audiovisual equipment (VCR, tape recorder, slide projector, camera, computer) to present book reports
Having reading contests with prizes and awards for reading books
Having a panel of students talk about or debate on a topic or situation from a book
Writing a formal book review
Dramatizing or acting a part of the book
Writing a script or play based on the story
Engaging in art activities related to the book
Keeping progress charts of books read
Developing advertisements for books

TABLE 11–1 • Most Frequently Circulated Information Books

Title	Author
Guinness Book of World Records	McWhirter
Drawing Horses and Foals	Bolognese
Scary Stories to Tell in the Dark	Schwartz
Headless Roommate and Other Tales of Terror	Cohen
Draw 50 Dogs	Ames
Draw 50 Airplanes, Aircraft and Spacecraft	Ames
Secrets of Ninja	Kim
Draw 50 Boats, Ships, Trucks and Trains	Ames
Superman—from 30's to 70's	—
Drawing Spaceships and Other Spacecraft	Bolognese
Drawing Dinosaurs and Other Prehistoric Animals	Bolognese
Dirt Bike Racing	Herda
BMX: A Guide to Motorcross	Coombs
Origami	Davidson
Bermuda Triangle and Other Mysteries of Nature	Dolan
The Martial Arts	Ribner
Unriddling	Schwartz
Six Missions of Texas	—
American Fighters of World War II	Anderton
Sharks	Blumberg
Ghostly Terrors	Cohen
Great Unsolved Cases	Madison
Crescent Color Guide to Dogs	Sayer
Garfield: The Complete Cat Book	Steneman

Knowing the types of books students prefer also aids in motivating students to read and in helping them find books of interest. Reed (1988) identified eight areas that abound with books written for teens: books dealing with the problems of adolescents, historical fiction, mystery, suspense, fantasy, science fiction, nonfiction, and poetry.

Carter (1987) looked more specifically at teenagers' interests in information books. The twenty-four most frequently circulated information books were the ones listed in Table 11–1.

Take a few minutes to check your knowledge of the favorite books of teens. The ten titles in Table 11–2 are from *Teens' Favorite Books: Young Adults' Choices 1987–1992* (1992) and have multicultural themes. This volume is a compilation of the favorite books of teenagers, chosen by teenagers.

Let's see how you did: 1 (i); 2 (h); 3 (b); 4 (f); 5 (a); 6 (j); 7 (e); 8 (c); 9 (d); 10 (g). Are you an expert on the favorite book selections of teenagers?

TABLE 11–2 • Teens' Favorite Books

Column A	*Directions:* Match each title in column A with its description in column B. Column B
_____ 1. *Lisa's War*	a. how disease changed the lives of fourteen young people
_____ 2. *The Adventures of High John the Conqueror*	b. glimpse of Japanese-American culture
_____ 3. *Molly By Any Other Name*	c. fantasy that teaches about culture and different values
_____ 4. *Skeeter*	d. Blackfoot Indian living in northern Montana
_____ 5. *How It Feels to Fight for Your Life*	e. Experiences of Christa McAuliffe with NASA
_____ 6. *Bloods: An Oral History of the Vietnam War by Black Veterans*	f. sixteen-year-olds learn about respect and race relations
_____ 7. *I Touch the Future*	g. Native American faces prejudice and pressure to assimilate
_____ 8. *Sing for a Gentle Rain*	h. popular legend among black slaves in the South
_____ 9. *Sweetgrass*	i. the Holocaust seen through the eyes of a Jewish teenager
_____ 10. *I Wear the Morning Star*	j. black veterans share their war experiences

MULTICULTURAL LITERATURE

Multicultural literature focuses on religious minorities (Jewish Americans, Amish, Buddhist Americans), people of different colors (Native Americans, Hispanic Americans, African Americans, Indonesian Americans, Asian Americans, European Americans); and regional cultures (Cajun, Appalachian). It also focuses upon depicting women and girls in stereotypic roles (Au, 1993).

Multicultural literature recognizes and supports the diverse backgrounds of students. It helps students gain insights into how people live, feel, think, and respond. At the same time it gives some students a sense of pride in their own culture, it also helps other students respect and appreciate diverse backgrounds. And multicultural literature provides a background for understanding how people of diverse backgrounds contribute to shaping American society (Au, 1993).

Literature can serve as the starting point for a lesson. It serves as the scaffold (background or schema) on which students explore their interests and add new knowledge (Diakiw, 1990).

We can integrate various genres of multicultural literature into our content areas—for example, biographies, folklore, historic nonfiction (people, places, history), and historic fiction. As we describe these various genres in the following sections, we will identify books you can use in your classroom. The suggestions were compiled from a number of different sources, including

> Banks, J.A. (1991). *Teaching strategies for ethnic studies.* (5th ed.). Boston: Allyn and Bacon.
>
> Kruse, G.M., & Horning, K.T. (1991). *Cultural literature for children and young adults: A selected listing of books 1980–1990: By and about people of color.* (3rd. ed.). Madison, WI: Cooperative Children's Book Center, University of Wisconsin.
>
> Nilsen, A.P., & Donelson, K.L. (1993). *Literature for today's young adults.* (4th ed.). New York: HarperCollins.
>
> Reed, A.J.S. (1988). *Comics to classics: A parents' guide to books for teens and pre-teens.* Newark, DE: International Reading Association.
>
> Sutherland, Z., & Arbuthnot, M.H. (1986). *Children and books.* (7th ed.). Glenview, IL: Scott, Foresman.
>
> *Teens' favorite books: Young adults' choices 1987–1992.* (1992). Newark, DE: International Reading Association.

The literature selections we list are presented alphabetically by title, with publication date, author, and publishing company included for your reference.

Biography

Biographies are a form of hero/heroine tales (Nilsen & Donelson, 1993). They tell us about the struggles, mistakes, feats, accomplishments, triumphs, and determination of people. They are about real people and what happened to them; they're about the history of peoples' lives. Autobiographies are written by the heros and heroines about themselves.

A good biography is accurate, free from the author's personal opinions. The author presents facts that can be verified; readers form judgments after considering the author's presentation. Some biographies you might consider are

Native Americans

> *Cherokee Chief: The life of John Ross* (1970). E. Clark. Crowell-Collier.
>
> *Chief Joseph, war chief of the Nez Perce* (1962). D. Russell and B. Ashabranner. McGraw Hill.
>
> *Eyes of darkness* (1985). J. Highwater. Lothrop, Lee & Shepard.
>
> *Geronimo, the last Apache war chief* (1952). E. Wyatt. Whitlesey.
>
> *Ishi: Last of his tribe* (1964). T. Kroeber. Parnassus.
>
> *In two worlds: A Yup'ik Eskimo family* (1989). A. Jenness and R. Rivers. Houghton Mifflin.
>
> *Indian chiefs* (1987). R. Freedman. Holiday House.
>
> *Lakota woman* (1990). M. Crow Dog and R. Erdoes. Grove Weidenfeld.
>
> *To live in two worlds; American Indian youth today* (1984). B. Ashabranner. Dodd, Mead.
>
> *Quanah Parker: Ambassador for peace* (1987). L. Hilts. Harcourt.

Sitting Bull, champion of his people (1946). S. Garst. Messner.

The story of Crazy Horse (1954). E. Meadowcroft. Grosset.

Suzette La Flesche: Voice of the Omaha Indians (1973). M. Crary.

Winged moccasins: The Story of Sacajawea (1954). F. J. Farnsworth.

Woman chief (1976). R. Sobol. Dial.

African Americans

Anthony Burns: The defeat and triumph of a fugitive slave (1988). V. Hamilton. Knopf.

Barbara Jordan: Speaking out (1977). J. Haskins. Dial.

Black people who made the Old West (1989). W. L. Katz. Crowell.

Extraordinary Black Americans: From colonial to contemporary times (1989). S. Altman. Children's Press.

Joe Louis: 50 years an American hero (1988). J. L. Barrow and B. Mader. McGraw-Hill.

Lena Horne (1983). J. Haskin. Coward-McCann.

Manchild in the promised land (1965). C. Brown. Macmillan.

Marching to freedom: The story of Martin Luther King, Jr. (1987). J. Milton. Dell.

Martin Luther King, Jr.: Free at last (1986). D. Adler. Holiday House.

The picture life of Whitney Houston (1988). G. Busnar. Franklin Watts.

Satchel Paige (1988). K. L. Humphrey. Franklin Watts.

Take a walk in their shoes (1989). G. T. Turner. Dutton.

Teammates (1990). P. Golenbock. Harcourt.

Hispanic Americans

Barrio boy (1971). E. Galarza. University of Notre Dame Press.

Cesar Chavez and La Causa (1986) M. Roberts. Children's Press.

Famous Puerto Ricans (1975). C. Hewlon. Dodd, Mead.

Hispanic voters: A voice in American politics (1988). J. Harlan. Franklin Watts.

Hunger of memory: The education of Richard Rodriguez (1982). R. Rodriguez. Godine.

Living up the street: Narrative recollections (1985). G. Soto. Strawberry Hill.

The picture life of Herman Badillo (1972). P. Allyn. Franklin Watts.

Pride of Puerto Rico: The life of Roberto Clemente (1988). P. W. Walker. Harcourt.

The snake in the sandtrap (1985). L. Trevino and S. Blair. Holt.

Asian Americans

Chinese women in America: A pictorial history (1986). J. Yung. University of Washington Press.

Daniel Inouye (1977). J. Goodsell. Crowell.

Heart of iron (1987). H. Hieb. Pacifica.

Isamu Noguchi: The life of a sculptor (1974). T. Tobias. Crowell.

The little weaver of Thai-Yen village (1987). Tran-Khan-Tuyet. Children's Press.

El Chino (1990). A. Say. Houghton Mifflin. (very easy reading)

Jewish Americans

Elie Weisel: Witness for life (1982). E. N. Stern. KTAV.
Guess who's Jewish in American history, 2nd ed. (1988). B. Postal and L. Koppman. Shapolsky.
The promised land, 2nd ed. (1969). M. Antin. Houghton Mifflin.

Folklore

Folklore is comprised of folktales, myths, legends, and hero tales. It originally was passed from generation to generation through oral language by storytellers.

Folklore is based on old dreams and great desires of people, and the images are magical. An example of this is the desire to travel. Greeks used the wings of birds; Germanic tribes used magical boots; Native Americans used the flight of an arrow; and Persians used flying carpets (Nilsen & Donelson, 1993).

Folklore presents us with emotions and actions on opposite ends of the continuum: good-evil, happiness-sadness, strength-weakness, envy-awe, heros-cowards, hard work-laziness, order-chaos. The hero or heroine eventually proves to be wise and brave and chooses good over evil (Nilsen & Donelson, 1993). The *folktale,* more specifically,

> starts briskly and continues to be filled with action; it often has humor; it appeals to children's sense of justice, since many tales reward good and punish evil; it has little nuance of characterization, so that characters are presented as entirely good, bad, obedient, lazy, and so on; it often includes rhyme or repetition; it is usually concise; it usually has a satisfying and definite conclusion. In other words, the folktale has all the things that children, especially small children, like. And if it has magic—and most do—so much the better. (Sutherland & Arbuthnot, 1986, p. 163)

The folktale often begins with "Once upon a time..." and is short, usually ending with everyone living "happily ever after." "The Elves and the Shoemaker," "The Three Billy Goats Gruff," and "The Gingerbread Boy" are three familiar folktales.

Fables are designed to teach a lesson or moral. The characters are usually animals who teach a lesson about human behavior. The animals don't have names the way we would name a pet; instead they are called by the type of animal they are. For example, "The Ant and the Grasshopper," the "Hare and the Tortoise," and "The Ugly Duckling" are classic fables.

Myths are longer than folktales and fables, and are more complex. They are ways to explain phenomena that human beings could not explain. Death, seasons, disease, and the solar system were explained by myths. In Greek mythology gods were brothers and sisters. Each god had certain powers. If a god were angry, a flood, earthquake, or disease might be the consequence.

Pourquoi tales are a type of myth that tell how or why something originated or came to be. "Why Mosquitoes Buzz in People's Ears" and "Why the Sun and the Moon Live in the Sky" are examples of pourquoi tales (*pourquoi* is French for "why").

Legends, epics and *hero tales* or *tall tales* have human heroes and may even contain a grain of historic basis; however, their deeds and feats became exaggerated greatly beyond the point of possibility. Their adventures make up a series of tales rather than just one story. Pecos Bill, Johnny Appleseed, and Paul Bunyan are three well-known American tall tale heroes.

Below, we've identified some example of folklore from various cultural groups.

Native Americans

Adventures of Nanabush: Ojibway Indian stories (1980). E. Coatsworth and D. Coatsworth. Atheneum.

Beyond the Clapping Mountains: Eskimo stories from Alaska (1943). C. E. Gillham. Macmillan.

Coyote (1983). J. Hayes. Mariposa.

Dance in the sky: Native American star myths (1987). J. G. Monroe and R. A. Williamson. Houghton Mifflin.

Earthmaker's tales: North American Indian stories about earth happenings (1989). G. W. Mayo. Walker.

Eskimo songs and stories (1973). E. Field. Delacorte.

The girl who married a ghost and other tales from the North American Indian (1978). E. S. Curtis. Four Winds.

Her seven brothers (1988). P. Globe. Bradbury.

Heroes and heroines in Tlingit-Haida legend (1989). M. L. Beck. Alaska Northwest.

How raven freed the moon (1987). A. Cameron. Harbour.

The mythology of North America (1985). J. Bierhorst. Morrow.

People of the short blue corn: Tales and legends of the Hopi Indians (1970). H. Courlander. Harcourt.

The talking stone: An anthology of Native American tales and legends (1979). D. DeWit. Greenwillow.

They dance in the sky: Native American star myths (1987). J. G. Monroe and R. A. Williamson. Houghton Mifflin.

The whistling skeleton: American Indian tales of the supernatural (1982). J. Bierhorst (ed.). Four Winds.

African and African American

The adventures of High John the Conqueror (1989). S. Sanfield. Orchard.

Aesop's fables (1967). V. Jones. Franklin Watts.

Apples on a stick: The folklore of Black children (1983). B. Michels and B. White. Coward-McCann.

Beat the story-drum, pum-pum (1980). A. Bryan. Atheneum.

The boy and the ghost (1989). R. D. San Souci. Simon & Schuster.

The hat-shaking dance, and other tales from the Gold Coast (1957). H. Courlander and A. Prempeh. Harcourt.

King's drum and other stories (1962). H. Courlander. Harcourt.

Lion and the ostrich chicks, and other African folktales (1986). A. Bryan. Atheneum.

Mother crocodile/Maman-caiman (1981). B. Diop. Delacorte.

The people could fly (1985). V. Hamilton. Knopf.

The river that gave gifts (1987). M. Humphrey. Children's Press.

The tales of Uncle Remus: The Adventures of Brer Rabbit (1987). J. Lester. Dial.

Hispanic

Dance of the animals (1972). P. Belpre. Warne.

Doctor Coyote: A native American Aesop's fable (1987). J. Bierhorst. Macmillan.

The hungry woman: Myths and legends of the Aztecs (1984). J. Bierhorst. Morrow.

The invisible hunters/Los cazadores invisibles: A legend from the Miskito Indians of Nicaragua/Una leyenda de los Indios Miskitos de Nicaragua (1987). R. and H. and O. Chow and M. Vidaure. Children's Press.

The king of the mountains: A treasury of Latin American folk stories (1960). M. A. Jagendorf and R. S. Boggs. Vanguard.

The mythology of Mexico and Central America (1990). J. Bierhorst. Morrow.

The mythology of South America (1988). J. Bierhorst. Morrow.

Once in Puerto Rico (1973). P. Belpre. Warne.

Asian

Chinese myths and fantasies (1961). C. Birch. Walck.

The dancing kettle and other Japanese folk tales (1949). Y. Uchida. Harcourt.

Japanese tales and legends (1959). H. and W. McAlpine (comps.). Walck.

The paper crane (1985). M. Bang. Greenwillow.

Pie-biter (1983). R. L. McCunn. Design Enterprises of San Francisco.

The rainbow people (1989). L. Yep (reteller). Harper.

The spring of butterflies and other folktales of China's minority peoples (1987). L. He. Lothrop, Lee & Shepard.

Toad is the uncle of heaven: A Vietnamese folk tale (1985). J. M. Lee. Holt.

Treasure Mountain: Folktales from Southern China (1982). C. E. Sadler (ed.). Atheneum.

Tye May and the magic brush (1981). M. G. Bang. Greenwillow.

Yeh-Shen: A Cinderella story from China (1988). A. L. Louie. Putnam.

Jewish

The case against the wind and other stories (1975). I. L. Peretz. Macmillan.

Greek and Roman

The Aeneid (1962). A. J. Church (ed.). Macmillan.

The children's Homer (1962). P. Colum. Macmillan.

The complete Greek stories of Nathaniel Hawthorne (1963). N. Hawthorne. Franklin Watts.

The golden shadow (1971). L. Garfield and E. Blishen. Pantheon.

The gorgon's head: The story of Perseus (1962). I. Serraillier. Walck.
Greek gods and heroes (1960). R. Graves. Doubleday.
Greek myths (1949). O. E. Coolidge. Houghton.
Greeks bearing gifts: The epics of Achilles and Ulysses (1976). B. Evslin. Four Winds.
The heroes (1963). C. Kingsley. Dutton.
The Iliad and the Odyssey of Homer (1964). A. J. Church (ed.). Macmillan.
The Odyssey of Homer (1951). A. J. Church. Macmillan.

People, Places, History

Mythology leads us to an understanding of people's fantasies and beliefs in the past. When we study people, places, and history, we study more recent history. Why did people migrate to the United States? What are their customs and beliefs? What were their home countries like? How do they feel? What are their thoughts?

Native Americans

American Indians today: Issues and conflicts (1987). J. Harlan. Franklin Watts.
Buffalo hunt (1988). R. Freedman. Holiday House.
Dancing teepees: Poems of American Indian youth (1989). V. D. H. Sneve (selector). Holiday House.
From Abenaki to Zuni: A dictionary of Native American tribes (1988). E. Wolfson. Walker.
Happily may I walk: American Indians and Alaska natives today (1986). A. Hirschfelder. Scribner's.
The igloo (1988). C. Yue and D. Yue. Houghton Mifflin.
Indian chiefs (1987). R. Freedman. Holiday House.
In two worlds: A Yup'ik Eskimo family (1989). A. Jenness and A. Rivers. Houghton Mifflin.
To live in two worlds; American Indian youth today (1984). B. Ashabranner. Dodd, Mead.
Tribal sovereignty: Indian tribes in U.S. history (1981). Daybreak.

African Americans

The Black Americans: A history in their own words (1984). M. Meltzer. Harper.
Black like me (1977). J. H. Griffin. Houghton Mifflin.
Black music in America: A history through its people (1987). J. Haskins. Crowell.
Black people who made the Old West (1989). W. L. Katz. Crowell.
Bloods: An oral history of the Vietnamese War (1985). W. Terry, III (ed.). Random House.
Breaking the chains: African-American slave resistance (1990). W. L. Katz. Atheneum.
The civil rights movement in America: From 1865 to the present (1987). P. McKissack and F. McKissack. Children's Press.
Roots (1976). A. Haley. Doubleday.

Hispanic Americans

An album of Puerto Ricans in the United States (1973). S. Brahs. Franklin Watts.

Chicanos: The story of Mexican Americans (1973). P. de Garza. Julian Messner.

Dark harvest: Migrant farmworkers in America (1985). B. Ashabranner. Dodd, Mead.

Freedom fighters (1980). L. Philipson and R. Llerena. Random House.

The Hispanic Americans (1982). M. Meltzer. Crowell.

Living up the street: Narrative recollections (1985). G. Soto. Strawberry Hill.

Los Chicanos: An awakening people (1970). J. Haddox. Western Press.

The Mexicans in America (1989). J. Pinchot. Lerner.

Mexico and the United States: Their linked destinies (1983). E. B. Fincher. Crowell.

The new Americans: Cuban boat people (1982). J. Haskins. Enslow.

The Puerto Ricans (1990). A. Tobier. Chelsea House.

The Puerto Ricans in America (1989). R. J. Larsen. Lerner.

Puerto Rico: Island between two worlds (1979). L. Perl. Morrow.

Pyramid of the Sun/Pyramid of the Moon (1988). L. E. Fisher. Macmillan.

Asian Americans

The Chinese-American heritage (1988). D. M. Brownstone. Facts on File.

Chinese Americans past and present: A collection of Chinese American readings and learning activities (1977). D. Wong and I. D. Collier. San Francisco Association of Chinese Teachers.

The Chinese of America (1982). J. Chen. Harper.

Chinese New Year (1987). T. Brown. Henry Holt.

Chinese women in America: A pictorial history (1986). J. Yung. University of Washington Press.

Coming to America: Immigrants from the Far East (1980). L. Perrin. Delacorte.

Cooking the Vietnamese way (1985). Chi Nguyen and J. Monroe. Lerner.

The eagle and the dragon (1985). D. Lawson. Crowell.

A family in China (1985). N. L. Fyson and R. Greenhill. Lerner.

Faithful elephants: A true story of animals, people and war (1988). Y. Tsuchiya. Houghton Mifflin.

Han Suyin's China (1988). H. Suyin. Universe.

Hmong folklife (1986). D. Willcox. Hmong Natural Association of North Carolina.

If I die in a combat zone (1987). T. O'Brien. Dell.

The journey (1990). S. Hamanaka. Orchard.

Vietnam: A history (1984). S. Karnow. Penguin.

The Vietnamese in America (1987). P. Rutledge. Lerner.

Jewish Americans

Anglish-Yiddish in American life and literature (1989). G. Bluestein. University of Georgia Press.

Call it sleep (1960). H. Roth. Pageant.

Feathers in the wind (1989). M. Chaikin. Harper.
The Jewish world (1984). D. Charing. Silver Burdett.
The Jews: Story of a people (1978). H. Fast. Dell.
Jews without money (1968). M. Gold. Avon.
The nine questions people ask about Judaism (1988). D. Prager and J. Telushkin. Simon & Schuster/Touchstone.
Rescue: The story of how gentiles saved Jews in the holocaust (1990). M. Meltzer. Harper.
Smoke and ashes: The story of the Holocaust (1990). B. Rogasky. Holiday House.
Sound the shofar: The story and meaning of Rosh Hashanah and Yom Kippur. (1986). M. Chaikin. Houghton Mifflin/Clarion.

Fiction

In ethnic fiction the characters are trying to balance two worlds. There is generally trouble fitting into the group or adult world, fear of being rejected, loneliness, and differences between generations. Children feel that their families are different from other families. There is an attempt to live in harmony with nature. Myths and legends appear in the literature. Often times bitterness and resentment enter into multicultural fictional literature. Teaching about the history of ethnic groups (biographies; myths; people, places, and history) lays a foundation for understanding fictional literature (Nilsen & Donelson, 1993).

Native Americans

Bearstone (1989). W. Hobbs. Atheneum.
Black star, bright dawn (1988). S. O'Dell. Houghton Mifflin
The brave (1991). R. Lipsyte. HarperCollins.
Ceremony (1977). L. M. Silko. Viking/Penguin
Eyes of darkness (1985). J. Highwater. Lothrop, Lee & Shepard.
Legend days (1984). J. Highwater. HarperCollins.
Night flying woman: An Ojibway narrative (1983). Minnesota Historical Society Press.
The Powwow highway (1990). D. Seals. Plume.
Racing the sun (1988). P. Pitts. Avon/Camelot.
The shadow brothers (1990). A. E. Cannon. Delacorte.
When the legends die (1963). H. Borland. Lippincott.
A woman of her tribe (1990). M. A. Robinson. Scribner's.

African Americans

Annie John (1985). J. Kincaid. Farrar, Straus & Giroux.
Betsey Brown (1985). N. Shange. St. Martin's.
Bright shadow (1983). J. C. Thomas. Avon.
Crystal (1987). W. D. Myers. Viking/Kestrel.
Denny's tapes (1987). P. C. McKissack. Knopf.
Fallen angels (1988). W. D. Myers. Scholastic.

Fast talk on a slow track (1991). R. Williamson-Garcia. Lodestar.
The gathering (1989). V. Hamilton. Greenwillow.
If Beale Street could talk (1974). J. K. Baldwin. Doubleday.
A little love (1984). V. Hamilton. Philomel.
Ludell (1975). B. Wildinson. Harper Collins.
Motown and Didi: A love story (1984). W. D. Myers. Viking/Kestrel.
The music of summer (1992). R. Guy. Delacorte.
Out from this place (1988). J. Hansen. Walker.
The shimmershine queens (1989). C. Yarbrough. Putnam.
Somewhere in the darkness (1992). W. D. Myers. Scholastic.
Which way freedom? (1986). J. Hansen. Walker.

Hispanic Americans

Across the great river (1989). I. B. Hernandez. Arte Publico.
Alan and Naomi (1977). M. Levoy. HarperCollins.
Barrio boy (1977). E. Galarza. University of Notre Dame Press.
Best friends tell the best lies (1989). C. Dines. Delacorte.
Famous all over town (1983). D. Santiago. Simon & Schuster.
Freedom flights (1980). L. Philipson and R. Llerena. Random House.
A heart of Azian: A novel (1988). R. Anaya. University of New Mexico Press.
The honorable prison (1988). L. B. de Jenkins. Penguin.
The me inside of me (1987). T. E. Bethancourt. Lerner.
Nilda (1973). N. Mohr. HarperCollins.
And now Miguel (1953). J. Krumgold. Crowell.
A shadow like a leopard (1981). M. Levoy. HarperCollins.
Stand and deliver (1989). N. Edwards. Scholastic.
A thief in the village, and other stories (1988). J. Berry. Orchard.
Throw a hungry loop (1990). D. Schenker. Knopf.

Asian Americans

The best bad thing (1983). Y. Uchida. Atheneum.
A boat to nowhere (1980). M. C. Wartski. Westminister Press.
Child of the owl (1977). L. Yep. Harper.
Children of the river (1989). L. Crew. Delacorte.
Desert exile: The uprooting of a Japanese American family (1982). Y. Uchida. University of Washington Press.
The floating world (1989). C. Kadohata. Viking/Penguin.
Her own song (1988). E. Howard. Atheneum.
Kim/Kimi (1987). H. Irwin. Macmillan.
The kitchen god's wife (1991). A. Tan. Putnam.
A long way from home (1980). M. C. Wartski. Westminster.
Molly by any other name (1990). J. D. Okomoto. Scholastic.
Mountain light (1985). L. Yep. Harper.
Rebels of the heavenly kingdom (1983). K. Paterson. Lodestar/Dutton.
Rice without rain (1990). M. Ho. Lothrop Lee & Shepard.

Several kinds of silence (1988). M. Singer. HarperCollins.
Shabanu: Daughter of the wind (1989). S. F. Staples. Alfred A. Knopf.
So far from the bamboo grove (1986). Y. K. Watkins. Lothrop, Lee & Shepard.
Tales from Gold Mountain: Stories of the Chinese in the New World (1990). P.
Yee. Macmillan.

Jewish Americans

Chernowitz! (1981). F. Arrick. Bradbury.
Daughters of the law (1980). S. F. Asher. Beaufort.
The fifth son (1985). E. Weisel. Simon & Schuster.
Gentlehands (1979). M. E. Kerr. Bantam.
Good-bye glamour girl (1984). E. Tamar. Lippincott.
Good if it goes (1984). G. Provost and G. Levine-Freidus. Bradbury Press.
The Holocaust: A history of courage and resistance (1974). B. Stadtler. Behrman
House.
I feel like the morning star (1989). G. Maguire. Harper.
Lisa's war (1991). C. Matas. Scribner's.
Pageant (1986). K. Laskky. Macmillan/Four Winds.
The return (1987). S. Levitin. Atheneum.
Rooftop secrets and other stories of anti-Semitism (1986). L. Bush. Union of
American Hebrew Congregations.
Silver days (1989). S. Levitin. Atheneum.
Tell us your secret (1989). B. Cohen. Bantam.

DISCUSSION QUESTIONS

Teachers often ask how they can stimulate students to talk about the books they've
read. This series of questions is recommended by Carter and Abrahamson (1990,
pp. 185–187) as a way to encourage students to talk about nonfiction literature.

1. How would this book be different if it had been written ten years earlier?
   ten years later?
2. Which illustrations do you wish you had taken or drawn yourself? Why?
   [What illustrations do you think would enhance the quality of the book?]
3. Compare this nonfiction book with another one written on the same topic.
   How do they differ? How are they alike? Which one do you like better (or
   believe more)? Why?
4. What segment, portion, or focus of this book would make a good docu-
   mentary? Why?
5. What steps do you think the author followed to research and write this
   book?
6. How would this book be different if it had been written for a fourth grader?
7. What kind of teacher do you think the author would make?
8. If you had a chance to interview the author(s) of this book, what would
   you ask?

9. Tell me three facts, theories, or incidents that you found particularily interesting. Now, assume you haven't read the book. Can you find this information? Why or why not? [Encourage students to try to locate it.]
10. Look at the title and the jacket of this book. What do they indicate the book will be about? Do they give a fair representation of the book's contents? [What other means might you use to select a book?]

As you read these nonfiction discussion questions, you probably noticed that many could be adapted to fiction. Combine these questions with the strategies highlighted in Chapters 5, 6 and 7 on comprehension, and you have a strong predicting and questioning component for your literature program.

STRATEGIES FOR USING LITERATURE

Many of the strategies described in Chapters 6 and 7 on comprehension and Chapter 10 on meeting students needs are appropriate for use with literature. Several additional strategies are described below.

Students can become exposed to the contents of an entire book in an hour. In the read-a-book-in-an-hour strategy Childrey (1980) recommends giving each student a chapter, or smaller section, of a book to read. (Each student in the class gets a section of the book to read. You can cut apart two paperback books rather than purchase a book for each student in the class.) Students read their sections silently and share, or summarize, the contents in sequential order with other students. When students have finished summarizing, each student in the class has heard a summary of the entire book. This will serve as an incentive for other students to read the book.

Encourage students to construct *data retrieval charts* as recommended by Banks (1991). These are a specific type of chart into which students supply researched information, obtained through their additional readings. The charts might contain information comparing conflicts within the cultural group and with other groups, special or unique values of the group, values shared with other groups, reasons for immigration, and level of cultural assimilation for different ethnic groups or individuals. These charts might compare the types, goals, ways, and reasons for the protests of various groups. The charts might compare the social, economic, and political situations of various ethnic groups in their lands before immigrating into the United States. These charts can serve as a source for discussion. Using the same types of charts, students can compare different characters in different stories.

Students can create Venn diagrams showing likenesses and differences. Venn diagrams are intersecting circles; the intersection shows the area both groups, people, or whatever you are comparing have in common. Figure 11–1 shows a Venn diagram outline.

Ninety-five different activities for stimulating student interest in reading are identified by Crawley and Merritt (1991, pp. 60–64). Here is a "baker's dozen" of their suggestions:

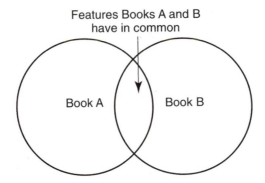

FIGURE 11–1   •   Venn Diagram Outline

   1.   Monthly topics. Set up a display of books, posters, or pictures about a specific topic each month.
   2.   Reading aloud. Read parts of stories or information books aloud to students to stimulate their interest. Stop at an interesting or exciting point.
   3.   Speakers. Ask community members to talk and share information about their work, interests, or hobbies.
   4.   Popular music. Generate opportunities for students to study the music and lyrics of popular music. They can study the lyric's meaning, read about the musicians (or read about the experiences the musician is describing).
   5.   Watching movies. Encourage students to watch movies about a specific book (or topic being studied in class).
   6.   Collages. Have students use cuttings of words and/or pictures from newspapers and magazines and construct a collage depicting the book read.
   7.   Autobiographies. Students can pretend to be a character and write an autobiography for the character.
   8.   Campaign speeches. What kind of speech do students think the character would make if she or he were running for president of the United States (or class president)? Student should write a speech for the character and deliver it before the class.
   9.   Crossword puzzles. Students can construct crossword puzzles using words from a factual book or several narrative books.
   10.   Epitaphs. Did a mean or evil person die in the story? Did a good or honest person die in the story? Have students write epitaphs that could have been printed on these characters' grave stones. (This could be done for living people also.)
   11.   Excuses. Did the story contain an episode in which a character did not do the right thing? Have students write an excuse the person may have given. (If a historical figure did not take the proper course of action, have students write an excuse for this character.)
   12.   Myths. Myths were once used to explain things that we now can explain through science. Let students create their own myths after reading several. (Students could also create myths explaining why political events occur.)

13. Tall tales. Tall tales are part of our American heritage. After reading several, have students try to write even taller tales. (Many of the events and decisions that have occurred in history lend themselves to tall tales.)

As students see the creations of fellow students, they will be directed toward other books.

DIRECTING STUDENTS TO BOOKS

Students often don't know where to turn when it comes to selecting books for personal reading. A simple way to assist students is to read a part of a book orally to them. Students of all ages (even adults) enjoy being read to.

Many of the strategies for using books discussed earlier can be used to direct students' attention to books. In addition to these strategies, Burmeister (1976) presents a *would-you-like-to-read-a-book-about* interest inventory that points students toward specific books. The following are adaptations of her inventory. We've included only four alternatives in each inventory as an example (see Examples 11.1 through 11.5). You will want to include a longer list of books—some easy reading and others more challenging for your students.

Each inventory begins with the following directions:

Directions: Circle YES or NO for each of the following questions. When you have finished, go to the bottom of the page to find the names of books that will interest you.

Example 11.1 Music Interest Inventory

Would you like to read about

YES NO 1. A composer and conductor who is very popular with common people and plays all types of music?

YES NO 2. Talented teen musicians trying to get to the top in rock 'n' roll?

YES NO 3. A rock singer who did something about hungry people around the world.

YES NO 4. The prestigious Juilliard School of Music?

These are the books you will enjoy reading if you answered yes to the numbered questions above.

1. J. Peyser. *Bernstein: A biography.*
2. T. Strasser. *Rock 'n' roll nights.*
3. B. Geldorf & P. Vallely. *Is that it?*
4. J. Kogan. *Nothing but the best: The struggle for perfection the Juilliard School.*

Example 11.2 History Interest Inventory

Would you like to read about

YES NO 1. The tragedy at Kent State University?
YES NO 2. Non-Jews who were victims of the Nazis?
YES NO 3. The ten days in Russia immediately after the Bolshevik takeover?
YES NO 4. The astronauts on the space shuttle *Challenger?*

These are the books you will enjoy reading if you answered yes to the numbered questions above.

1. J. A. Michener. *Kent State: What happened and why.*
2. I. R. Friedman. *The other victims: First-person stories of non-Jews persecuted by the Nazis.*
3. J. Reed. *Ten days that shook the world.*
4. D. Cohen & S. Cohen. *Heroes of the Challenger.*

Example 11.3 Poetry Interest Inventory

Would you like to read

YES NO 1. Dream poems?
YES NO 2. Poetry about a Hispanic neighborhood in Los Angeles?
YES NO 3. A collection of poems on all kinds of subjects?
YES NO 4. Poems about teenage experiences?

These are the books you will enjoy reading if you answered yes to the numbered questions above.

1. N. Larrick (ed.). *Bring me all your dreams.*
2. G. Soto. *Neighborhood odes.*
3. F. McCullough (selector). *Earth, air, fire and water.*
4. J. Viorst. *If I were in charge of the world and other worries.*

Example 11.4   Sports Interest Inventory

Would you like to read about

YES   NO   1. A woman who was great in almost all sports?
YES   NO   2. Yogi Berra, the famous baseball player?
YES   NO   3. Women who were outstanding in sports?
YES   NO   4. A fictional character who has to go to Japan to play baseball?

These are the books you will enjoy if you answered yes to the numbered questions above.

1. W. O. Johnson & N. P. Williamson. *"Whatta-Gal:" The Babe Didrickson story.*
2. Y. Berra. *It ain't over.*
3. F. Sabin. *Women who win.*
4. D. Klass. *The Atami Dragons.*

Example 11.5   Science, Animals Interest Inventory

Would you like to read about

YES   NO   1. Rescuing and caring for whales?
YES   NO   2. A person who studied wolves and what he found out?
YES   NO   3. A lioness and the woman who cared for her?
YES   NO   4. Lives of bears and how they were studied around Yellowstone Park?

These are the books you will enjoy if you answered yes to the numbered questions above.

1. K. Mallory & A. Conley. *Rescue of the stranded whales.*
2. R. Peters. *Dance of the wolves.*
3. J. Adamson. *Born free: A lioness of two worlds.*
4. M. Calabro. *Operation grizzly bear.*

In addition to using interest inventories, you can listen to what students say and talk about to gain insight into their interests. The questions they ask in class may give you insight.

Being a model is the best way to encourage your students to read. Let them see you reading. Read to them. Tell them about interesting books related to the topics you are studying. Provide time for your students to read. And make books available to them.

CONCLUSION

The amount of time students spend on outside reading greatly enhances their reading achievement and their achievement in content classes. Vocabulary, syntactic competence, and reading rate increase significantly as the amount of reading increases.

There are numerous reasons why some teenagers do not read. Among these reasons are (1) equating reading with failure, (2) difficulty with concentration, (3) the "need" for extrinsic rewards, and (4) the desire to be part of a group that doesn't value reading.

To help in selecting books (prereading), some of the activities students preferred were watching stories on TV or video, participating in book fairs, having parts of books read aloud to them, and hearing authors speak. They preferred sharing their books by talking with friends, developing AV productions, and having reading contests and prizes.

Studies have shown that students *do* like to read nonfiction. *The Guinness Book of World Records* is their favorite nonfiction book.

Multicultural literature focuses on religious minorities, people of different colors, and regional cultures. Presenting women in nonstereotypic roles also is included in multicultural literature. Multicultural literature helps students gain insight into how other people live, feel, think, and respond. It shows how people of all cultures are alike, and also how they are different.

Biography and folklore are two genres of multicultural literature. Biographies tell about people, their struggles and their successes. Folklore is made up of folktales, myths, legends, and hero tales (tall tales).

People, places, and history make up a third category of multicultural literature. We find out why people migrate to the United States, what their customs and beliefs are, and what they feel and think.

Fiction also provides us with multicultural awareness. The characters often face the conflict of trying to balance the beliefs and customs of their homeland with those of their new land.

There are numerous questions and activities you can use with your students to captivate their interest. Data retrieval charts, Venn diagrams, collages, writing autobiographies, writing excuses, and writing myths are only a few of the many activities cited.

Students can be directed to books in many ways. Interest inventories, reading aloud to students, and book sharing among students are several means.

POSTREADING

INTEGRATING WRITING

In your journal describe a teacher you had, and tell what she or he did to encourage students to read beyond classroom textbooks. How did you feel in this teacher's class? Describe a book you enjoyed reading while in middle or high school, and recall what made it so enjoyable.

REVIEW

Make a list of words and concepts related to Chapter 11. Organize these into a graphic organizer. Be able to explain why you organized them as you did.

PRACTICE

Do Enabling Activity 29 in Appendix A.

12

STUDENTS WITH SPECIAL NEEDS

"Recently, I read that about a fifth of our children live in poverty and a third grow up without adequate job skills," commented Joe.

"I've been reading about the drug abuse, child abuse, and poverty in our country and the effects they have on children. It's hard to believe that so many children are living at the poverty level," sighed Lynn.

"I didn't realize that there were so many at-risk students in a country like ours until I attended the last staff development meeting," added Toni.

"I know it's all hard to believe, but today's students aren't the same as the students I taught twenty years ago," replied Joe, "They seem to have so many more problems."

"I wonder what students twenty years from now will be like?" questioned Toni as the bell rang.

DISCUSS

What kinds of problems have you noticed among today's students? Should the classroom teacher be responsible for meeting the needs of the diverse population that we find in our schools? How can you meet the diverse needs of your students?

PREORGANIZE

Go through the chapter and make a skeletal outline of the major headings and subheadings. This will provide you with a chapter organizer. Predict the contents of the text under one of these subheadings.

OBJECTIVES

After reading this chapter, you should be able to

1. identify health and safety obstacles to success in school and their impact upon learning.
2. describe the language use of multicultural groups.
3. identify language interference problems of multiculturally diverse groups.
4. explain the provisions of Public Law 94-142 and its important implications for education.
5. specify the characteristics of students having special education needs and tell what classroom adjustments can be made for them.

If you were in the insurance business, what people would you insure? Would you insure people with physical or mental problems? Obviously not. You would insure people who were healthy. You would be in great risk of financial loss if you insured only high-risk customers (Vacca & Padak, 1990). Students with special needs are the "high-risk customers" of education. These are the students who are at risk—students affected by health and safety obstacles, culturally different students, and students with special education needs. These are the students who will probably not graduate from high school without educational intervention. Gifted and talented students, on the other hand, pose another set of challenges, and they too can become at-risk students.

These students account for the variations in student achievement we discussed in Chapter 1. They are the ones who require assignments of varying levels of difficulty and who especially need the alternative strategies we have presented throughout this book.

The changing demographics and social conditions of our country are creating major challenges for our schools and society at large. Who are these at-risk students? What challenges face our schools?

HEALTH AND SAFETY OBSTACLES

Some children face obstacles to success in school because of factors outside their own control. These involve health and safety issues. Let's look at a few statistics that shed light on the problem of at-risk students (Stevens & Price, 1992).

- Approximately 350,000 children each year are exposed to drugs, including alcohol, before they are born.
- Each year, some 37,000 prematurely born babies leave the hospital weighing less then 3 1/2 pounds. Many of these children will have severe learning problems.
- Three to four million children have been exposed to lead at damaging levels.
- Over 300,000 children are homeless each year.
- Between 15,000 and 30,000 children are infected with HIV.
- Over two million children are abused.

These conditions are not limited to any one social, economic, or cultural group—they cross all population lines.

Drug Abuse

The major cause of mental retardation in the Western world is fetal alcohol syndrome (FAS). Children and adolescents suffering from FAS have three characteristics: problems with the central nervous system (for example, hyperactive, poor attention, learning disabilities), facial and physical abnormalities, and low weight and short height. These children also are impulsive, communicate poorly, and associate with children younger than themselves. In adolescence they have trouble with depression and anxiety (Burgess & Streissguth, 1992).

At this time there is not much research on the effects of prenatal exposure to cocaine and other drugs. Griffith (1992) presents an overview of drug use and points out factors that interfere with a clear picture of the effects of drugs on children. Mothers taking drugs often receive little or no prenatal care and have poor nutrition.

Postnatal factors that result from drug use by parents also affect the child. Parents' behavior toward the child is unpredictable, and the child is often neglected by having poor medical care, poor nutrition, and an unstimulating learning environment.

Individually, these children have other problems. About 30 percent of children exposed to drugs have delayed language development. Children may have low tolerance levels for frustration and become easily over stimulated. They may withdraw or have difficulty controlling their behavior.

Aggressive Medical Treatment

Many children are alive and entering our schools today because of advances in medical treatment. These advances, however, are not without problems for families and schools. In fact, these treatments can create educational problems for children and later adults. Bartel and Thurman (1992) present an overview of children and these aggressive medical treatments.

More than half of all childhood cancers are the result of brain and nervous system tumors and leukemia. About 1 out of every 800 to 1,000 children is a survivor of cancer and has undergone such treatments as systemic drug therapy, radiation, and chemotherapy. The survival rate of children with leukemia has increased from three months of life in the 1950s to 80 percent being free of symptoms five years after diagnosis in the 1990s. Children who survive these cancers do have related problems though. The treatments often result in a decline in academic ability and cognitive functioning. These children have difficulty following directions, take more time at tasks, and learn slowly. They express themselves less, are less active, and have difficulty concentrating.

Low birth weight is another problem associated with aggressive medical practices. Each year 255,000 babies—or about 6.8 percent of all infants—are born with low birth weights (2.2 pounds or less). These infants tend to be more easily irritated, less easy to understand in the initial means of communication, and have less regular patterns of eating and sleeping. As a result of the children's under size and the parents' frustration in meeting their needs, these children grow to school-age amid a great deal of stress.

Lead Exposure

Estimates show that 16 percent of all American children (3 to 4 million) have blood levels of lead that are toxic to the neurological system. And we now know that lead poisoning has lasting effects. These high-lead-content blood levels are experienced by upper-class white children as well as poorer children. Lead "poisoning" is a very serious cause of learning problems and failure in school (Needleman, 1992).

Needleman (1992) continues that elevated lead levels (often found in bones and teeth) are associated with poorer language development, lower IQ scores, and poorer attention. These children have difficulty following directions, have trouble sticking to a task, are more easily distracted, and are less independent than other children.

Poverty and Homelessness

The Committee for Economic Development (CED) reported in 1989 that

over 20 percent of all children under eighteen currently live in families whose incomes fall below the poverty line, and 25 percent of all children under six are now living in poverty....

Children of single parents tend to do worse in school than those with two parents living at home, and their dropout rate is nearly twice as high. In 1985, 66 percent of black children, over 70 percent of Hispanic children, and nearly half of all white children lived in poverty. (p. 9)

The CED further reports that

over 50 percent of all welfare expenditures in this country go to families in which the mother began her parenting as a teenager....[and that] the United States has the highest rate of teenage pregnancy among all developing countries—seven times that of the Netherlands, three times that of Sweden, and more than twice that of Great Britain and Canada. (p. 25)

We are reminded by the Youth and America's Future Commission (1988) that poverty is highly correlated with school failure. The factors of minority status, being in a single-family home, or coming from a single-parent home are not the major reasons for school failure, although they may contribute to it. *Poverty* is the major cause of school failure.

Linehan (1992) reports on the number of homeless families and the effects of homelessness on children. The number of homeless families has increased over the years. Most of these families are headed by a single mother. Between 68,000 and half a million children are homeless each night in the United States. These figures do not include the estimated 14 million people who do not go to shelters (they live with relatives).

Homeless children often experience frequent moving, many school changes, tight and overcrowded places to live, and a lack of basic living necessities (adequate food, clothing, transportation, medical care). As a result, children often do not attend school, may be unable to participate in school activities (parties, trips), may come to school late, and may have very poor self-concepts.

HIV Infection

Human immunodeficiency virus (HIV) affects the central nervous system of children. Problems in all areas of development may occur as a result of HIV—motor, language, cognitive, sensory, and social. In 1991 there were 3,426 known cases of HIV in children under thirteen; the actual number of children with HIV infection may be three times higher (Seidel, 1992).

Seidel (1992) indicates that other factors besides HIV infection may account for the developmental delays of these children. Inadequate prenatal care, improper nutrition, parents on drugs, and low birth weights are some factors.

Child Abuse

Children may be physically, sexually, and/or emotionally abused. Children who experience physical and verbal abuse may exhibit impulsive behavior, excessive physical activity, and short attention spans. Their sequential memory may be weak. They may have difficulty with cause-effect relationships because their parents control them and don't allow them to experiment with and explore their environment. They may be timid and fearful. They have difficulty making a distinction between their feelings and behavior. Communicating with words is a struggle and they use gestures to keep people at a distance. Games and recess time become stressful because of the rules imposed and practice required (Craig, 1992).

Early intervention for children facing health and safety obstacles is essential. Teaching communication skills, enhancing social skills, and targeting daily living skills are the challenges of parents, educators, and community leaders.

MULTICULTURAL DIVERSITY

The Commission on Work, Family and Citizenship (1989) projects that during the 1990s more than 30 percent of the young people in the United States will be from minority groups.

> More than 15 percent of all youth will be black, about 4.5 percent Native American and Asian and Pacific Islander, and perhaps 12 percent Hispanic....For example, nearly 875,000 youth, mostly from Mexico and the Caribbean,...applied for resident status under the provisions of the Immigration Reform and Control Act of 1986. (p. 3)

The commission goes on to report that the educational level of young immigrants is often much lower than that of native-born youth of the same cultural group. For example, 76.9 percent of the American-born Mexican youth completed high school and 6.4 percent college in contrast to 21.5 percent and 1.1 percent, respectively, of new immigrants.

The way language is used in the home, and language interference problems that arise when students change from one language to another, may affect school success. Teachers awareness of these differences will enhance students' chances of success.

A survey of literature generated at California State University (1986) describes differences in the language uses of Chinese American and Mexican American families. Chinese Americans label, or name, secondary items (like shoes, house, specific vegetable names) for children. If children label an item incorrectly (call a cat a dog), the adults quickly supply the correct label without judgment. Discussions in the home often make reference to correct behavior, and showing emotions is discouraged. Children are encouraged to talk about events, happenings, or experiences with family members; however, outside the home children are expected to listen. Parents talk to their children about events that are happening or will happen. They talk about and read books with their children and tell their children stories about people and events in history.

Mexican American families attach labels to primary items, such as family members' names and the names of pictures on television. Labeling secondary items is less likely to occur. Parents rarely ask children to talk about events that happened in the past if they already know about them. Children, however, are encouraged to talk with other adults about happenings that would be news to them. Adults very seldom talk about what they are doing at the moment, but they do talk about and plan things in the future. Scary stories usually are told by children and adults. Books are not usually available in the home because they are not promoted commercially in Mexico.

In addition to the way language is used in the home, we can look at the language interference that occurs when students move from one language to another. It is beneficial for teachers to understand some of the language interferences of multicultural groups so that they will recognize why students communicate orally and in writing as they do. In Figures 12–1, 12–2, and 12–3, we summarize some of the language differences between English and Spanish, Creole, and black English, respectively.

Creole is based on the French language for its vocabulary but on African languages for its structure. Figure 12–2 presents some of the differences between Creole and English. Many of these differences are the same as those faced by Spanish-speaking students.

In the same manner that Spanish and Creole have their unique characteristics that interfere with speaking English, nonstandard English (often referred to as black English) has its unique characteristics that cause interferences. Figure 12–3 presents some of these linguistic differences.

As you review these language interferences, think about your students' reading and writing. Are all miscues in reading the result of students not knowing the words? Or might they be the result of students not hearing or having difficulty making the sounds of English? Are all writing errors the result of not knowing how to form a sentence or paragraph? Or might they be the result of using language structures that differ from those of English?

FIGURE 12–1 • Language Interferences of Spanish

Phonology

1. No short vowel sounds.
2. Consonant sound substitutions

English		*Spanish Substitution*	
b	(box)	v	(vox)
j	(jet)	y	(yet)
j	(jet)	ch	(chet)
m	(Sam)	ng	(sang)
n	(run)	ng	(rung)
s	(sell)	z	(zell)
sh	(ship)	ch	(chip)
th	(than)	d	(Dan)
th	(they)	s	(say)
w	(wait)	g	(gate)

3. Difficulty with final consonant sounds because only a limited number occur in Spanish. Consonants that cause difficulty: b, g, h, k, m, p, s, and v.
4. Difficulty with final consonant digraphs. Consonant digraphs that cause difficulty: voiced th, unvoiced th, sh, and ch.
5. Difficulty with certain initial consonant blends: sk, sm, sn, sp, st, scr, shr, spl, spr, and str.

Grammar

1. In Spanish *no* is used to mean both "not" and "no."

   English: She did not go.
   Spanish: She no go.

2. The words *do, does,* and *did* are not used to form questions.

   English: Did you go shopping?
   Spanish: You go shopping? (raising intonation)

3. Adjectives follow nouns.

   English: The box is heavy.
   Spanish: The box heavy.

FIGURE 12–1 • *Continued*

4. *To be* is not used to express temperature, age, or state of being.

> *English:* I am 18 years old.
> *Spanish:* I have 18 years.

5. The prepositions *in* and *on* are not used. Instead, *en* is used.

> *English:* The pot is on the stove.
> *Spanish:* The pot is en the stove.

6. The comparative and superlative suffixes *er* and *est* are not used. Instead, *more* and *the most* are used.

> *English:* John is the biggest.
> *Spanish:* John is the most big.

7. Adjectives come after nouns.

> *English:* The big dog.
> *Spanish:* The dog big.

8. Articles are used with professional titles.

> *English:* I saw Dr. Lynn.
> *Spanish:* I saw the Dr. Lynn.

FIGURE 12–2 • **Language Interferences of Creole**

Phonology

1. No short vowel sounds.
2. Consonant sound substitutions.

English		Creole Substitution	
r	(ripe)	w	(wipe)
sh	(shin)	ch	(chin)
th	(think)	sh	(sink)
th	(them)	z	(zem)
n	(run)	ng	(rung)

3. Difficulty with final consonant digraphs because only a limited number are used in Creole. Difficulty with b, f, g, h, k, m, p, s, and v.
4. Difficulty with final consonant digraphs: unvoiced th, voiced th, sh, and ch.
5. Difficulty with certain initial consonant blends: sk, sm, sn, sp, st, scr, shr, spl, spr, and str.

Grammar

1. Plurals are not made by adding *s*. Instead *yo* is placed after the noun.
2. There are not variant forms of pronouns (such as, *they, them, their, he, she, it*). *He* is used to refer to males, females, and objects.
3. The verb *to be* is not used.
4. Definite articles (*the*) are used after nouns, not before.

FIGURE 12–3   •   Language Interferences of Black English

Phonology

1. The final consonants *d, t,* and *k* are omitted.

English	*Black English*
told	tol
lift	lif
risk	ris

2. Plural and past tense endings are omitted.

English	*Black English*
rocks	rock
boots	boot
stopped	stop
barked	bark

3. The *r* and *l* sounds are omitted at the ends of words.

English	*Black English*
tore	toe
door	doe
stool	stoo
mail	may

4. Various consonant sounds are substituted for *th*.

English	*Black English*	
this	dis	(the sound of *d* at the beginning)
mother	muver	(the sounds of *v, dd,* or *tt* in the middle)
	mudder	
	mutter	
with	wif	(the sound of *f* at the end of words)

Grammar

1. Double negatives are used.

   English: I don't have any bananas.
   Black English: I don't have no bananas

2. *S* is added to irregular plurals.

   English: men, feet
   Black English: mens, feets

3. The root word is used for third-person agreement.

   English: John walks every morning.
   Black English: John walk every morning.

4. The pronouns *they* and *them* are substituted for *their* and *those*.

   English: They carried their balloons.
                     Send me those letters.

FIGURE 12–3 • *Continued*

Black English: They carried they balloons.
Send me them letters.

5. Omissions and substitutions are made for the verb *to be*.

English: Sam is running
Sam is tired. (at this time)
Sam is tired. (all the time)
They (we, you) were running.
Black English: Sam running.
Sam be tired.
Sam bes tired.
They (we, you) was running.

6. The word *done* is substituted for *have*.

English: I have completed my homework.
Black English: I done my homework.

Source: Adapted from J. R. Harber & J. N. Beatty (1978), *Reading and the Black English-speaking child.* (Newark, Del.: International Reading Association.); and N. R. Bartel, J. J. Grill, & D. N. Bryen (1973), Language characteristics of Black children: Implications for assessment, *Journal of School Psychology, 11,* 351–364.

Within the learning structure, provide many concrete experiences for students. Use picture books containing visual representations of the written text. Provide many oral experiences prior to reading. Concentrate on survival words (*food, door,* and the like) before moving to the abstract. During writing assignments, provide sentence patterns that students may copy, substitute words in, and expand on. Provide a "buddy" who speaks both English and the student's primary language.

SPECIAL EDUCATION NEEDS

Meeting the needs of people with "special needs" was not always a priority or goal of society. At one time these people where placed in so-called poorhouses. Later they were relegated in residential schools (Templeton, 1991). Placing such children and adults in residential schools was common until the 1960s.

In 1975, Congress passed Public Law 94-142—The Education of All Handicapped Children Act. This law mandated that all students should receive free public education in the "least restrictive environment." It specified that children who can benefit from placement in a regular classroom should be placed there for part, or all, of the school day. This law led the way to what we presently call mainstreaming.

Public Law 99-457 extends the provisions of Public Law 94-142, calling for servicing children from birth to five years old if they are classified as at-risk.

We can classify students receiving special services into the following categories: children with learning disabilities, physically challenged, mentally challenged, and gifted. We will consider each of these groups in this section.

People with Learning Disabilities

Learning disabled (LD) students have been referred to by numerous labels. Some of these labels include dyslexic, brain injured, and minimal brain dysfunctional. These are children of normal intelligence who have severe difficulty with language and/or mathematics. It is estimated that 3 to 5 percent of school-age youth have learning disabilities.

If you were to observe the reading of students with learning disabilities, you would notice that they reverse words, lose their place, confuse similar words and letters, and repeat words during reading. In spelling they place letters in the wrong order, reverse words and letters, and have difficulty with phoneme-grapheme relationships. In handwriting they may form letters incorrectly—even when looking at them; they also have difficulty staying on the line, copying from the board, and completing written assignments on time. They may be quite withdrawn, easily distracted, disorganized, unable to follow directions, and may have difficulty relating to others.

Letting students use typewriters and computers for written work is beneficial, as is allowing students to tape record assignments. Provide many prereading experiences for students prior to reading (see Chapter 6). And after reading, provide many opportunities for students to use the information (see Chapter 7).

Physically Challenged

Physical challenges (visual, auditory, and other physical challenges) do not have to be a handicap to learning. Many of today's advances in technology can ameliorate or help students cope with their challenges. Three categories of physical challenges will be outlined in this section: visual, auditory, and other physical challenges.

Visually Challenged

Visually challenged students range from those who are totally blind and must rely solely on their auditory and tactile senses, to students who cannot see as well as other students with their vision corrected. These are students whose vision cannot be totally corrected with glasses.

You probably have heard of the terms *myopia* (nearsightedness, or the ability to see things best at a close distance), *hyperopia* (farsightedness, or the ability to see things best in the distance), and *strabismus* (cross-eyedness). These are several of the visual challenges that affect the reading achievement of some students, but not others. It is an individual matter.

Figure 12–4 presents a checklist you can use to help ascertain if a student is visually challenged. Remember, one or two symptoms do not mean a student has a visual problem, but a number of symptoms in combination with their intensity may indicate referral to an ophthalmologist.

Within the classroom these students might need special lighting, special magnifiers, braille materials, audiotapes, or large-print books. Other adjustments might include providing well-lighted areas for working, avoiding glare whenever possible, using large letters when writing on the board, giving students shortened

---

FIGURE 12–4 • Checklist for Vision

_____ closing or covering one eye

_____ red and watery eyes

_____ squinting

_____ complaints of blurred vision

_____ complaints of double vision

_____ tilting the head

_____ frequent blinking

_____ complaints of headaches

_____ losing place frequently

_____ skipping lines when reading

_____ frequent omissions of words

_____ holding books too close

_____ avoidance of close work

_____ not being able to see the board

_____ errors in copying from the board

_____ errors in copying from books and papers

_____ trouble staying on lines when writing

---

assignments, giving students breaks when doing close work, or letting students tape record assignments. Instead of writing, students might well use typewriters or computers.

Auditorially Challenged

Auditory, or hearing, losses vary in type and severity. Students in your classes may range from mild loss to total hearing loss. Students with a mild loss may be able to hear sounds in the distance. Those with mild to severe losses need hearing aids and special training in lip reading, making the phonemes of our language, using the intonational system of our language, or controlling the loudness of their speech.

Students with auditory losses may have difficulty with the learning process because of inaccurate hearing and the loss of high-frequency consonant sounds. You will recall from Chapter 1 that consonant sounds are more important in word attack than vowel sounds. Inaccurate hearing may result in the mispronunciation of words and the inability to follow class discussions or directions.

Figure 12–5 presents a checklist for observing the hearing of students. Remember, these do not always indicate a hearing loss, but in combination they may be signs that the child should be tested by an audiologist.

After referral to an audiologist, you can make classroom adjustments for these students by standing close to the student when speaking, avoiding standing in front of windows, being sure the student can see your lips when speaking, not facing the

FIGURE 12–5 • Checklist for Hearing

_____ inattention during class

_____ inappropriate responses during class

_____ asking questions that have already been answered

_____ inability to follow oral directions

_____ frequent requests to have directions repeated

_____ cupping the ear with hand

_____ turning one ear toward the speaker

_____ focusing on speaker's lips

_____ frowning while listening

_____ speaking in an excessively loud voice

_____ speaking in a monotone

_____ speech difficulties

_____ complaints of dizziness

_____ complaints of earaches

_____ discharges from the ear

chalkboard when talking, giving the student a seat in the front of the room or near the group speaking, using visual activities whenever possible, giving the student written directions for activities, and speaking loudly and clearly. Wearing bright lipstick will help students see your lips. Assign the student a "pal" to repeat directions if necessary.

Other Physical Challenges

Children with many types of physical challenges (e.g., muscular dystrophy, cystic fibrosis, spinal injuries) that inhibit movement are being integrated into the regular classroom. These students often need special seating and assistance with writing and speaking. You may need to alter physical activities or give alternate assignments. Computers can help with fine-motor writing activities.

Mentally Challenged

The classification of students by mental differences is usually expressed as an IQ score. IQ is expressed by the formula

$$(MA - CA) \times 100 = IQ$$

in which, MA = mental age; CA = chronological age; and IQ = intelligence quotient. Mental age refers to the student's present development in comparison to other students of the same age. Chronological age is the student's present age. If a student's mental age is lower than his or her chronological age, the IQ will be below 100. The following guides are used to classify students' learning level according to IQ.

Classification of Learner	*IQ Range*
Gifted or talented	130 and above
Average	90–110
Slow (borderline)	71–85
Mild retardation (educable)	56–70
Moderate retardation (trainable)	41–55
Severe or profound retardation	40 and lower

In this section we will discuss slow learners.

Slow learners account for about 14 percent of the school population. These students are more concrete learners, have shorter attention spans, and need help organizing. Gunning (1992) refers to these students as "more so" students. Basically, they need the same instruction as average students, but "more so"—more guidance, more reinforcement, more practice, more patience, and more materials at their instructional levels.

These students need to have you break down learning tasks into smaller units. They need close supervision to catch difficulties as they work through tasks. And they need minimal distractions (Rubin, 1985). These students also need a great deal of concept development work, direct, purposeful experiences, survival vocabulary (for reading signs, restaurant menus), and listening and speaking activities.

SUGGESTIONS AND INSIGHTS FOR WORKING WITH AT-RISK STUDENTS

Stevens and Price (1992) make several suggestions for school-family cooperation in working with at-risk students.

- Make school libraries open after school hours. Include materials on child care, and provide opportunities for a library forum in which parents can share concerns, interests, and skills.
- Show parents how to reinforce skills taught in school in meaningful, authentic situations—for example, writing thank-you letters, calculating the cost of a pizza with two toppings before ordering it.
- Use portfolio assessment (discussed in Chapter 3) to form a basis for communication and to show examples of student work.
- Show how school activities can be incorporated into community issues.
- Provide referral services to support parents in meeting the needs of their children.

Hill (1991, p. 310) gives us these insights for understanding at-risk students.

- Failure hurts.
- Being forced to do something in front of others—particularly something "simple"—can be humiliating.
- Failure prompts impulses to escape, distract, cheat, and attack.
- Failure can come from simply not knowing how to think about a task.
- Wanting to learn and being able to learn are two different things.
- Being forced to do something is painful but may be a necessary first step if you are going to improve.
- When you are thinking poorly, it helps if people try to understand how you are thinking.
- Taking time to talk about the way you think can change the way you think.
- Learning different specific strategies for thinking is motivating.
- Success and learning cross-fertilize one another.
- Nothing is more important than being accepted and affirmed for who you are.

GIFTED AND TALENTED STUDENTS

Gifted and talented students present another challenge for teachers. Public Law 97-35 specifies gifted students as giving "evidence of high performance capability in areas such as intellectual, creative, artistic, leadership capacity, or specific academic fields." IQ, however, is the primary determiner of being classified as gifted.

Gifted students should not simply be doing more of the same things that others in the classroom are doing, nor should they be expected to have the same interests as adults or behave like adults. Utilizing materials that capitalize on our literary heritage is advantageous. Provide opportunities for gifted students to engage in higher levels of abstract thinking. Let students pursue topics of study in depth. Have them branch out into more diverse research methods and materials, including interviews. Teach these students the study skills and time management strategies they need to tackle the independent learning they are so capable of (Hoskisson & Tompkins, 1987). If not challenged, these students are at risk of dropping out of school from boredom.

If we take the time to understand at-risk students, they can become "students of promise."

CONCLUSION

Health and safety obstacles that affect their lives and learning must be overcome by students. The use of drugs and alcohol by parents before children are born, the effects of aggressive medical treatment, exposure to lead, poverty and home-lessness, HIV infection, and child abuse—these are conditions the students did not create yet must contend with day after day.

The multicultural diversity of our country is increasing. The way language is used in the homes of students, and the language differences caused by shifting from one language to another, affect academic progress.

Public Law 94–142 mandates that all students having special needs be taught in the "least restrictive environment." This law led the way to what we presently call mainstreaming.

Learning disabled youth comprise about 3 to 5 percent of our population. LD students confuse words, put letters in the wrong places, write letters backwards, and have trouble keeping their writing on lines.

Physical challenges include visual impairment, hearing impairment, and other challenges that impair movement.

Learners are often classified according to their rate or capacity for learning, called IQ. Gifted students have IQs of 130 and above. Slow, or borderline, students have IQs of 71–85. Our average student's IQ is between 90 and 110.

POSTREADING

INTEGRATING WRITING

In your journal describe one or two experiences you have had with mainstreaming. Describe ways you know of to help students who have special needs succeed.

REVIEW

Make a list of words and concepts related to Chapter 12. Organize these into a graphic organizer. Be able to explain why you organized them as you did.

PRACTICE

Do Enabling Activity 30 in Appendix A.

REFERENCES

Aaronson, E. (1978). *The jigsaw classroom*. Beverly Hills: Sage Publications.

Aaronson, S. (1975). Notetaking improvement: A combined auditory, functional and psychological approach. *Journal of Reading, 19,* 8–12.

Allen, A. A. and Mountain, L. (1992). When inner city black children go on-line at home. *The Computing Teacher, 20* (3), 35–37.

Alvermann, D. E., Dillon, D. R., O'Brien, D. G., and Smith, L. C. (1985). The role of the textbook in discussion. *Journal of Reading, 29,* 50–57.

Anderson, J. (1983). Lix and Rix: Variations on a little-known readability index. *Journal of Reading, 26,* 490–496.

Anderson, R. C., and Pearson, P. D. (1984). A scheme-theoretical view of basic processes in reading. In P. D. Pearson (ed.), *Handbook of reading research*. New York: Longman.

Anderson, T. H. (1980). Study strategies and adjunct aids. In R. J. Spiro, B. C. Bruce, and W. F. Brewer (eds.); *Theoretical issues in reading comprehension: Perspectives from cognitive psychology, articifial intelligence, linguistics and education*. Hillsdale, N.J.: Erlbaum.

Applebee, A. N., Langer, J. A., and Mullis, I. (1988). *Who reads best? Factors relating to reading achievement in grades 3, 7, and 11*. Princeton: Educational Testing Service.

Armbruster, B. B., Osborn, J. H., and Davison, A. I. (1985). Readability formulas may be dangerous to your textbooks. *Educational Leadership, 42* (4), 18–20.

Arthur, S. V. (1981). Writing in the content areas. In E. K. Dishner, T. W. Bean, and J. E. Readence (eds.), *Reading in the content areas: Improving classroom instruction*. Dubuque: Kendall/Hunt.

Asch, S. E. (1969). Reformulation of the problem of association. *American Psychologist, 24,* 92–102.

Au, K. H. (1993). *Literacy instruction in multicultural settings*. Fort Worth: Harcourt Brace Jovanovich.

Ausubel, D. P. (1968). *Educational psychology: A cognitive view*. New York: Holt, Rinehart & Winston.

———. (1963). *The psychology of meaningful verbal learning*. New York: Grune & Stratton.

———. (1960). The use of advance organizers in the learning and retention of meaningful verbal materials. *Journal of Educational Psychology, 51,* 267–272.

Ausubel, D. P. and Youssef, M. (1965). The effect of spaced repetition on meaningful retention. *Journal of General Psychology, 73,* 147–150.

Baker, R. L. (1971). *The use of information organizers in ninth grade social studies classes.* Ph.D. dissertation, Syracuse University.

Banks, J. A. (1991). *Teaching strategies for ethnic studies.* 5th ed. Boston: Allyn and Bacon.

Banks, N. (1975). *Quiz book on the American revolution.* New York: Bantam Books.

Bartel, N. R., and Thurman, S. K. (1992). Medical treatment and educational problems in children. *Phi Delta Kappan, 74,* 57–61.

Bean, T. W., and Pardi, R. (1979). A field test of a guided reading strategy. *Journal of Reading, 23,* 144–147.

Bean, T. W., and Peterson, J. (1981). Reasoning guides: Fostering reading in content areas. *Reading Horizons, 21,* 196–199.

Bean, T. W., Singer, H., Sorter, J., and Frazee, C. (1986). The effect of metacognitive instruction in outlining and graphic organizer construction on students' comprehension in a tenth-grade world history class. *Journal of Reading Behavior, 18* (2), 153–169.

Beck, I. L., McKeown, M. G., and Omanson, R. C. (1987). The effects and uses of diverse vocabulary instructional techniques. In M. G. McKeown and M. E. Curtis (eds.), *The nature of vocabulary acquisition,* 147–163. Hillsdale, N.J.: Lawrence Erlbaum.

Berkowitz, S. J. (1986). Effects of instruction in text organization on sixth-grade students' memory for expository reading. *Reading Research Quarterly, 21,* 161–178.

Berry, S. M. (1986). Tired of just reading the text and answering questions? If so, write books. *English in Texas, 17* (2), 18–20.

Best, A. (1992). Crossroads. *The Computing Teacher, 20* (3), 5.

Blake, H., and Spennato, N. A. (1980). The directed writing activity: A process with structure. *Language Arts, 57,* 317–318.

Blanchard, J. S., and Mason, G. E. (1985). Using computers in content areas reading instruction. *Journal of Reading, 29,* 112–117.

Blanchard, J. S., Mason, G. E., and Daniel, D. (1987). *Computer Applications in Reading.* 3rd ed. Newark, Delaware: International Reading Association.

Blanchowicz, C. L. Z. (1985). Vocabulary development and reading: From research to instruction. *The Reading Teacher, 38,* 876–881.

Blanton, W., Farr, R., and Rudman, J. J. (1972). *Reading tests for the secondary grades: A review and evaluation.* Newark, Del.: International Reading Association.

Bloom, B., et al. (1956 & 1984). *Taxonomy of educational objectives:* Book 1 *Cognitive domain.* New York: Longman.

Bormuth, J. R. (1968). Cloze test readability: Criterion reference scores. *Journal of Educational Measurement, 5,* 189–196.

Brandt, R. (1987). On cooperation in schools: A conversation with David and Roger Johnson. *Educational Leadership, 3,* 14–19.

Brophy, J. (Spring 1981). Teacher praise: A functional analysis. *Review of Educational Research,* p. 26. Washington, D.C.: American Educational Research Association.

Brophy, J., and Good, T. (1974). *Teacher-student relationships: Causes and consequences.* New York: Holt, Rinehart & Winston.

Brozo, W. G. (1986). Making the connection: Writing in the content areas. *Journal of Reading, 29,* 357–359.

Bruner, J. S. (1961). The act of discovery. *Harvard Educational Review, 37,* 21–32.

Burgess, D. M. and Streissguth, S. T. (1992). Fetal alcohol syndrome and fetal alcohol effects: Principles for education. *Phi Delta Kappan, 74,* 24–26, 28, 30.

Burmeister, L. E. (1976). Vocabulary development in content areas through the use of morphemes. *Journal of Reading, 19,* 481–487.

Burns, P. C., Roe, B. D., and Ross, E. P. (1984). *Teaching reading in today's elementary schools.* 3rd ed. Boston: Houghton Mifflin.

Calkins, L. M. (1983). *Lessons from a child*. Exeter, N.H.: Heinemann.

Capuzzi, D. (1973). Information intermix. *Journal of Reading, 16,* 453–458.

Carr, E. M. (1985). The vocabulary overview guide: A metacognitive strategy to improve vocabulary comprehension and retention. *Journal of Reading, 28,* 684–689.

Carter, B. (1987). *A content analysis of the most frequently circulated information books in three junior high libraries*. Doctoral dissertation, University of Houston.

Carter, B., and Abrahamson, R. F. (1990). *Nonfiction for young adults; from delight to wisdom*. Phoenix: Oryx Press.

Carter, B. B. (1974). Helping seventh graders to understand figurative expressions. *Journal of Reading, 20,* 553–558.

Carver, R. P. (1992). Reading rate: Theory, research, and practical implications. *Journal of Reading, 36* (2), 84–95.

Casale, U. P. (1985). Motor imaging: A reading-vocabulary strategy. *Journal of Reading, 28,* 619–621.

Castallo, R. (1976). Listening guides: A first step toward notetaking and listening skills. *Journal of Reading, 19,* 289–290.

Caughran, A., and Mountain, L. H. (1962). *Reading Skillbook 1*. New York: American Book Company.

Cheek, M. C., and Cheek, E. H. (1980). *Diagnostic prescriptive reading instruction*. Dubuque: Wm. C. Brown.

Childrey, J. A., Jr. (1980). Read a book in an hour. *Reading Horizons, 20,* 174–176.

Clary, L. M. (1991). Getting adolescents to read. *Journal of Reading, 34* (5), 340–345.

———. (1986). Twelve "musts" for improved reading comprehension. *Reading Horizons, 26,* 99–104.

Clary, L. M., and Smith, S. J. (1986). Selecting basal reading series: The need for a validated process. *The Reading Teacher, 39,* 390–394.

Clewell, S. F., and Haldemos, J. (1983). Organizational strategies to increase comprehension. *Reading World, 22,* 314–321.

Coffman, G., and Sharpe, R. A. (1993). Understandings of literacy portfolios. *The Abstract, 13* (1), 9–13.

Commission on Reading. (1985). *Becoming a nation of readers*. Washington, D.C.: U.S. Department of Education.

Conley, M. W. (1992). *Content reading instruction: A communication approach*. New York: McGraw-Hill.

Coon, G. E. (1976). Homophones. *Reading Teacher, 29,* 652.

Cooper, J. M., Hansen, J., Martorella, P. H., et al. (1977). *Classroom teaching skills: A handbook*. Lexington, Mass.: D. C. Heath.

Couch, L. L. (1983). Anatomy of a writing assignment, or how dieting can improve your students' writing. *English Journal, 72* (5), 29–31.

Craig, S. E. (1992). The educational needs of children living with violence. *Phi Delta Kappan, 74,* 67–68, 70–71.

Crawley, S. J., and Merritt, K. (1991). *Remediating reading difficulties*. Dubuque: Wm C. Brown.

Crawley, S. J., and Mountain, L. (1981). Opinion polls and values clarification. *The Social Studies, 72*(6), 271–272.

Cunningham, D., and Shablak, S. L. (1975). Selective reading guide-o-rama: The content teacher's best friend. *Journal of Reading, 18,* 380–382.

Cunningham, J. W., Cunningham, P. M., and Arthur, S. (1981). *Middle and secondary school reading*. New York: Longman.

Cunningham, P., Crawley, S., and Mountain, L. (1983). Vocabulary scavenger hunts: A scheme for schema development. *Reading Horizons, 24,* 45–50.

Cunningham, P. M., and Cunningham, J. W. (1976). Improving listening in content area subjects. *National Association of Secondary School Principals Bulletin, 60*(404), 26–31.

———. (1976). SSSW, better content writing. *The Clearing House, 49,* 237–238.

Dale, E. (Dec. 1965). Vocabulary measurement: Techniques and major findings. *Elementary English,* 895–901, 948.

———. (1969). *Audio visual methods in teaching.* 3rd ed. Holt, Rinehart & Winston.

Dale, E., and Raths, L. (1945). Discussion in the secondary school. *Educational Research Bulletin, 24,* 1–6.

Darch, C. B., Carnine, D. W., and Kameenui, E. J. (1986). The role of graphic organizers and social structure in content area instruction. *Journal of Reading Behavior, 18*(4), 275–295.

Davis, C. A., and Irwin, J. W. (1980). Assessing readability: The checklist approach. *Journal of Reading, 24,* 124–131.

DeCecco, J. P. (1968). *The psychology of learning and instruction: Educational phychology.* Englewood Cliffs, N.J.: Prentice-Hall.

DeFina, A. A. (1992). *Portfolio assessment: Getting started.* New York: Scholastic.

DeVries, D. L., and Slavin, R. W. (1978). Teams-games-tournament: A research review. *Journal of Research and Development in Education, 12,* 28–38.

Diakiw, J. Y. (1990). Children's literature and global education: Understanding the developing world. *The Reading Teacher, 43* (4), 296–300.

Dishner, E. K., Bean, T. W., and Readence, J. E. (1981). *Reading in the content areas: Improving classroom instruction.* Dubuque: Kendall/Hunt.

Dishner, E. K., and Readence, J. E. (1977). A systematic procedure for teaching main idea. *Reading World, 16,* 292–298.

Dockterman, D. A. (1991). *Great teaching in the one-computer classroom.* Cambridge, Mass.: Tom Snyder Productions.

Donlan, D. (1980). Locating main ideas in history textbooks. *Journal of Reading, 24,* 135–140.

Dudycha, G. J. (1957). *Learn more with less effort.* New York: Harper & Row.

Dueck, K. (1986). Classroom notebook writing: RAFT. *Kappa Delta Pi Record, 22* (2), 64.

Duffelmeyer, F. A. (1985). Teaching word meanings from an experience base. *The Reading Teacher, 39,* 6–9.

Duffy, G. G., and Roehler, L. R. (1984). Improving reading instruction through the use of responsive elaboration. *The Reading Teacher, 40,* 514–520.

———. (1986). The subtleties of instructional mediation. *Educational Leadership, 43*(7), 23–27.

Dunn, R., and Dunn, K. (1978). *Teaching students through their individual learning styles: A practical approach.* Reston, Va.: Reston.

Dweck, C., et al. (1978). Sex differences in learned helplessness. II: The contingencies of evaluative feedback in the classroom; and III: An experimental analysis. *Developmental Psychology, 14,* 268–276.

Eanet, M. G., and Manzo, A. V. (1976). REAP: A strategy for improving reading/writing/study skills. *Journal of Reading, 19,* 647–652.

Earle, R. A., and Barron, R. F. (1973). An approach for teaching vocabulary in content subjects. In H. L. Herber and R. F. Barron (eds.), *Research in reading in the content areas: Second year report.* Syracuse: Syracuse University Reading and Language Arts Center, 84–100.

Edwards, P. (1973). Panorama: A study technique. *Journal of Reading, 17,* 132–135.

Edwards, T. L. (1977). *Puzzles.* New York: Waldman.

Eichholz, G., and Barbe, R. (1961). An experiment in vocabulary development. *Educational Research Bulletin, 40,* 1–7, 28.

Ekwall, E. E., and Shanker, J. L. (1983). *Diagnosis and remediation of the disabled reader.* 2nd ed. Boston: Allyn and Bacon.

Ellis, S. S., and Whalen, S. F. (1990). *Cooperative learning: Getting started.* New York: Scholastic.

Espy, W. (1972). *The game of words.* Columbus, Ohio: Charles Merrill.

Estes, T. H. (1970). *Use of guide materials and small group discussion in reading ninth grade social studies assignments.* Ph.D. dissertation, Syracuse University.

Faw, H. W., and Walker, T. G. (1976). Mathemagenic behaviors and efficiency in learning from prose materials: Review, critique, and recommendations. *Review of Educational Research, 46,* 691–720.

Fay, L. (1965). Reading study skills: Math and science. In J. A. Figurel (ed.), *Reading and Inquiry.* Newark, Del.: International Reading Association.

Fletcher, H. (1979). *Puzzles, puzzles and more puzzles.* New York: Platt & Munk.

Flood, J. (1986). The text, the student, and the teacher: Learning from exposition in middle schools. *The Reading Teacher, 39,* 784–791.

Flood, J. and Lapp, D. (1990). Reading comprehension instruction for at-risk students: Research based practices that can make a difference. *Journal of Reading, 33*(7), 490–496.

Florio, S., and Clark, C. M. (1982). The functions of writing in the elementary school. *Research in Teaching of English, 16,* 115–120.

Frager, A. M. (1993). Affective dimensions of content area reading. *Journal of Reading, 36* (8), 616–622.

Fry, E. (1968). A readability formula that saves time. *Journal of Reading, 11,* 513–516, 575–578.

———. (1977). Fry's readability graph: Clarifications, validity, and extension to level 17. *Journal of Reading, 21,* 242–252.

———. (1978). *Skimming and scanning.* Providence: Jamestown.

Frymier, J. (1985). *Motivation to learn.* West Lafayette, Ind.: Kappa Delta Pi.

Fulwiler, T. (1980). Journals across the disciplines. *English Journal, 69* (9), 14–19.

Garner, R., and Kraus, C. (1981–82). Good and poor comprehender differences in knowing and regulating reading behaviors. *Educational Research Quarterly, 6* (4), 5–12.

Garner, R., and Reis, R. (1981). Monitoring and resolving comprehension obstacles: An investigation of spontaneous text lookbacks among upper-grade good and poor comprehenders. *Reading Research Quarterly, 16,* 569–582.

Gauthier, L. R. (1990). Helping middle school students develop language facility. *Journal of Reading, 34* (4), 274–276.

———. (1991). Using journals for content area comprehension. *Journal of Reading, 34*(6), 491–492.

Gentile, L. M., and McMillan, M. M. (1977). Why won't teenagers read? *Journal of Reading, 20* (8), 649–654.

Geva, E. (1983). Facilitating reading comprehension through flowcharting. *Reading Research Quarterly, 18,* 384–405.

Glenn, A. D., and Lewis, V. J. (1982). Analyzing the textbook to improve student reading and learning. *Reading World, 21,* 293–298.

Goodman, K. S. (1970). Behind the eye: What happens in reading. In K. S. Goodman and O. S. Niles (eds.), *Reading process and program.* Urbana, Ill.: National Council of Teachers of English.

Grant, R. (1993). Strategic training for using text headings to improve students' processing of content. *Journal of Reading, 36* (6), 482–488.

Graves, D. H. (1983). *Writing: Teachers and children at work.* Exeter, N.H.: Heinemann.

Graves, M. F. (1986). Vocabulary learning and instruction. In E. Z. Rothkopf (ed.), *Review of Research in Education, 13,* 49–90. Washington, D.C.: American Educational Research Association.

Gunning, T. (1992). *Creating reading instruction for all children.* Boston: Allyn & Bacon.

Guthrie, J. T. (1973). Reading comprehension and syntactic responses in good and poor readers. *Journal of Educational Psychology, 65,* 294–299.

Guthrie, J. T., et al. (1974). The maze technique to assess, monitor reading comprehension. *The Reading Teacher, 28,* 161–168.

Hanf, M. B. (1971). Mapping: A technique for translating reading into thinking. *Journal of Reading, 14,* 225–230, 270.

Hansell, T. S. (1978). Stepping up to outlining. *Journal of Reading, 22,* 248–252.

Hansen, J., and Hubbard, R. (1984). Poor readers can draw inferences. *The Reading Teacher, 37,* 586–589.

Harker, W. J. (1977). Selecting instructional materials for content area reading. *Journal of Reading, 21,* 126–130.

Harris, J. (1985). The cloze procedure: Writing applications. *Journal of Teaching Writing, 4,* 105–111.

Hash, R. J. (1974). *The effects of a strategy of structured overviews, levels guides and vocabulary exercises on student achievement, reading comprehension, critical thinking and attitudes of junior high school classes in social studies.* Ed.D. dissertation, Syracuse University.

Hash, R. J., and Bailey, M. B. (1978). A classroom strategy: Improving social studies comprehension. *Social Education, 42,* 24–26.

Hennings, D. G. (1982). A writing approach to reading comprehension—Schema theory in action. *Language Arts, 59,* 8–17.

Herber, H. L. (1970). *Teaching reading in content areas.* Englewood Cliffs, N.J.: Prentice-Hall.

___. (1978). *Teaching reading in content areas.* 2nd ed. Englewood Cliffs, N.J.: Prentice-Hall.

Herber, H. L. and Herber, J. N. (1993). *Teaching reading in content areas with reading, writing, and reasoning.* Boston: Allyn and Bacon.

Hill, M. (1992). The new literacy. *Electronic Learning, 12* (1), 28–33.

Hipple, T. W., Wright, R. G., Yarbrough, J. H., and Bartholomew, B. (1983). Forty-plus writing activities. *English Journal, 72* (3), 73–76.

Hirsch, E. D., Jr. (1987). *Cultural literacy: What every American needs to know.* New York: Harper & Row.

Hittleman, D. R. (1983). *Developmental reading K–8: From a psycholinguistic perspective.* 2nd ed. Boston: Houghton Mifflin.

Hoffman, J. V. (1979). Developing flexibility through ReFlex action. *The Reading Teacher, 33,* 223–229.

Hofler, D. B. (1983). Outlining—Teach the concept first. *Reading World, 32,* 176–177.

Hoskisson, K. and Tompkins, G. E. (1987). *Language Arts Content and Teaching Strategies.* Columbus, OH: Merrill.

Hughes, D. C. (1973). An experimental investigation of the effects of pupil responding and teacher reacting on pupil achievement. *American Educational Research Journal, 10,* 21–37.

Jevitz, L., and Meints, D. W. (1979). Be a better book buyer: Guidelines for textbook evaluation. *Journal of Reading, 21,* 126–130.

Jiganti, M. A., and Tindall, M. S. (1986). An interactive approach to teaching vocabulary. *The Reading Teacher, 39,* 444–448.

Johnson, D. D., Pittelman, S. D., and Heimlich, J. E. (1986). Semantic mapping. *The Reading Teacher, 39,* 778–783.

Johnson, D. D., and Johnson, B. von H. (1986). Highlighting vocabulary in inferential comprehension instruction. *Journal of Reading, 29,* 622–625.

Karlin, R., and Karlin, A. R. (1984). Writing for reading. *Reading Horizons, 24,* 124–128.

Kirsch, I., and Jungeblut, A. (1986). *Literacy: Profiles in America's young adults.* Princeton, N.J.: National Assessment of Educational Progress.

Klausmeier, H., Ghatala, E. S., and Frazer, D. A. (1974). *Conceptual learning and development.* New York: Academic.

Koenke, K. (1972). Reading evaluation by the high school teacher. *Journal of Reading, 16,* 220–225.

Kruse, G. M., and Horning, K. T. (1991). *Cultural literacy for children and young adults: A selected listing of books 1980–1990: By and about people of color.* 3rd ed. Madison, Wis.: Cooperative Children's Book Center, University of Wisconsin.

Kutina, R. (1981). Graphic puzzles. *American Way, 12,* 69.

Langer, J. A. (1981). From theory to practice: A prereading plan. *Journal of Reading, 25,* 152–156.

Lewis, J. S. (1979). Directed discovery learning: Catalyst to reading in the content areas. *Journal of Reading, 22,* 714–719.

Lindquist-Sandmann, A. (1987). A metacognitive strategy and high school students: Working together. *Journal of Reading, 30,* 326–332.

Linehan, M. F. (1992). Children who are homeless: Educational strategies for school personnel. *Phi Delta Kappan, 74,* 61–66.

Linn, R. L., Graue, M. E., and Sanders, N. M. (1990). Comparing state and district test results to national norms: Interpretations of scoring "above the national average." CSE Technical Report No. 308. Los Angeles: UCLA Center for Research on Evaluation, Standards, and Student Testing.

Livaudais, M. F. (1985). *A survey of secondary (grades 7–12) students' attitudes toward reading motivational activities.* Doctoral dissertation, University of Houston.

Lyons, B. (1981). The PQP method of responding to writing. *English Journal, 70*(3), 42–43.

Macklin, M. D. (1978). Content area reading is a process of finding personal meaning. *Journal of Reading, 22,* 212–215.

Mangieri, J. N. (1977). The GRADE technique. *Journal of Reading, 29,* 622–625.

Manis, M. (1966). *Cognitive processes.* Belmont, Calif.: Wadsworth.

Manzo, A. V. (1975). Guided reading procedure. *Journal of Reading, 18,* 287–291.

———. (1979a). The Request procedure. *Journal of Reading, 13,* 123–126, 163.

———. (1979b). The Request procedure. In C. Pennock (ed.), *Reading comprehension on four linguistic levels.* Newark, Del.: International Reading Association.

———. (1980). Three "universal" strategies in content area reading and languaging. *Journal of Reading, 22,* 146–149.

Mathison, C. (1989). Activating student interest in content area reading. *Journal of Reading, 33* (3), 170–176.

McAndrews, D. A. (1983). Underlining and notetaking: Some suggestions from research. *Journal of Reading, 27,* 103–108.

———. (1986). Evaluating textbooks in the context of teaching and learning. *Forum for Reading, 17,* 73–79.

McClain, L. J. (1981). Study guides: Potential assets in content classrooms. *Journal of Reading, 24,* 321–325.

McConnell, S. (1992/93). Talking drawings: A strategy for assisting learners. *Journal of Reading, 36* (4), 260–269.

McDaniel, N., and Mountain, L. (1993). There's a portfolio in your future. *The Abstract, 13* (1), 5–6.

McKenna, M. (1976). Synonymic versus verbatim scoring of the cloze procedure. *Journal of Reading, 20,* 141–143.

McLaughlin, G. H. (1969). SMOG grading—A new readability formula. *Journal of Reading, 12,* 639–645.

McNeil, J. D. (1984). *Comprehension: New directions for classroom practice.* Glenview, Ill.: Scott, Foresman.

Meyer, B. J. F., Brandt, D. M., and Bluth, G. J. (1980). Use of top-level structure in text: Key for reading comprehension of ninth grade students. *Reading Research Quarterly, 16,* 72–103.

Micklos, J. (1980). The facts, please, about reading achievement in American schools. *Journal of Reading, 24,* 44–45.

Miller, G. A., and Gildea, P. M. (1987). How children learn words. *Scientific American, 257* (3), 94–99.

Miller, K. K., and George, J. E. (1992). Expository passage organizers: Models for reading and writing. *Journal of Reading, 35* (5), 372–377.

Mims, M., and Gholson, B. (1977). Effects of type and amount of feedback upon hypothesis sampling among 7–8 year old children. *Journal of Experimental Psychology, 24,* 358–371.

Moore, D. W., and Readence, J. E. (1984). A quantitative and qualitative review of graphic organizer research. *Journal of Educational Research, 78,* 11–17.

Moore, M. A. (1981). C2R: Concentrate, read, remember. *Journal of Reading, 17,* 337–339.

Morgan, C. R., and Deese, J. (1969). *How to Study.* 2nd ed. New York: McGraw-Hill.

Mountain, L. (1978). *ATTENTION SPAN STORIES: Star trip.* Providence: Jamestown Publishers.

———. (1978). *ATTENTION SPAN STORIES: Time trip.* Providence: Jamestown Publishers.

———. (1992–93). Doing homework on a telecommunications network. *Journal of Educational Technology Systems, 21* (3), 103–107.

———. (1982). *English word fun.* Wilkinsburg, Pa: Hayes.

———. (1993). Home-to-school network interactions between teacher-education students and children. *Educational Technology, 33* (2), 41–43.

———. (1993). Math synonyms. *The Reading Teacher, 46* (5), 451–452.

———. (1985). Word puzzles for vocabulary development. *Reading Horizons, 26* (1), 16–24.

Murray, D. M. (1968). *A writer teaches writing: A practical method of teaching composition.* Boston: Houghton Mifflin.

———. (1968). *Learning by teaching: Selected articles on writing and teaching.* Montclair, N.J.: Boynton/Cook.

Muther, C. (1984–85). How to evaluate a basal textbook: The skills trace. *Educational Leadership, 42* (4), 79–80.

———. (1985). Reviewing research when choosing materials. *Educational Leadership, 42* (5), 86–87.

————. (1985). What every textbook evaluator should know. *Educational Leadership, 42*(4), 4–8.

Nagy, W. E., and Anderson, R. (1984). How many words are there in printed English? *Reading Research Quarterly, 19,* 304–330.

National Assessment of Educational Progress. (1986). *Literacy: Profiles of America's young adults.* Princeton: Educational Testing Service.

————. (1988). *Reading report card.* Princeton: Educational Testing Service.

Needleman, H. L. (1992). Childhood exposure to lead: A common cause of school failure. *Phi Delta Kappan, 74,* 35–37.

Nelson-Herber, J. (1986). Expanding and refining vocabulary in content areas. *Journal of Reading, 29,* 626–633.

Newell, G. E. (1984). Learning from writing in two content areas: A case study/protocol analysis. *Research in the Teaching of English, 18,* 265–287.

Nichols, J. N. (1985). The content reading-writing connection. *Journal of Reading, 29,* 265–267.

————. (1980). Using paragraph frames to help remedial high school students with written assignments. *Journal of Reading, 24,* 228–231.

Nilsen, A. P., and Donelson, K. L. (1993). *Literature for today's young adults.* 4th ed. New York: Harper Collins.

Noe, K. S., and Standal, T. C. (1984–85). Computer applications of readability formulas: Some cautions. *Computers, Reading and Language Arts, 2* (2), 32–33.

Nolte, R. Y., and Singer, H. (1985). Active comprehension: Teaching a process of reading comprehension and its effects on reading achievement. *The Reading Teacher, 39,* 24–31.

Nurnberg, M., and Rosenblum, M. (1966). *All about words.* New York: Mentor Books, New American Library.

Orlando, V. P. (1980). Training students to use a revised version of SQ3R: An instructional strategy. *Reading World, 20,* 65–70.

Orleans, S., and Orleans, J. (1977). *Pencil puzzles 3.* New York: Grosset & Dunlap.

Paivio, A. (1971). *Imagery and verbal processes.* New York: Holt, Rinehart & Winston.

Palincsar, A. S. (1986). Metacognitive strategy instruction. *Exceptional Children, 53,* 118–124.

Palincsar, A. S., and Brown, A. L. (1986). Interactive teaching to promote independent learning from text. *The Reading Teacher, 39,* 771–777.

Palmatier, R. A. (1973). A notetaking system for learning. *Journal of Reading, 17,* 36–39.

————. (1971). Comprehension of four notetaking procedures. *Journal of Reading, 14,* 234–240, 258.

Pauk, W. (1974). *How to study in college.* 2nd ed. Boston: Houghton Mifflin.

————. (1963). On scholarship: Advice to high school students. *The Reading Teacher, 17,* 72–78.

————. (1974). Preparing for exams. *Reading World, 23,* 286–287.

————. (1984). The new SQ3R. *Reading World, 23,* 274–275.

Pearson, P. D. (1976). A psycholinguistic model of reading. *Language Arts, 53,* 319–322.

————. (1985). Changing the face of reading comprehension instruction. *The Reading Teacher, 34,* 914–920.

Pearson, P. D., and Johnson, D. D. (1972). *Teaching reading comprehension.* New York: Holt, Rinehart & Winston.

Peterson, H. A., et al. (1935). Some measurements of the effects of reviews. *Journal of Educational Psychology, 26,* 65–72.

Petros, T., and Hoving, K. (1980). The effects of review on young children's memory of prose. *Journal of Experimental Child Psychology, 30,* 33–43.

Petrosky, A. R. (1982). From story to essay: Reading and writing. *College Composition and Communication, 23,* 19–36.

Piercey, D. (1982). *Reading activities in content areas: An ideabook for middle and secondary schools.* 2nd ed. Boston: Allyn & Bacon.

Prell, J. M., and Prell, P. A. (Nov. 1986). Improving test scores—Teaching test-wiseness: A review of literature. *Phi Delta Kappan Research Bulletin.*

Rankin, E. F., and Culhane, J. W. (1969). Comparable cloze and multiple-choice comprehension test scores. *Journal of Reading, 13,* 193–198.

Raphael, T. E. (1982). Question-answering strategies for children. *The Reading Teacher, 36,* 186–190.

———. (1984). Teaching learners about sources of information for answering comprehension questions. *Journal of Reading, 27,* 303–311.

———. (1986). Teaching question answer relationships, revisited. *The Reading Teacher, 39,* 516–522.

Raphael, T. E., and Pearson, P. D. (1985). Increasing students' awareness of sources of information for answering questions. *American Educational Research Journal, 22,* 217–235.

Ravitch, D., and Finn, C. E., Jr. (1987). *What do our 17-year olds know?* New York: Harper & Row.

Readence, J. E., Baldwin, R. S., and Richelman, R. J. (1983). Instructional insights into metaphors and similes. *Journal of Reading, 27,* 109–112.

Readence, J. E., Bean, R. W., and Baldwin, R. S. (1981). *Content area reading: An integrated approach.* Dubuque: Kendall/Hunt.

Readence, J. E., and Searfoss, L. W. (1980). Teaching strategies for vocabulary development. *English Journal, 69* (7), 43–46.

Redfield, D. R., and Rousseau, E. W. (1981). A meta-analysis of research on teacher questioning behavior. *Review of Educational Research, 51,* 237–245.

Reed, A. J. S. (1988). *Comics to classics: A parents' guide to books for teens and pre-teens.* Newark, Del.: International Reading Association.

Reynolds, A. G., and Flagg, P. W. (1977). *Cognitive psychology.* Cambridge, Mass.: Winthrop.

Reynolds, H. J., and Glaser, R. (1964). Effects of repetition and spaced review upon retention of a complex learning task. *Journal of Educational Psychology, 55,* 297–308.

Richgels, D. J., and Hansen, R. (1984). Gloss: Helping students apply both skills and strategies in reading content textbooks. *Journal of Reading, 27,* 312–317.

Robinson, F. (1961). *Effective study.* Rev. ed. New York: Harper & Row.

Rodrigues, R. J. (1983). Tools for developing prewriting skills. *English Journal, 72*(2), 58–60.

Roe, B. E., Stoodt, B. D., and Burns, P. C. (1983). *Secondary school reading instruction.* 2nd ed. Boston: Houghton Mifflin.

Rowe, M. B. (1974). Wait-time and rewards as instructional variables, their influence on language, logic, and fate control: Part One—Wait-time. *Journal of Research in Science Teaching, 11,* 81–94.

Rubin, D. (1985). *Teaching Elementary Language Arts.* 3rd ed. Columbus, Ohio: Merrill.

Rundus, D. J. (1971). Analysis of rehearsal processes in free recall. *Journal of Experimental Psychology, 89,* 63–77.

Schwartz, E., and Sheff, A. (1975). Student involvement in questioning for comprehension. *The Reading Teacher, 29,* 150–154.

Schwartz, R. M., and Raphael, T. E. (1985). Concept of definition: A key to improving students' vocabulary. *The Reading Teacher, 39,* 198–205.

Seidel, J. F. (1992). Children with HIV—related development difficulties. *Phi Delta Kappan, 74,* 38–40, 56.

Shafer, R. E. (ed.). (1979). Applied linguistics and reading. Newark, Del.: International Reading Association.

Sharan, S. (1980). Cooperative learning in small groups: Recent methods and effects on achievement, attitudes, and ethnic relations. *Review of Educational Research, 50,* 241–271.

Shefelbine, J. (1991). *Encouraging your junior high student to read.* Newark, Del.: International Reading Association.

Shepherd, D. L. (1982). *Comprehensive high school reading methods.* 3rd ed. Columbus, Ohio: Charles E. Merrill.

Sherer, P. A. (1977). Those mystifying metaphors: Students can read them. *Journal of Reading, 20,* 559–562.

Shugarman, S. L., and Hurst, J. B. (1986). Purposeful paraphrasing: Promoting a nontrivial pursuit for meaning. *Journal of Reading, 29,* 396–399.

Simpson, M. L., Stahl, N. A., and Hayes, C. G. (1989). PROPE: A research validation. *Journal of Reading, 33,* 22–28.

Sinatra, R. C., Berg, D., and Dunn, R. (1985). Semantic mapping improves reading comprehension of learning disabled students. *Teaching Exceptional Children, 17*(4), 310–314.

Sinatra, R. C., Stahl-Gemake, J., and Berg, D. N. (1984). Improving reading comprehension of disabled readers through semantic mapping. *The Reading Teacher, 38,* 22–29.

Sinatra, R., Stahl-Gemake, J., and Morgan, N. W. (1986). Using semantic mapping after reading to organize and write original discourse. *Journal of Reading, 30,* 4–13.

Sirotnik, E. A. (1985). Evaluating computer software. *Educational Leadership, 42*(4), 39–42.

Slavin, R. E. (1987b). *Cooperative learning: Student teams.* Washington, D.C.: National Education Association.

———. (1985). Cooperative learning: Applying contact theory in desegregated schools. *Journal of Social Issues, 41*(3), 45–62.

———. (1987a). Cooperative learning and the cooperative school. *Educational Leadership, 45* (3), 7–13.

———. (1980). Cooperative learning. *Review of Educational Research, 50,* 315–342.

———. (1978). *Using student team learning.* Baltimore: Center for Social Organization of Schools, Johns Hopkins University.

Smith, C. C., and Bean, T. W. (1980). The guided writing procedure: Integrating content reading and writing. *Reading World, 19,* 270–274.

Smith, F. (1973). *Psycholinguistics and reading.* New York: Holt, Rinehart & Winston.

———. (1988). *Understanding reading.* 4th ed. Hillsdale, N.J.: Lawrence Erlbaum.

Smith, L. (undated). Selected unpublished papers on concept development, Augusta (Georgia) College.

Smith, M. K. (1941). Measurement of the size of general English vocabulary through the elementary grades and high school. *Genetic Psychology Monographs, 24,* 313–324.

Smith, R., and Elliott, P. G. (1979). *Reading activities for middle and secondary schools.* New York: Holt, Rinehart & Winston.

Solon, C. (1980). The pyramid diagram—College study skills tool. *Journal of Reading, 23,* 594–597.

Spache, G. D. (1962). Is this a breakthrough? *The Reading Teacher, 15,* 258–263.

Spiegel, D. L. (1981). Six alternatives to the directed reading activity. *The Reading Teacher, 34,* 914–920.

Spires, H. A., and Stone, P. D. (Oct. 1989). The directed notetaking activity: A self questioning approach. *Journal of Reading,* 36–39.

Spitzer, H. F. (1939). Studies in retention. *Journal of Educational Psychology, 30,* 641–656.

Spivack, J. F. (ed.). (1982). *Careers information.* White Plains, N.Y.: Knowledge Industry.

Spring, H. T. (1985). Teacher decision making: A metacognitive approach. *The Reading Teacher, 3,* 290–295.

Spyridakis, J., and Standal, T. (1987). Signals in expository prose: Effects on reading comprehension. *Reading Research Quarterly, 22* (3), 285–298.

Staton, T. F. (1982). *How to study.* 7th ed. Nashville, Tennessee: How to Study, P.O. Box 40273.

Stevens, R. (1912). The question as a measure of classroom practice. *Teachers College Contributions to Education,* no. 48. New York: Teachers College Press, Columbia University.

Stevens, L. J., and Price, M. (1992). Meeting the challenge of educating children at risk. *Phi Delta Kappan, 74,* 18-20, 22-23.

Stewart, R. A., and Cross, T. L. (1991). The effects of marginal glosses on reading comprehension and retention. *Journal of Reading, 35* (1), 4–12.

Stieglitz, E. L., and Stieglitz, V. S. (1981). SAVOR the word to reinforce vocabulary in the content areas. *Journal of Reading, 25,* 46–51.

Stotsky, S. (1982). The role of writing in developmental reading. *Journal of Reading, 25,* 330–340.

Stoodt, B. D. (1981). *Reading instruction.* Boston: Houghton Mifflin.

Strange, M., and Allington, R. L. (1977). Considering text variables in content area reading. *Journal of Reading, 21,* 149–152.

Sutherland. Z., and Arbuthnot, M. H. (1986). *Children and books.* 7th ed. Glenview, Ill.: Scott, Foresman.

Taba, H. (1967). *Teacher's handbook for elementary social studies.* Reading, Mass: Addison-Wesley.

Taylor, B. M. (1982). Text structure and children's composition and memory for expository material. *Journal of Educational Psychology, 74,* 323–340.

Taylor, B. M., and Beach, R. W. (1984). The effects of text structure instruction on middle grade students' comprehension and production of expository text. *Reading Research Quarterly, 19,* 134–146.

Taylor, B. M., and Samuels, S. J. (1983). Children's use of text structure in the recall of expository material. *American Educational Research Journal, 20,* 517–528.

Taylor, W. S. (1953). Cloze procedures: A new tool for measuring readability. *Journalism Quarterly, 30,* 415–433.

———. (1956). Recent developments in the use of cloze procedure. *Journalism Quarterly, 33,* 42–48, 99.

Tchudi, S. N., and Yates, J. (1983). *Teaching writing in the content areas: Senior high school.* Washington, D.C.: National Education Association.

Teens' favorite books: Young adults' choices 1987-1992. (1992). Newark, Del.: International Reading Association.

Templeton, S. (1991). *Teaching the integrated language arts.* Boston: Houghton Mifflin.

Thelen, J. N. (1986). Vocabulary instruction and meaningful learning. *Journal of Reading, 29,* 603–609.

Thomas, E. L., and Robinson, H. A. (1972). *Improving reading in every class: A sourcebook for teachers.* Boston: Allyn & Bacon.

Thomas, K. J. (1978). The directed inquiry activity: An instructional procedure for content reading. *Reading Improvement, 15,* 138–140.

Tierney, R. J., Readence, J. E., and Dishner, K. E. (1990). *Reading strategies and practices: A compendium.* 3rd ed. Boston: Allyn and Bacon.

Tomas, D. (1977). A survey of research on the teaching of vocabulary. Unpublished paper, University of Houston.

Tovey, D. R. (1976). The psycholinguistic guessing game. *Language Arts, 53,* 319–322.

Traxler, A. E. (1938). Improvement of vocabulary through drill. *English Journal, 27,* 491–494.

Turner, T. N. (1976). Figurative language: Deceitful mirage or sparkling oasis for reading. *Language Arts, 53,* 758–761.

Tyson, E., and Mountain, L. (1982). A riddle or pun makes learning words fun. *The Reading Teacher, 36,* 170–173.

Vacca, R. M. (1981). *Content area reading.* Glenview, Ill.: Scott, Foresman.

Vacca, R. T., and Padak, N. D. (1990). Who's at Risk in Reading, *Jounal of Reading, 33,* 486–488.

Vaughan, S., Crawley, S., and Mountain, L. (1979). A multilple-modality approach to word study: Vocabulary scavenger hunts. *The Reading Teacher, 32,* 434–437.

Weber, R., and Shake, M. C. (1988). Teachers' rejoinders to students' responses in reading lessons. *Journal of Reading Behavior, 20,* 285–299.

Weil, M., and Joyce, B. (1978). *Information processing models for teaching.* Englewood Cliffs, N.J.: Prentice-Hall.

White, T. G., Graves, M. F., and Slater, W. H. (1990). Growth of reading vocabulary in diverse elementary schools: Decoding and word meaning. *Journal of Educational Psychology, 82*(2), 281–290.

Wiesendanger, W. D. (1986). Durkin revisited. *Reading Horizons, 26,* 89–97.

Williams, C. K. (1973). *The differential effects of structured overviews, levels guides and organizational pattern guides upon the reading comprehension of twelfth grade students.* Ed.D. dissertation, State University of New York at Buffalo.

Wilson, R. M. (1981). *Diagnostic and remedial reading for classroom and clinic.* 4th ed. Columbus, Ohio: Charles E. Merrill.

Winograd, P. N. (1984). Strategic difficulties in summarizing texts. *Reading Research Quarterly, 19,* 404–425.

Wolpert, E. (1972). Length, imagery values and word recognition. *The Reading Teacher, 26,* 180–186.

Wong, B. Y. L. (1986). Metacognition and special education: A review of a view. *The Journal of Special Education, 20* (1), 9–29.

Wong, B. Y. L., and Jones, W. (1982). Increasing metacomprehension in learning-disabled and normally-achieving students through self-questioning training. *Learning Disability Quarterly, 5,* 228–240.

Wood, K. D. (1992). Fostering collaborative reading and writing experiences in mathematics. *Journal of Reading, 36* (2), 96–103.

Appendix

ENABLING ACTIVITIES

CHAPTER 2

Activity 1

SMOG Readability

Calculate the readability of the following books using the SMOG readability formula.

> *Book 1:* The number of polysyllabic words found in each of the three samples was 18, 15, and 20.
>
> *Book 2:* The number of polysyllabic words found in each of the three samples was 8, 11, and 9.

Activity 2

Fry Readability

Calculate the readability of the following textbook sample* using the Fry Graph.

Passage 1

> On May 25, 1961, President John Kennedy pledged the United States to landing a man on the moon. He said that in ten years an astronaut should land on the moon. He should also come back to earth safely.
>
> In July of 1969 three astronauts began their trip to the moon. Armstrong, Aldrin and Collins left earth in Apollo 11.
>
> On July 20, Armstrong and Aldrin entered their lunar module. It took about three hours to put on their special space suits. Then the exciting time came. About five hundred million people watched their TV sets. The men from Apollo 11 took their first steps on the moon.

*From S. Crawley and L. Mountain, *Cloze attention to comprehension, Book E* (Hamden, Conn.: Learning Systems Corp., 1984), pp. 1, 7–8, 11–12. Reprinted by permission of Learning Systems Corp.

Passage 2

The Inca Empire was a large and great civilization in South America. The government decided what work the people would do. It decided what crops farmers would plant and what buildings and roads would be built. The ruler's word was law. Several royal families helped him rule. The ruler owned all the land. It was each person's duty to serve the state. The ruler in return saw to it that everyone had food, clothes, shelter and protection.

The Incas were good farmers. They built canals for irrigation. Their use of terraces increased the amount of farming space. They also raised llamas for food, clothing, and transportation.

Passage 3

The story of people on earth begins during the Ice Age. There are many things we do not know about the Ice Age, but we do know a few things. For example, we know that there was a great deal of water frozen in what we call glaciers. As a result, the oceans were about three hundred feet lower than they are today. We also know that the glaciers moved from high ground to low ground.

During the Ice Age the temperature became warmer at times and the ice melted a little. The ice never completely melted, though. Another time of cold weather came, and the ice froze again.

At one time there was so much water frozen in glaciers that there was land where there is now ocean. Initially bridges were formed between these lands. Later these lands became separated by ocean.

Activity 3

SMOG and Rix Readability

Calculate the readability of the previous selection using the SMOG and Rix formulas. Do you find any differences in readability? Why or why not?

Activity 4

Writing to a Specific Readability Level

In order to understand the challenges that textbook authors and publishers face, rewrite the following passage so that the readability of the passage is grade 5. (The passage presently has a readability of grade 9 using the Fry graph.) What did you notice as you tried to lower the readability of the passage?

Our faces tell much about us. They convey information to observers about how we feel, who we are, and what we are thinking. The standard we hold for beauty is not defined; yet it has controlled the destiny of men.
The face is often utilized to identify status and character. We may be young or old, friendly or distant, sensitive or insensitive, expressionless or animated. We can be identified as part of a family or race.

Scientists have discovered that children must learn to distinguish faces. Scientists are studying how people use faces to express emotions. They have used fossil records to learn about early man. Scientists are discovering much more about faces than you ever imagined.

Activity 5

Subjective and Objective Evaluation
Select a textbook in your content area. Evaluate it using the guidelines outlined in Chapter 2.

CHAPTER 3

Activity 6

Cloze Test
Complete and score the following cloze test.

Wilson Taylor developed the cloze procedure. The cloze procedure derived _____ name from "closure" which _____ to the tendency of _____ beings to complete an _____ pattern.

To construct a _____ test you should select _____ passage about 250 words _____ length. The passage should _____ be dependent upon previously _____ material or material that _____ later in the chapter. _____ every fifth word. (Do _____ delete words from the _____ and last sentences in _____ passage). When you finish _____ words you will have _____ fifty blank spaces. Replace _____ deleted word with spaces _____ equal length.

To administer _____ test, give students a _____ of the test with _____ blank spaces. The students _____ the material silently and _____ the deleted word for _____ blank space.

In scoring _____ test, only exact replacements _____ the original word are _____ as correct answers. Words _____ are spelled incorrectly are _____ as correct answers. If _____ student scores 41 to _____ percent correct, the material _____ at the student's instructional _____. If a score of _____ to 100 percent is _____ by a student, the _____ is at the independent _____. A score of 40 _____ or less indicates that _____ material is at the _____ frustration level. The textbook is too difficult for students scoring 40 percent or less on the cloze test.

Number correct = ____

Percent correct = ____

Reading level = ____

Note: Percent correct equals the number correct divided by the total number of possible answers. This selection contained forty possible answers.

CHAPTER 4

Activity 7

Figurative Language

Identify the type of figurative language used in each of the following examples:

1. I almost jumped out of my skin. _____

2. The chef was as neat as a pin. _____

3. The cashier is a peach. _____

4. You did well in the stockmarket this week. You lost your shirt.

   _____

5. The car gasped as it lurched up the hill. _____

6. It was a bittersweet lesson. _____

7. "Hoot! Hoot!" cried the owl. _____

Activity 8

Context Clues

Using your knowledge of semantic clues, determine the meaning of the italicized word in each of the following examples. Then identify the type of context clue used.

1. The *sagacious* employer studied the applications of prospective employ-ees, while the obtuse competitor hired anyone on the spot.

   Meaning: _____

   Type of clue: _____

2. The speaker was so *garrulous* that people said his mouth ran like a leaky faucet.

Meaning: _____

Type of clue: _____

3. The delicate, pale purple that contrasts with the yellows and pinks is *mauve.*

   Meaning: _____

   Type of clue: _____

4. Our trip to Japan was exciting. Some of the sights included Halsingborg, Hirosaki, Hiroshima, *Toyota,* and Tokyo.

   Meaning: _____

   Type of clue: _____

5. The *occult* or abstruse explanation left everyone speechless.

   Meaning: _____

   Type of clue: _____

6. Suddenly the wind began to howl; the room began to shake; and the lights blinked on and off. But, as quickly as the episode started, it stopped. The experience was frightening and *enigmatic.*

   Meaning: _____

   Type of clue: _____

7. A member of the Smith family has *myasthenia gravis.* The voluntary muscles progressively become weaker without atrophy.

   Meaning: _____

   Type of clue: _____

8. The Clays kept talking about their big home, summer cottage, expensive antiques, and children attending Yale. They were real *braggadocios.*

   Meaning: _____

   Type of clue: _____

Activity 9

List-Group-Label

Your students have just finished studying Canada. You began a list-group-label lesson with your students and they brainstormed the names below. Categorize the names the way you think your students might categorize them. (Some of the names may go into more than one category.)

Alberta, British Columbia, Charlottetown, Edmonton, Fredericton, Halifax, Manitoba, Montreal, New Brunswick, Newfoundland, Northwest Territories, Nova Scotia, Ontario, Prince Edward Island, Quebec, Regina, St. John, St. John's, Saskatchewan, Toronto, Vancouver, Victoria, Whitehorse, Winnipeg, Yellowknife, Yukon Territory

Activity 10

Vocabulary Overview

Develop your own vocabulary overview using the following words: *birds, aviary, oology, ornithology, mew.* (You may have to review the meanings of these terms before constructing the guide.)

Activity 11

Vocabulary Reinforcement

Try the following activity. What thought process do you have to go through to complete the activity?

Directions: Using the clues on the right, unscramble the words and write them correctly on the line provided.

_____	1.	nblealytiiar	A factor to consider in textbook selection
_____	2.	aasehtmc	Mental framework of thinking
_____	3.	ddeoginc	Sounding out words
_____	4.	atmsncies	Linguistic term for meanings of words
_____	5.	uoslrec	Tendency of human beings to complete an incomplete pattern
_____	6.	yitauc	Keenness of vision or hearing
_____	7.	occntesp	Mental constructs of categories
_____	8.	ucvtdiine	Going from specific to general
_____	9.	pybroeleh	Overstatement
_____	10.	oyomronx	Example: brightly subdued

Activity 12

Vocabulary Reinforcement

Try this activity. Is the thought process different from the thought process used in Activity 11?

Directions: Unscramble the words below. One letter belongs in each space.

1. emipesmhu   _ _ _ _ _ _ _ _ _
2. mniatoelraoi   _ _ _ _ _ _ _ _ _ _ _
3. hhooprmga   _ _ _ _ _ _ _ _ _
4. neoopamoati   _ _ _ _ _ _ _ _ _ _
5. rnmoyca   _ _ _ _ _ _ _
6. eanoopijrt   _ _ _ _ _ _ _ _ _ _
7. oxmnyroo   _ _ _ _ _ _ _ _
8. eromtaph   _ _ _ _ _ _ _ _

CHAPTER 5

Activity 13

Levels of Comprehension—Questions

Read the passage below. Then develop three literal, two interpretive, and two critical/creative questions that you could ask students.

One day we came to the royal city, where I was brought before the queen and her court. I bowed before her, and she held out her little finger for me to kiss.

Thanks to Glumdalclitch, I had learned enough of the language to talk to the queen. She was very kind. She bought me from the farmer and asked Glumdalclitch to stay as my nurse and teacher.

One morning my little nurse put me on the window sill to get some air while she washed my clothes. As soon as she left, some wasps as big as turkeys came flying in. Their droning was louder than bagpipes.

As they flew around me, deafening me with their noise, I was fearful that they would sting me to death. So I drew my sword, ready to defend myself. One came at me and I ran him through. Then another, and again I put my sword to good use. When I killed the third wasp, the rest of them flew away.

Another time, when I needed to defend myself, my sword was of no use to me. I was alone in the garden, and a small white spaniel came sniffing up to me. So quickly did the dog take me up in his mouth that there was no time to call for help. Wagging his tail, he ran straight to the gardener and set me gently on the ground. He had been so well trained that he carried me between his teeth without breaking my skin.

The gardener picked me up and asked me if I were all right. I was so frightened and out of breath that for a moment I could not answer. But soon I realized that I was not hurt. From then on, however, I did not go into the garden alone.

After a while I even worked out a way to read the books of Brobdingnag. The book I wished to read would be opened for me and propped up against the wall. Then a tall ladder would be placed in front of it. I would climb to the top of the ladder where I could begin reading the page. As I finished the first few lines, I would descend a step and read on, going in the way to the bottom of the page. The paper was as thick and stiff as cardboard so I could turn the pages for myself.

Even though I was quite happy in Brobdingnag, I could not help wishing sometimes to be in a country where I did not have to live in fear of being stepped on.*

*"Gulliver in the Land of the Giants," pp. 209–210 in *Jamestown Heritage Readers, Book F* (Teacher's Edition), by L. Mountain, S. Crawley, and E. Fry. Copyright 1991 by Jamestown Publishers, Providence, Rhode Island. Reprinted by permission.

Activity 14

Levels of Comprehension—Statements
Using the passage in activity 13, develop three literal, two interpretive, and two applied level statements.

CHAPTER 6

Activity 15

Advance Organizer
Write your own comparative advance organizer for a concept studied in your content area.

Activity 16

Think Sheet
The book *Nonfiction for Young Adults from Delight to Wisdom* (Carter & Abrahamson, 1990, Oryx Press) contains the following chapter and subtopics. Write your predictions for each heading and subheading.

Accuracy

Qualifications
Scholarship
Fact and Opinion
Sensationalism
Stereotyping
Anthropomorphism and Teleology

Activity 17

Structured Question Guide and Process Sheet
Alone, and then in a group, complete the following structured question and process sheet.

Question: Are computers more of an advantage or disadvantage in our everyday lives?

Part 1
Place a check beside the items you use that are computer assisted or run by computers.

___ microwave	___ car
___ dishwasher	___ talking vending machines
___ refrigerator	___ photocopy machines
___ clothes washer	___ automatic teller machines (ATM)

___ price scanner (at store)   ___ typewriter

___ CD player   ___ television

___ VCR   ___ clock

Add others you can think of.

Part 2

Possible uses of computers are listed in column A. In column B, list the benefits to people. In column C, list their drawbacks. In column D, rank these from 1 to 7 according to degree of benefit (1 = greatest benefit).

A Uses of Computers	*B* Benefits	*C* Drawbacks	*D* Rankings
Teaching			
Entertainment			
Unvaried work			
Word processing			
Problem solving (simulations)			
Repetitive drill			
Budgeting			
Other: _____			

Part 3

Compare your answers with those of others in your group.

1. Did members of your group have similar benefits listed? Which were the same for most members?
2. Were similar drawbacks listed by members of your group? What were these drawbacks?
3. Did anyone in your group list additional uses of computers? What were these uses?
4. Compare your rankings in column D with others in your group. How were they alike or different?
5. Can computers do things that people can't do?
6. Can people do things that computers can't do?

CHAPTER 7

Activity 18

Organizational Patterns

Identify the organizational pattern used in each of the following sentences.

1. Zono School considered property destruction and fighting as major disciplinary problems; on the other hand, Ringho School considered the throwing of paper on the floor as its major disciplinary problem.

    Pattern: _____

2. Before the Soviet-born youth was given political asylum in the United States, a court hearing had to be held.

    Pattern: _____

3. We must remember to buy almonds, chocolate chips, and butterscotch chips while shopping.

    Pattern: _____

4. To compare the three, a conservative doesn't know how to walk; a radical tries to walk in the air; and a reactionary walks backward.

    Pattern: _____

5. Wiley Post completed the first around-the-world flight because of his plane (*The Winnie Mae*), his skill, and his determination.

    Pattern: _____

6. A course entitled "Strategies in the Supermarket" was offered after the cost of food began to skyrocket.

    Pattern: _____

Activity 19

Three Levels Guide

Construct a three levels guide using the following poem.

> *A centipede ran happily*
> *Until a frog in fun*
> *Asked, "Pray, which leg comes after which?"*
> *This threw his mind in such a pitch*
> *He stood distracted in the ditch*
> *Considering how to run.*

Activity 20

RADAR

Form a group of three to four people and complete the following RADAR activity.

> *Step 1:* **Read.** Read the following material on the circulatory system. As you're reading, mentally compare the circulatory system to an irrigation system.

As you intake food, it goes through the digestive system and enters the blood stream, or circulatory system, through the intestines.

There is a special vein, the portal vein, that carries the blood from the intestines to the liver.

The liver serves as a filtering system for foods that are dissolved in the blood. Only certain foods are selected for distribution.

Blood from the liver flows into a vein called the vena cava inferior. This vein brings oxygen-poor blood from the lower part of the body to the heart.

Another vein, the vena cava superior, brings oxygen-poor blood from the upper part of the body to the heart.

Blood from the vena cava veins enters the right auricle of the heart. It is then pumped into the right ventricle.

The blood goes from the right ventricle into the pulmonary artery. The pulmonary artery then carries the oxygen-poor blood to the lungs.

The oxygen-poor blood gives up carbon dioxide in the lungs and takes on oxygen. It then becomes oxygen-rich blood.

The pulmonary vein brings the oxygen-rich blood back to the heart.

Within the heart, the left auricle pumps the blood into the left ventricle. This oxygen-rich blood is pumped to other parts of the body by the heart's left ventricle.

Step 2: **Analogize.** Explain how the circulatory system and an irrigation system are alike.

Step 3: **Discuss.** Discuss which comparisons you liked best and why. Include both physical features and processes in your discussion.

Step 4: **Apply.** Discuss the kinds of problems that might occur in these systems. What can be done to control these problems?

Step 5: **Research.** You might want to research points brought out in step 4.

Activity 21

Graphic Organizer

Read the selection below. Select approximately ten terms and develop a graphic organizer. (An array might be interesting to develop.)

The deck of the ship was rocking under his feet. Salty ocean spray was blowing in Joe's face. And there was no land in sight.

"Our captain is out of his mind," the sailor grumbled. "He's going to make us sail this ship right off the edge of the world, hunting for a new route to India."

"We can't sail off the edge of the world," said Joe. "The world is round."

"That's what you say," answered the sailor. "And that's what our captain, Christopher Columbus, says too. But I don't think you're right."

"You just wait," said Joe, grinning. "You'll find out that Columbus and I are right." It was almost too good to be true, he and Columbus!

An old sailor climbed down the rigging and came over to them. He was rubbing his eyes and frowning. "When I was on the lookout just now, I thought I saw a dark line on the horizon. It looked like a coastline. But these old eyes have fooled me before, after so long a time at sea. You climb up, young fellow," he said to Joe. "And tell me if I'm seeing things."

Joe climbed to the crow's nest and peered at the horizon. Sure enough, he could see something far in the distance. It just had to be land. Joe's heart beat faster. America was about to be discovered.

"I see something too," he shouted to the old sailor. "It must be a coastline. I'll get the captain."*

Activity 22

Circle of Knowledge
Using the names of states and their capitals engage in a circle of knowledge activity.

CHAPTER 8

Activity 23

Study Plan
Develop a daily schedule for your own studying. Share it with members of the class.

Activity 24

Mnemonic Device
Select a topic from your content area. Describe a mnemonic device you can introduce to your students. Explain how students can use it to remember the information they should recall.

CHAPTER 9

Activity 25

Writing Organizer
Refer again to the writing organizer example in Chapter 9. Outline or organize the words at the end of the selection into a story sequence. Use this outline as a guide to developing the next episode of the story. Write the next episode.

---

*From *ATTENTION SPAN STORIES: Time Trip* by Lee Mountain, p. 25. Copyright 1978 by Jamestown Publishers, Rhode Island. Reprinted by permission.

Activity 26

Brainwriting

Select a current events topic. Working in small groups, complete a brainwriting exercise.

Activity 27

Student Summary Writing

Write a five-minute summary of what was discussed in class today.

CHAPTER 10

Activity 28

Cooperative Learning

Working in groups, prepare a teams-games-tournament that could be used as a review for this text, *Strategies for Guiding Content Reading.*

CHAPTER 11

Activity 29

Interest Inventory

Develop an interest inventory similar to those described in Chapter 11. Use at least fifteen books related to your content area. Remember, design the inventory for middle and high school students, not college students.

CHAPTER 12

Activity 30

Students with Special Needs

Investigate the services provided in your area for students with special needs. How are students mainstreamed? What provisions are made for students who are mainstreamed?

B

ANSWERS TO
ENABLING ACTIVITIES

CHAPTER 2

Activity 1

SMOG Readability

Book 1: The number of polysyllabic words found in each of the three samples was 18, 15 and 20. Readability is grade 10.

$$18 + 15 + 20 = 53$$
$$\sqrt{47} = 7$$
$$7 + 3 = \mathbf{10}$$

Book 2: The number of polysyllabic words found in each of the three samples was 8, 11, and 9. Readability is grade 8.

$$8 + 11 + 9 = 28$$
$$\sqrt{25} = 5$$
$$5 + 3 = \mathbf{8}$$

Activity 2

Fry Readability

Only syllables above one in each word have been accented. Therefore, *and* would not have any accent mark above it because it has only one syllable. *Table* would have one accent mark above it because it contains one syllable beyond one.

Passage 1

On May 25, 1961, President John Kennedy pledged the United States to landing a man on the moon. He said that in ten years an astronaut should land on the moon. He should also come back to earth safely.

In July of 1969 three astronauts began their trip to the moon. Armstrong, Aldrin and Collins left earth in Apollo II.

On July 20, Armstrong and Aldrin entered their lunar module. It took about three hours to put on their special space suits. Then the exciting time came. About five hundred million people watched their TV sets. The men from Apollo II took their first steps on the moon.

Passage 2

The Inca Empire was a large and great civilization in South America. The government decided what work the people would do. It decided what crops farmers would plant and what buildings and roads would be built. The ruler's word was law. Several royal families helped him rule. The ruler owned all the land. It was each person's duty to serve the state. The ruler in return saw to it that everyone had food, clothes, shelter and protection.

The Incas were good farmers. They built canals for irrigation. Their use of terraces increased the amount of farming space. They also raised llamas for food, clothing, and transportation.

Passage 3

The story of people on earth begins during the Ice Age. There are many things we do not know about the Ice Age, but we do know a few things. For example, we know that there was a great deal of water frozen in what we call glaciers. As a result, the oceans were about three hundred feet lower than they are today. We also know that the glaciers moved from high ground to low ground.

During the Ice Age the temperature became warmer at times and the ice melted a little. The ice never completely melted, though. Another time of cold weather came, and the ice froze again.

At one time there was so much water frozen in glaciers that there was land where there is now ocean. Initially bridges were formed between these lands. Later these lands became separated by ocean.

	Number of Sentences	Number of Syllables
Passage 1:	9.3	146
Passage 2:	11.3	147
Passage 3:	7.2	133
Totals:	27.8	426

$$27.8 \div 3 = 9.3 \qquad\qquad 426 \div 3 = 142$$

Plot 9.3 sentences and 142 syllables on the Fry graph. Readability = grade 6

Activity 3

SMOG and Rix Readability

SMOG

$$10 + 10 + 6 = 26$$

$$\sqrt{25} = 5; \ 5 + 3 = 8$$

Readability = grade 8

Rix

Number of sentences: $10 + 12 + 10 = 32$;
Number of long words: $14 + 21 + 11 = 46$
Rix score = $46 \div 32 = 1.4$

Readability = grade 5

All three readability scores are different, although the Fry (grade 6) and Rix (grade 5) are only one grade apart. Each formula measures readability differently. Fry and Rix measure instructional level readability, whereas SMOG measures independent level readability.

Activity 4

Writing to a Specific Readability Level
Answers will vary.

Activity 5

Subjective and Objective Evaluation
Answers will vary.

CHAPTER 3

Activity 6

Cloze Test

Wilson Taylor developed the cloze procedure. The cloze procedure derived _its_ name from "closure" which _refers_ to the tendency of _human_ beings to complete an _incomplete_ pattern.

To construct a _cloze_ test you should select _a_ passage about 250 words _in_ length. The passage should _not_ be dependent upon previously _learned_ material or material that _comes_ later in the chapter. _Delete_ every fifth word. (Do _not_ delete words from the _first_ and last sentences in _the_ passage). When you finish _deleting_ words you will have _approximately_ fifty blank spaces. Replace _each_ deleted word with spaces _of_ equal length.

To administer _the_ test, give students a _copy_ of the test with _the_ blank spaces. The students _read_ the material silently and _supply_ the deleted word for _each_ blank space.

In scoring _the_ test, only exact replacements _of_ the original word are _counted_ as correct answers. Words _that_ are spelled incorrectly are _counted_ as correct answers. If _a_ student scores 41 to _60_ percent correct, the material _is_ at the student's instructional _level_ .If a score of _61_ to 100 percent is _obtained_ by a student the _material_ is at the independent _level_. A score of 40 _percent_ or less indicates that _the_ material is at the _student's_ frustration level. The textbook is too difficult for students scoring 40 percent or less on the cloze test.

Number correct = _____

Percent correct = _____

Reading level =   _____

Note: Percent correct equals the number correct divided by the total number of possible answers. This selection contained forty possible answers.

CHAPTER 4

Activity 7

Figurative Language

1. hyperbole
2. simile
3. metaphor
4. irony
5. personification
6. oxymoron
7. onomatopoeia

Activity 8

Context Clues

1. *sagacious*
   Meaning: discerning, keen, and farsighted in judgment
   Type of clue: comparison/contrast

2. *garrulous*
   Meaning: talkative
   Type of clue: familiar expressions or figures of speech

3. *mauve*
   Meaning: pale purple color
   Type of clue: direct definition or explanation

4. *Toyota*
   Meaning: city in Japan
   Type of clue: words in a series

5. *occult*
   Meaning: not easily understood, obtuse
   Type of clue: synonym or restatement

6. *enigmatic*
   Meaning: puzzling
   Type of clue: mood or tone

7. *myasthenia gravis*
   Meaning: a disease that causes the voluntary muscles to become progressively weaker
   Type of clue: explanation through example

8. *braggadocios*
   Meaning: those who brag
   Type of clue: inference

Activity 9

List-Group-Label

Provinces	*Capital*	*Largest City or Town*	*Territory*
Alberta	Edmonton	Edmonton	Northwest Territories
British Columbia	Victoria	Vancouver	Yukon Territory
Manitoba	Winnipeg	Winnipeg	Yellowknife
New Brunswick	Fredericton	St. John	Whitehorse
Newfoundland	St. John's	St. John's	
Nova Scotia	Halifax	Halifax	
Ontario	Toronto	Toronto	
Prince Edward Island	Charlottetown	Charlottetown	
Quebec	Quebec	Montreal	
Saskatchewan	Regina	Regina	

Activity 10

Vocabulary Overview
Answers will vary. The answers might fit around the following basic outline.

Birds

aviary   ornithology
mew   oology

Activity 11

Vocabulary Reinforcement

1. learnability
2. schemata
3. decoding
4. semantics
5. closure
6. acuity
7. concepts
8. inductive
9. hyperbole
10. oxymoron

Activity 12

Vocabulary Reinforcement

1. euphemism
2. amelioration
3. homograph
4. onomatopeia
5. acronym
6. pejoration
7. oxymoron
8. metaphor

How are activities 11 and 12 different? In activity 11, the meaning of the word was provided. In activity 12, you only had to recall what the word looked liked, not its meaning.

CHAPTER 5

Activity 13

Levels of Comprehension—Questions
Possible questions might include

Literal

1. Who taught Gulliver to speak the language?
2. What deafened Gulliver?
3. Who carried Gulliver to the gardener?

Interpretive

1. What evidence is there that the giants were educated?
2. In what ways was Gulliver creative?

Critical/Creative

1. How would living in a land of tiny people differ from living in a land of giants?
2. How would you have behaved if you were in Gulliver's place?

Activity 14

Levels of Comprehension—Statements
Possible statements might be

Literal

1. The dog was well trained.
2. Gulliver climbed a ladder to read a book.
3. Gulliver lived in fear.

Interpretive

1. Life in the land of giants was challenging.
2. Gulliver was well cared for.

Applied

1. A person's size does not determine his or her willpower.
2. Life has many challenges.

CHAPTER 6

Activity 15

Advance Organizer
Answers will vary.

Activity 16

Think Sheet
Answers will vary.

Activity 17

Structured Question Guide and Process Sheet
Answers will vary.

CHAPTER 7

Activity 18

Organizational Patterns

1. Comparison/contrast
2. Time order
3. Listing or enumeration
4. Comparison/contrast
5. Cause/effect
6. Time order

Activity 19

Three Levels Guide

A possible guide might look like this.

Read the following statements. Place a check on the numbered line if the statement tells what the author said.

___1. It's a bright day.
___2. The centipede was once happy.
___3. The centipede became distracted.

Read the following statements. Place a check before them if they tell what the author meant by what was written.

___1. The centipede became confused.
___2. A frog began to tease the centipede.
___3. The ditch was too high for the centipede to get out.

Read the following statements. Place a check before them if the ideas they contain can be supported by information in the poem. Can these generalizations be drawn? Be ready to give evidence from everyday life and the selection to support your answers.

___1. Events in life can cause distraction and confusion.
___2. Life is just a bowl full of cherries.
___3. Life's small questions can create big problems or concerns.

Activity 20

RADAR

Step 2: The analogy between circulation and irrigation might compare these features.

a. use pumping system
b. fluids work through system, system recycles
c. vessels are like pipes with one way flow system
d. need to maintain consistent pressure with valves and overflow valves (spleen)
e. filter system
f. fuels support life; fertilizer carried with water (feeding)

Step 4: What can be done to control these problems?

Problems	*Possible Solutions*
blockage	replace valves, pipes, and vessels
bad fuel pump	replace motor or heart
low or high pressure	take medication (use cleaning agents)
clogged valves and pipes	change water or blood
poison	
broken vessels and pipes	
poor nutrients	
leaky valves	
bad water or disease	

Activity 21

Graphic Organizer
Answers will vary.

Activity 22

Circle of Knowledge
States and Capitals

Ala.	Montgomery	Mont.	Helena
Alaska	Juneau	Nebr.	Lincoln
Ariz.	Phoenix	Nev.	Carson City
Ark.	Little Rock	N.H.	Condord
Calif.	Sacramento	N.J.	Trenton
Colo.	Denver	N. Mex.	Santa Fe
Conn.	Hartford	N.Y.	Albany
Del.	Dover	N.C.	Raleigh
Fla.	Tallahassee	N. Dak.	Bismarck
Ga.	Atlanta	Ohio	Columbus
Hawaii	Honolulu	Okla.	Oklahoma City
Idaho	Boise	Oreg.	Salem
Ill.	Springfield	Pa.	Harrisburg
Ind.	Indianapolis	R.I.	Providence
Iowa	Des Moines	S.C.	Columbia
Kan.	Topeka	S.Dak.	Pierre
Ky.	Frankfort	Tenn.	Nashville
La.	Baton Rouge	Tex.	Austin
Maine	Augusta	Utah	Salt Lake City
Md.	Annapolis	Vt.	Montpelier
Mass.	Boston	Va.	Richmond
Mich.	Lansing	Wash.	Olympia
Minn.	St. Paul	W.Va.	Charleston
Miss.	Jackson	Wis.	Madison
Mo.	Jefferson City	Wy.	Cheyenne

CHAPTER 8

Activity 23

Study Plan
Answers will vary.

Activity 24

Mnemonic Device
Answers will vary.

CHAPTER 9

Activity 25

Writing Organizer
Answers will vary.

Activity 26

Brainwriting
Answers will vary.

Activity 27

Student Summary Writing
Answers will vary.

CHAPTER 10

Activity 28

Cooperative Learning
Answers will vary.

CHAPTER 11

Activity 29

Interest Inventory
Answers will vary.

CHAPTER 12

Activity 30

Services for Special Needs Students
Answers will vary.

AUTHOR INDEX

Aaronson, E. , 188
Aaronson, S. , 228
Abrahamson, R. F., 254
Allen, A. A., 230
Allington, R. L., 21
Alvermann, D. E., 224
Anderson, J., 26
Anderson, R., 51
Anderson, T. H., 201
Applebee, A. N., 4
Arbuthnot, M. H., 245
Armbruster, B. B., 18, 28
Arthur, S. V., 83, 211, 233
Asch, S. E., 51
Asimov, I., 54
Au, K. H., 244
Ausubel, D. P., 123, 128, 131, 180

Bailey, M. D., 150
Baker, R. L., 150
Baldwin, R. S., 34, 54, 188
Ball, H. G., 28
Banks, J. A., 245, 255
Barbe, R., 51
Barron, R. F., 126
Bartel, N. R., 265
Bartholomew, B., 220
Beach, R. W., 201
Bean, R. W., 34, 188
Bean, T. W., 145, 204
Beck, I. L., 78

Berg, D. N., 145
Berkowitz, S. J., 145
Berry, S. M., 220
Best, A., 14
Blake, H., 205
Blanchard, J. S., 21, 230
Blanchowicz, C. L. Z., 52
Blanton, W., 32
Bloom, B., 104, 107, 108, 113, 166
Bluth, G. J., 154
Bormuth, J. R., 33
Brandt, D. M., 154, 225
Brophy, J., 115, 117
Brown, A. L., 118
Bruner, J. S., 131
Burgess, D. M., 265
Burmeister, L. E., 87, 257
Burns, P. C., 181

Calkins, L. M., 202
Cappuzzi, D., 226
Carnine, D. W., 145
Carr, E. M., 71
Carter, B. B., 54, 243, 254
Carver, R. P., 173
Casale, U. P., 74
Castallo, R., 188
Caughran, A., 181
Childrey, J., 255
Clark, C. M., 200
Clary, L. M., 21, 123, 241

SUBJECT INDEX